Capitalist Workingman's Paradises Revisited

Capitalist Workingman's Paradises Revisited

Corporate Welfare Work in Great Britain, the USA, Germany and France in the Golden Age of Capitalism, 1880-1930

Erik de Gier

Routledge
Taylor & Francis Group
LONDON AND NEW YORK

First published in 2016 by Amsterdam University Press Ltd.

Published 2025 by Routledge
4 Park Square, Milton Park, Abingdon, Oxon OX14 4RN
605 Third Avenue, New York, NY 10158

Routledge is an imprint of the Taylor & Francis Group, an informa business

ISBN: 9789089645814 (hbk)
ISBN: 9781041176558 (pbk)
ISBN: 9781003692058 (ebk)
NUR 762 / 906

Cover design: Gijs Mathijs Ontwerpers, Amsterdam

DOI: 10.5117/9789089645814

Table of contents

List of illustrations

Acknowledgements

Various persons contributed to the writing of this book. Firstly, I am grateful to Professor Marcel van der Linden (International Institute of Social History, IISH, Amsterdam), who, at an initial stage, was willing to discuss the idea of the book with me. Furthermore, various persons commented on parts of the manuscript: Dr. Lout Bots (Radboud University, Nijmegen) commented on the first two chapters of the manuscript. Professor Joseph White (Pittsburgh University) commented more specifically on chapter 2, regarding secular and purist origins of enlightened capitalism, as well as the chapter on Great Britain. Dr. Jill M. Jensen (Penn State University) did the same with respect to the chapter on the United States. Subsequently, Professor Jacques van Hoof (Radboud University and Leiden University) and Dr. Jill M. Jensen (Penn State University) extensively reviewed the whole manuscript. I am certain that their comments contributed substantially to the quality of the definite manuscript.

I also want to thank Saskia Gieling, Louise Visser and Jaap Wagenaar, the responsible editors at Amsterdam University Press (AUP), who made possible the printing and publishing of this book. Thanks, finally, to the various institutions willing to provide me with the illustrative material included in the book.

Preface

During my tenure as a professor of comparative labour market policies between 2008 and 2013 at Radboud University, Nijmegen, the Netherlands, I felt struck by two major international developments that most probably are going to change the actual and future world of work in a fundamental way for a long time to come. On the one hand, far-reaching flexibilization of work and labour contracts has become a predominant trend in the last decades on both internal and external labour markets in almost all EU countries, and the United States. On the other hand, we can observe in the same period a gradual breakdown of the stable postwar social compact that resulted in collective welfare states, guaranteeing sustainable work and worker security, in most of these countries.

Both developments are interrelated and reinforce each other in a positive way. In the end, this might result in new forms of serious marginalization or precarization of large groups of workers, not only low and semi-skilled. Other major consequences might be a decoupling of loyalty of workers to the firms in which they work, degradation of work and working conditions, and, ultimately, also a decrease of productivity and quality of products and services rendered by workers.

Taken together, this appears to be too high a price for developments that, at first sight, appear gainful for economies and firms.

As a labour sociologist, I felt challenged by contributing to finding solutions to the negative consequences of flexibilization of the world of work and the related retrenchment of the welfare state. Not by walking the usual beaten track, but by applying the nowadays too often neglected path of history-oriented sociology of work. More specifically, the method applied in this book summarizes, interprets and compares in an accessible and comprehensive way the available relevant, mostly country-specific, secondary literature on this theme. This implies also the most important added value of this book. The result is a still intriguing, somewhat forgotten, chapter of paternalistic employer welfare work in the golden age of capitalism by the end of the nineteenth and beginning of the twentieth centuries in the four most important industrialized countries at that time: Great Britain, The United States, Germany, and France. I hope this book is not only interesting for academics, but also for employers, workers, and policymakers.

Eventual omissions and inaccuracies in the book remain the responsibility of the author.

Erik de Gier
Heilig Landstichting, the Netherlands, Spring 2016

1 Introduction[1]

In one of his last works before he passed away, renowned French author Émile Zola sketched a utopian *cité idéale,* or ideal steel manufacturing company town, by 1900. He compared this new fictitious town, La Crêcherie, with the adjacent, more traditional company town, Beaucourt. In contrast to Beaucourt, workers at La Crêcherie had better working conditions, better wages, shorter working hours and could also access a number of additional welfare work benefits, like attractive family houses with gardens, green parks, schools, cooperative shops, pensions, etc. Moreover, to prevent a monotonous work life, workers at La Crêcherie had to rotate tasks several times a day. Generally, workers and their families at la Crêcherie were happier and healthier than the workers at Beaucourt. Zola's novel was not a complete figment. He based his utopia on Fourier's ideas concerning the Phalanstère, a collectively organized utopic living and working community. Zola also undertook extensive research in the important French coalmines of Anzin in the North of France, as well as in a large steel complex in the industrial city Saint Etienne. What Zola had in mind at that time was to influence social reformers, progressive employers and politicians in the French Third Republic, and likewise define a new ideal for French labour relations at the turn of the nineteenth century.[2] In fact, Zola's *cité idéale* better expressed the progressive mood of the past in France – as well as in many other capitalist countries – because avant-garde company towns had already been built in France and elsewhere from the 1850s.[3]

In the golden age of enlightened capitalism between 1880 and 1930 many, mainly larger, companies in various sectors (e.g. textiles, railroads, coalmining, metallurgy, electro technics, food, chemical industry) in various

1 A first initial version of this chapter was presented at the international conference 'Social Boundaries of Work. Changes in the sphere of work in the 21st century capitalism', University of Wroclaw, 14-15 November 2014; and subsequently published in Warsaw Forum of Economic Sociology (WFES). See De Gier 2015, pp. 117-129.

2 Zola (1901), *Travail.* See also Zola (1885), *Germinal.* The research at Anzin was done before writing *Germinal,* a novel about a dramatic labour conflict at a mine complex in the North of France. The French Left received *Travail* well, but not uncritically. The practical impact of his book on French industrial relations remained limited.

3 Albeit with one exception. In 1917, famous French architect Tony Garnier published a design of the ideal *cité industrielle,* a modernist future company town to be realized in the big industrial region in the Southeast of France. Garnier based his design on the ideas of both Fourier and Zola.

industrialized countries introduced remarkably comprehensive welfare work programmes. These programmes encompassed all kinds of provisions, such as workingman's housing, cheap mortgage loans, profit sharing schemes, saving schemes, pension saving schemes, schools, healthcare services, shops, sports facilities, and worker participation. Employers, often supported by social reformers, had various short-term as well as long-term economic and moral aims to introduce welfare work programmes in their companies. The most important were: creating a stabile workforce by preventing a high turnover; binding workers and worker families to the company; preventing strikes and labour unrest; keeping unions out; moralizing and disciplining the workforce; improving the motivation and productivity of workers; betterment of worker's health; and, finally, improving hygiene in the workplace, but also inside the workingman's home. Often, company welfare work programmes protected workers from the cradle to the grave. Before the First World War, the provision of workingman's housing, profit sharing, saving schemes, pensions, schools, and health services were the most important issues of welfare work. After the First World War, until the 1930s, the interest of employers and reformers largely shifted to worker participation and to combining welfare work with efficiency and the organization of work (scientific management and Fordist work policies). As a result, traditional paternalism was gradually replaced by what has been coined neo-paternalism. Then, the Great Depression of the 1930s caused a rapid and sudden decline of welfare work and enlightened capitalism in the majority of the American and European companies involved. Today, a number of welfare work programmes still exist, albeit in a different guise and packed in Human Resource Management (HRM) programmes. Moreover, after the Second World War, many countries incorporated a large part of former company welfare work into newly created collective welfare state provisions, such as housing, pensions, education, and health services.

In this book, I will deal with the unfolding, further development and performance of the vanguard of corporate welfare work in a comparative way in the four most important capitalist countries, mainly in the period between 1880 and 1930.[4] These countries are Great Britain, the United States, Germany, and France. In Germany, fast becoming – alongside the United States and Great Britain – one of the most important industrial nations in the world, corporate welfare work got a rather unique additional dimension

4 Of course, at that time, there were also many firms that performed poorly with respect to welfare work. See for example, in this respect, Green 2010. Green also pays attention to what he calls 'satanic mills' alongside 'industrial Edens' that shaped the American economy.

thanks to explicit and close links with new factory architecture, product design, product quality, quality work, and joy in work. Of course, corporate welfare work also unfolded in many other industrializing countries at almost the same time, but by focusing on the four most important capitalist countries of that period I hope to discern some important systematic similarities and differences in the development of enlightened corporate welfare work between 1880 and 1930.

One of the main reasons for a retrospective survey is the recently initiated dismantling of collective welfare state provisions in many Western countries, causing significant voids in social and worker protection. At the same time, the personal responsibility of workers for their own work and welfare is stressed in increasingly flexible work settings, but often in an austere environment of corporate welfare work provisions. As American sociologist Richard Sennett has made clear in his impressive evaluation of the 'new capitalism' of our time, this development could easily come at the expense of workers' remaining craftsmanship and, likewise, personal security.[5]

Ultimately, the question is whether we can still learn from this past experience of welfare work at the time of enlightened capitalism, a period in which a substantial number of enlightened or progressive employers in the four countries under examination took care of workers' welfare, sometimes, as noted above, 'from the cradle to the grave'?

The period 1880-1930 may be considered as a blooming period of enlightened capitalism throughout the North-Atlantic world, including the United States, Canada, Australia, and Europe. Setting aside the severe economic crisis of the 1880s, this period was characterized by steady, long-term strong economic growth in these parts of the world. It was also a time of progressive politics and social reforms. Think, in this respect, of the Progressive Era in the United States, the late Victorian reform period in Great Britain, the first phase of the Third Republic in France and of pre-First World War Wilhelmine Germany and its postwar successor, the Weimar Republic. Moreover, it was also an intensive period of policy learning across borders and continents, with the intention of taming the negative social consequences of unbridled capitalism. In particular, there was an extensive mutual exchange of ideas and practical experiences with respect to social and employment policies between America and Europe, promoted, for

5 Sennett 1998; 2006; 2008.

example, by the world exhibitions on both continents and mutual fishing expeditions by employers, reformers and social scientists.[6]

The economic roots of enlightened capitalism are located in both the first and the second industrial revolutions. The first industrial revolution, characterized by the invention of the steam engine and the introduction of the market economy, as well as the rapid development of new transport systems, took off in the eighteenth century and in the first half of the nineteenth century, initially in England and subsequently also in other countries. It marked the transition of agricultural labour into industrial labour through the introduction of the factory system and mechanization of work. This caused a huge demand for labour and migration from countryside to town, and to places with an abundant availability of natural resources needed by the new industries. In order to be attractive to agricultural workers and artisans, new and growing companies were urged to introduce welfare work as well as to provide company housing in places where adequate workingman's housing was lacking. Welfare work in this period was by nature paternalistic, primarily directed at moral education and disciplining of the new workforce as well as at the prevention of labour unrest. Religious or utopian motives on the employer's side also often played a role.

The second industrial revolution took off at the beginning of the twentieth century, first in the United States and then also prominently in Germany. This second industrial revolution is characterized by the invention of electricity, new materials, medicine, cars, scientific management and Fordism, and marks the transition of traditional paternalism to neo-paternalism, in which managerial capitalism, rather than family capitalism, was to play a decisive role. The second industrial revolution did not imply a decisive end to traditional paternalistic welfare work. On the contrary, it just implied a shift within traditional welfare work programmes and, in addition, an extension of traditional welfare work programmes with Taylorist and Fordist policies at the company level.[7]

In addition to economic and political roots, enlightened capitalism also had religious and ideological roots. The Protestant ethic was not only interwoven with the onset and development of capitalism itself, but also with the development of enlightened capitalism. A good example is the extensive welfare work policy of a small cohesive network of family-related Calvinistic Mulhousian textile entrepreneurs in mid-nineteenth-century Alsace. At a very early stage, this group of entrepreneurs built, not only

6 Rodgers 1998.

7 See for example Hobsbawn 1989; 1996.

for mere economic reasons, one of the most extensive company towns or *cités ouvrières* in France, consisting of, at that time, attractive single-family houses surrounded with gardens and provided with several amenities. These entrepreneurs also developed other welfare work programmes like pension schemes, a mutual aid fund, medical services and cooperative shops. Moreover, such programmes had a significant influence on social reforms at the state level in France, such as the legislation of child labour. Subsequently, the so-called Mulhousian Welfare Work Model was widely emulated by other French employers. Another example is the welfare work programmes introduced by Quaker entrepreneurs in England and the United States. The Cadbury family, for example, created its own exemplary and widely admired 'workingman's paradise' at Bournville, near Birmingham, by the end of the nineteenth century, more or less copied by, for example, Quaker chocolate manufacturer Milton Hershey in Pennsylvania, chocolate manufacturer Menier in France and steel manufacturer Krupp in Germany (Margarethenhöhe).

Non-purist, secular examples are Robert Owen's ideas on the future of human society and Fourier's ideas of a phalanstère, a communist living and work community. Owen first practised his ideas in his cotton factory and company town New Lanark in Scotland. Later, Owen attempted in vain to create sustainable idealistic living and working communities in the New World. Fourier never realized his phalanstère, but had a strong influence on many temporary attempts, mostly by European immigrants, to create phalanstère-like communities in the New World. In France, Fourier inspired Jean-Baptiste Godin, a stove manufacturer, building a so-called Familistère, adjacent to its already existing factory. This Familistère was designed in accordance with Fourier's phalanstère and contained a great number of apartments for his workers and their families. On the same site, Godin built a school, a large theatre, bathing and washing facilities, a restaurant and an indoor swimming pool. Fourier also inspired the futuristic, but never realized *cité ouvrière,* designed by renowned French architect Tony Garnier between 1901 and 1917.

Britain has been the cradle of corporate welfare capitalism. Already in the initial stage of the first industrial revolution, from the mid-eighteenth century onwards, a significant number of entrepreneurs introduced welfare work programmes, including company housing in new factory villages adjacent to their factories. Apart from eighteenth-century New Lanark, Saltaire in West Yorkshire constructed after 1851 was exemplary. Sir Titus Salt, a wealthy self-made textile manufacturer employing some 3,000 workers, constructed factory village Saltaire. The ultimately 800 workingman's dwellings with gardens in Saltaire were built in wide streets, with spacious squares and with recreational grounds. All houses had access to water, gas and lavatories. Salt also built churches, a hospital, a community centre, factory schools and a park. At that time, however, the dominant entrepreneurial doctrine was 'laissez-faire'. A more comprehensive social doctrine or concise idea of social policy remained lacking.

The apex of welfare work in Britain was reached by the end of the nineteenth century when in-majority Quaker entrepreneurs in the realm of the chocolate and food industry (Cadbury, Rowntree, Fry) developed sometimes-bulky welfare work programmes. For example, the social reform-oriented Cadbury brothers moved their factory in Birmingham to a green site on the city's outskirts. There, they constructed their new 'factory in a garden' and also built the romantic workingman's village Bournville with about 300 red-brick cottages with front- and back gardens in tree-lined streets. This industrial garden village was also provided with churches, schools, a meetinghouse, shops and a library. Cadbury's business philosophy was based on benevolence, efficiency, equal treatment and social justice. The working conditions in the factory were significantly better compared to factories in neighbouring Birmingham. Monotonous work in the factory was combatted, for example, by introducing shorter working hours and encouraging the workers to make use of the educational provisions. A works council was also introduced.

Another notable British example is Port Sunlight; built in Cheshire by William Hesketh Lever, co-founder of soap manufacturer Lever Brothers. Like the Cadbury's, Lever built a model industrial colony consisting of 720 houses in old English style with gardens by 1909. Lever's aim was to create one big 'Sunlight-family'. In order to achieve this, Lever promoted all kinds of social clubs for his workers, such as a music band, a historical society, a choir and a horticultural society. Workers worked eight hours per day, instead of the usual twelve hours. Wages were rather generous. In addition, workers received sickness benefits, pensions and could make use of medical services. There was also a well-developed system of profit sharing, called 'prosperity sharing'. Unions were also allowed, as well as collective agreements.

If Britain has been the cradle of corporate welfare work, the United States may be characterized as the land of the creation of an almost infinite number of company towns and welfare work initiatives, where the big mistakes and negative effects of the Industrial Revolution in England should and could be avoided. The American government defined welfare work in 1916 in rather broad terms as "anything for the comfort and improvement, intellectual and social, of the employees, over and above wages paid, which is not a necessity of the industry nor required by law." In practice, this encompassed provisions such as company housing, education, recreation, profit sharing, stock ownership, medical care, sickness benefits, pensions, social work, grievance procedures and worker participation. Like Britain, the United States has some fine examples of early welfare work initiatives by enlightened paternalistic employers, such as the exemplary construction of Pullman City. However, the apex of American corporate welfare capitalism was reached between 1910 and 1929, when employers not only built a number of so-called 'new' company towns, but also widely supported the view that cooperation between management and labour would be beneficial to both the well-being of workers and the efficiency and productivity of firms.

George Pullman, owner of the Pullman Palace Car Factory, designed both a new factory and company town near Chicago in the 1880s. The town was laid out as a geometric iron grid. Pullman based his town on his aesthetic conviction of the commercial value of beauty. The factory was constructed adjacent to, albeit separated from, the town next to a major boulevard. The town also had greens, a lake, a public park and a number of public buildings, such as a church, schools, a hotel, a market building with shops and a multipurpose community building. Houses were for rent and had access to gas, water and sewerage. The town had almost 13,000 inhabitants by 1893.

Pullman ran the town autocratically as a private company and saw the company town as an economic investment. Factory wages were average, but temporarily sick workers received full payment. Disabled workers were offered suitable employment. On the other hand, unions were not allowed. The big 'Pullman strike' of 1894, protesting a severe wage cut, foreboded the gradual demise of the company town in the late 1890s as well as the end of Pullman's overly paternalistic welfare work system. Pullman's model remained exceptional in the American context and did not really get a successful follow-up. Nevertheless, the evolution of 'new' company towns from 1910 onwards signified an extraordinary step forward in the evolution of American welfare work. In contrast to former, more traditional company towns, a 'new' company town was designed and planned for the first time in American history by professional independent architects, landscape architects and planners, like Grosvenor Atterbury and John Nolen. They designed and planned more than 40 'new' company towns between 1910 and 1930. 'New' company towns were usually more varied than traditional company towns, with various housing types, the application of inexpensive new construction materials like concrete and standardization of the building process. As future residents, the workers themselves were also involved in the design and planning of the 'new' company towns. An illustrative example of a 'new' company town is Indian Hill at Worcester, Massachusetts designed by Grosvenor Atterbury for the Norton Grinding Company (machine tools). This company was already in the vanguard of American welfare capitalism and employed 3,500 workers by 1915. Norton's welfare work encompassed a hospital, factory safety, sanitation programmes, worker dining rooms and cafeterias, paid vacations, pensions, recreational facilities and a mutual benefit society. The new town was built for skilled and supervising employees. Influenced by existing New England company towns, colonial cottages and European garden cities, Atterbury designed a romantic and picturesque town in a Dutch colonial style, including a town square with shops and with single-family houses with five to seven rooms.[8]

Although Germany had much in common with the other three countries dealt with in this book with respect to welfare work in the golden age of enlightened capitalism, it differed in one striking aspect with Britain, the United States and France. This was the conscious intention of politicians, policymakers, industrialists, designers, architects, economists, and social scientists to base German industry on the concept of 'quality work'. Quality work encompassed important interrelated aspects of product quality, joy in work, and the quality of work itself. To enable this, after 1900 an intensive collaboration developed between the newly founded German Werkbund (DWB), consisting of prominent members of the various groups mentioned above, and a number of individual industrialists. At stake was the realization of what was called *Deutsche Arbeit* (German Work)[9]. Of course, also in Britain, the United States and France, sometimes renowned architects were involved in the design of company housing and factory buildings, as was the case, for example, with the 'new' American company towns mentioned above. However, in no other country was the involvement of architects, designers, politicians, and employers so intensively organized and so comprehensive as in Germany after 1900 until the rise of the national socialist dictatorship in the 1930s.

A particularly good example of more traditional welfare work in Germany is the Krupp Steel Works at Essen in the Ruhr-Region. Krupp developed into a nationally important entrepreneurial family dynasty in a rather

8 See about the American 'new' company towns Crawford 1995.

9 See, in this respect, the important work of British historian Joan Campbell: Campbell 1989.

short timespan. It was Friedrich Krupp, son of founder of the firm Alfred Krupp, who decided to build worker colonies and worker settlements from the 1860s onwards. Krupp was not the only German firm that constructed workingman's housing, but it is no exaggeration to say that by the end of the nineteenth century the firm outpaced any other German company with respect to company housing, both in quantitative and qualitative terms. By that time, Krupp had become the nationwide model-builder of company housing for at least coalmines, steel producers, and some other companies.[10] Perhaps the apotheosis was the construction of Krupp's industrial garden village Margarethenhöhe in Essen, from 1906. Inspired by Cadbury's Bournville, Margarethenhöhe, designed by renowned Werkbund architect Georg Metzendorf, became a romantic workers garden village with cottages in meandering, tree-lined streets and a central square. The village also had a hotel, a big grocery shop, a post office, a church, etc. Although Margarethenhöhe was not exclusively built for Krupp workers, the village rapidly became Krupp's international welfare work showpiece.

Krupp's welfare work programmes were much more extensive than only offering company housing for rent to his workers. They also encompassed secure employment, high wages, sickness and industrial accidents insurance, old age pensions, hospitals, a lending library, company shops (*Konsumanstalt*), social institutions, and recreational facilities. The Krupp-workforce became one big and privileged 'Kruppianer' family.

With respect to the development of German work or quality work after the turn of the century, Krupp was no longer in the vanguard of enterprises that played a key role in the new neo-paternalistic welfare work in Germany. This role was reserved for other companies in the new industries, such as the manufacturing and chemical industries in emerging urban and regional industrial centres. In the Main-Rhine Region of Ludwigshafen, chemical giants such as BASF and Bayer would play an important role in this respect, also in collaboration with Werkbund members. In Berlin, also called the 'first Technopolis' or 'first Silicon Valley', giant electro-technical corporations such as AEG and Siemens became very prominent in welfare work.[11]. Renowned architects, such as AEG's Peter Behrens, designed new factory buildings and company housing. In the case of company housing in Berlin and also in some other urban centres where the supply of workingman's housing was scarce, third-party building companies, often with the financial

10 In 1914, about 20 per cent of all 10,000 Krupp workers and their families lived in Krupp worker colonies near Essen.

11 Osterhammel 2010: 398.

involvement of the principal company, took prime responsibility for building workingman's housing. Henceforth not the single-family house was the standard workingman's home, but apartments in blocks. Siemensstadt, for example, the big company town near the site of the Berlin Siemens head office and factory buildings, was designed by in-company architect Hans Hertlein and built in the 1920s by various independent building companies. Various renowned Werkbund architects, such as Walter Gropius, the later director of the famous arts school Bauhaus at Weimar, designed the different apartment houses. In the subsequent cases, former romantic ideas about building single-family cottages were exchanged for functional ideas and the New Objectivity style (*Neue Sachlichkeit*). The AEG-apartment blocks, designed by Peter Behrens, also offered functionally designed furniture and timesaving kitchen and household devices.

France, the fourth industrial country under examination, is, to some extent, another special case. Although not the cradle of welfare work, France, like Britain, was an early performer of paternalistic welfare work in the nineteenth century. Exemplary in this country, particularly with respect to company housing was, as has been noted, the Mulhousian model or *solution Mulhousienne,* which included an almost exclusive choice for single-family houses with gardens instead of apartment housing built in company towns (*cités ouvrières*). At first sight, the Mulhousian model did not differ that much from the preference for cottages and single-family houses also existing in other countries. However, France's industrial revolution was somewhat retarded by successive political upheaval, such as the French Revolution of 1789 and its aftermath. Therefore, the transition from an agricultural society into an industrializing society took place in France in a relatively short time span compared to other countries. Consequently, a substantial part of the new industrial labour force maintained a farming background for quite a long time. So, by offering single-family houses with gardens, industrial work would become more attractive for (former) agricultural workers. In this way, employers could better serve the well-being of workers too. By 1876, some 1,000 houses were realized at Mulhouse. By 1895, this number had risen to 1,240 dwellings with 10,000 inhabitants.

A second principal difference with most other industrializing countries was the rather early stage, the 1850s, at which the comprehensive Mulhousian model was developed. Moreover, not a single entrepreneur was involved, but rather a strong network of family-related social reform oriented Calvinistic textile entrepreneurs in the Mulhouse region; for example, Dollfus, Koechlin, Schlumberger, and Zuber. This group, united in the

'Société Industrielle de Mulhouse', not only introduced sometimes-common welfare work programmes in its companies, but also promoted industrial development, innovation, and public welfare in the Mulhouse region. In addition to workingman's housing, welfare work here encompassed: factory bakeries; cooperative shops; savings banks and regional pension savings banks for factory workers; mutual aid provisions; free medical services; libraries; a swimming pool; a gymnasium; a theatre; and, last but not least, a number of vocational training schools.

Also in France, textile entrepreneurs built many company towns in the North as well as coal mining societies and metallurgical industries. A striking example of the latter is the Schneider Metal Works and Mining Company established at Le Creusot in the Burgundy region. In a relatively short period, form 1836 onwards, the Schneider dynasty developed the most important metallurgical industry in France, comparable at a national scale to the Krupp Works at Essen, Germany. From the outset, welfare work played an important role in the Schneider enterprise. In this case, not primarily by building company housing, but by offering various educational provisions and other welfare work programmes. To make the company less vulnerable to external labour market influences, the Schneider Company developed its own school system, ultimately encompassing primary, secondary, tertiary, and vocational education. Company jobs were primarily offered to those who had taken part in the Schneider school system.

With regard to housing, workers were stimulated to build and even to design their own dwellings. Schneider offered financially attractive loans to enable this. Other welfare work on behalf of the so-called 'Creusotiens' workers family encompassed: old age pensions; allowances for large families; a provident fund to support sick and injured workers and survivors; a hospital; a home for the elderly; churches; sports facilities; cooperative stores; a company restaurant, etc. Welfare work at Schneider was extremely effective in the sense that, compared to other companies and industries in France, the Schneider Company remained almost immune to any labour conflict until the 1930s. Indeed, only one strike occurred between 1880 and 1930, in 1899.

As has been remarked, in all four countries enlightened capitalism almost came to an end during the years of the Great Depression in the 1930s. It only partly revived in a somewhat comparable way after the Second World War. More importantly, from the 1950s onwards, the welfare state adopted the main basic elements of former paternalistic corporate welfare work. Today, in most western industrialized countries, including the United

States, Britain, Germany, and France, a structural downsizing of welfare state capitalism is occurring with the risk of leaving significant voids in worker protection and worker security. Although today's flex-capitalism differs fundamentally from the paternalistic capitalism of the past, the question arises whether companies must retake some of their past welfare work responsibilities and, if so, in what form? Could companies learn from the past paternalistic welfare work of companies such as Cadbury, AEG, Siemens, or the extraordinary group of Mulhousian textile companies? Would it be helpful, for example, to reintroduce renewed mutual aid funds at the company, sectorial, or regional level with responsibilities shared by employers and workers? And, would it also be helpful to involve workers more directly in redesigning quality work, including product quality? It is tempting to answer these questions in the affirmative. However, it is obvious that the overly paternalistic pitfalls of the past must be avoided. What is needed, in sum, is a fundamental redesign of welfare work in the context of future, rather austere collective welfare states and highly flexible companies. The result could be innovated hybrid comprehensive welfare work programmes that mix company responsibility, the personal responsibility of individual workers, and collective state responsibility. Its content must be based on a balanced combination of quality work, product quality, and work- and income security.

In sum, this book deals with the phenomenon of enlightened capitalism and social engineering, between approximately 1880 and 1930.

Although there have been many company towns and worker colonies as expressions of paternalistic welfare work in the industrialized capitalist world, the focus in this book is on enlightened capitalism and social engineering in Great Britain, the United States, Germany, and France.[12] There are some important reasons for this selective choice.

Firstly, in the golden age of capitalism, the four selected countries could be considered as the most important industrialized or industrializing countries of the North-Atlantic world. They constituted the vanguard.

Britain is the country where modern industrialized capitalism took off. It is the country of the first industrial revolution. Britain is also the country where a religious inspiration of enlightened capitalism was most pronounced. Moreover, what makes Britain an interesting case is the relationship of enlightened capitalism with a nineteenth-century Victorian public morale and, as a corollary, its relationship with the Arts and

12 See for a recent historic global overview Borges & Torres 2012.

Crafts Movement. Also in the United States the religious inspiration in the case of enlightened capitalism has been strong. As in Britain, puritanism and Quakerism played a significant role. More in general, the American nineteenth-century factory system evolved over time into so-called 'welfare capitalism'. In addition to industrial firms, welfare capitalism was introduced in large department stores in big cities on the East Coast, such as New York, Boston, and Philadelphia.

In Germany, as in the Anglo-Saxon world, enlightened capitalism was inspired significantly by religious ideas. In this country, however, it was not so much Quakerism, but ideas about social reform based on Christian-social and also social liberal principles, first embodied by the 'Heimatschutz Movement' and later by its successor the 'Deutsche Werkbund' (DWB). What makes Germany a particularly interesting case is the early interest in this country in the architecture of factory buildings in combination with attention to the design and quality of products and the working conditions of workers. Also in Germany, the English example of Bournville played a significant role. At the turn of the nineteenth century, Margarethe Krupp, spouse of steel magnate Friedrich Alfred Krupp, travelled to Bournville and subsequently emulated Bournville's concept in the new garden city Margarethenhöhe in Essen.

In France, enlightened capitalism goes back as far as the ideas of utopian-socialists, such as Charles Fourier, and the Phalanstère style of building that he propagated.

A second reason for selecting the United States, Great Britain, Germany, and France is that enlightened capitalism in these four countries had some interesting similarities, such as its social-religious and purist inspirations, the role and significance of industrial architecture, product design, and welfare work. Another important common denominator is the idea of the garden city, as designed originally by English Quaker Ebenezer Howard. Also relevant is the role played by applied-arts movements such as the English Arts and Crafts Movement and the Deutsche Werkbund (DWB).[13]

Thirdly, the four-countries-choice offers the possibility of comparing developments with respect to welfare work between a number of important European countries, as well as between Europe and the United States. As contended, this is interesting because there has been a lively transatlantic interaction and exchange of social policy ideas in the golden age

13 De Gier 2012.

of capitalism. In this respect, Britain and Germany acted as the primary models and also as rivals of the United States.[14]

The next chapter (chapter 2) sketches the relevant cultural background of enlightened capitalism. This chapter deals, in particular, with purist and profane origins of enlightened capitalism. Subsequently, chapters 3, 4, 5 and 6 deal with the flowering period of enlightened capitalism and corporate welfare work in Great Britain, the United States, Germany, and France, respectively.

Chapter 7 is devoted to a brief inter-country comparison. In combination with the introductory chapter, chapter 7 can also be read separately as a summary of the book.

Finally, chapter 8 raises the question of whether, and what we could learn from past experience with respect to the future of corporate welfare work and the welfare state.

14 Rodgers 1998: 3-4.

2 Secular and purist origins of enlightened capitalism

2.1 Introduction

The first industrial revolution took off in Britain. This is one of the main reasons that, with some notable exceptions, enlightened capitalism on a larger scale first took shape on the British Isles before dispersing to the continent and to America. One such continental exception was the model saltworks manufacture La Saline Royale d'Arc-et-Senans in the French Jura, near the city of Besançon. Designed by Louis XV's famous court architect Claude-Nicolas Ledoux, La Saline Royale was constructed between 1775-1793. The Royal Saltworks started operating in 1778 and remained productive until 1895. Ledoux considered La Saline as an expression of his *cité idéale,* in which working, living, and hierarchical worker control were integrated equally.[1] After a more ambitious first plan concerning the ideal city of Chaux, rejected by the king, Ledoux's definite design for La Saline consisted of an assembly of eleven independent, symmetrical buildings located on a semi-circle containing an inner square with four fountains. The most impressive building was the large director's house, which featured a front colonnade of six impressive columns overseeing and dominating the whole inner site as well as the equally monumental entrance of La Saline Royale. Ledoux's ideas about la cité idéale were strongly influenced by the Enlightenment. He was, for example, a contemporary of other influential French Enlightenment spirits, such as Diderot, Turgot, Malesherbes, Necker, and Condorcet. Like many others in this time period, he was also touched by a certain Anglomania related to the first English Industrial Revolution.

Though fully state sponsored, La Saline Royale can undoubtedly be considered as an early forerunner or illustrative example of later industrial capitalist workingman's paradises, including a number of enlightened company towns. According to Rabreau, it is both an allegory of the Enlightenment and an industrial monument.[2]

Rabreau's statement refers to the fact that in addition to material aspects, spiritual aspects go hand in hand with the development of enlightened capitalism. Therefore, in the remaining part of this chapter, I will pay

1 Rabreau 2002.

2 *Ibid.:* 84-87.

further attention to the secular origins of enlightened capitalism as well as to religious purist origins.

Many of the relevant aspects culminate in the ideas and actions of Welshman and entrepreneur Richard Owen (1771-1858). Before becoming known as a utopian socialist, alongside French utopian socialists Fourier, Cabet, and Saint-Simon, he was the owner and manager of the textile mills and model factory village of New Lanark in Scotland. To some extent, Owen achieved his social utopia in New Lanark. In this respect, he was not completely unique. Other contemporary English entrepreneurs founded comparable model villages. Owen's uniqueness lies more in the fact that his ideas were rooted in both the Enlightenment as well as in purist motives. He narrowly collaborated with Quakers in England and the United States. Moreover, his later social experimentation, particularly in the United States, was based on communitarian ideas. Below, I will deal in more detail with the ideas and motives of Owen, Jeremy Bentham (as an important representative of English Utilitarianism), French utopian-socialism and finally, with religious purist ideals.

2.2 Robert Owen's social reforms

Crucial to understanding Owen's social engineering is his principal idea, rooted in Enlightenment thinking, that man's character is largely determined by environmental influences. According to Owen, "the character of man is formed for him, and not by him."[3] As such, man is malleable and able to be led in the 'right' direction by a combination of educational efforts and disciplinary action. This had to be set in a framework of a complete reform of the existing labour system.[4] Thus, Owen stood opposite the protestant ethic, based on the idea that man has to work hard and in a disciplined way during his lifetime in order to earn afterlife salvation.

In Britain, the mills of New Lanark were one of the first impressive examples of enlightened capitalism. The mills were operative from 1786 and, prior to Owen, initially owned by his future father-in-law David Dale. Other comparable contemporary initiatives were, for example, Finlay's Deanston mill, Richard Arkwright's mills at Cromford, and the cotton mills constructed by the Strutts of Derby at Milford and Belper.[5] In all cases, it

3 Owen 1991.
4 Kolakowski 1976: 220-227.
5 Fitton & Wadsworth 1958.

concerned the construction of factory villages in the textile industry with additional worker welfare policies.

Finlay's Deanston Mill encompassed a company shop with low cost merchandise, a model farmhouse, a school, and a sick fund. Prize competitions contributed to cleanliness in the factory.[6]

In the context of their time, the Strutts and the Arkwrights were good employers. The Strutts, Unitarians, supported religious and political freedom as well as the improvement of the life and living conditions of the labouring classes. In 1807, they founded Sunday schools for their factory children at Belper and Milford. These children initially made long working days of twelve hours per day, six days a week. Gradually, the number of working hours for children was reduced. At the same time, the recruitment age increased. Factory discipline was important. Fines were introduced to reduce absenteeism, theft, destruction or damage of mill property, and misconduct outside working hours. Almost all mill workers were paid on the basis of piecework and payment in kind. The Strutts arranged company housing for their workers. In 1832, Belper consisted of 1,482 houses, twenty per cent of which were owned by the Strutts. Against wage deductions they supplied their workers with coal, milk, meat, and vegetables. There was a women's sick club.[7]

Later examples of factory villages were Saltaire (1851) and J.J. Cash Ltd.

Sir Titus Salt founded Saltaire, a Victorian model village near Bradford, in 1851. It consisted of brick stone houses for the workers, washhouses, bathhouses, and other worker facilities such as a school, a hospital, a library and reading room, a billiard room, etc. As C. & R. Bell argue, Saltaire is generally considered as an important development in the history of nineteenth-century city planning in Britain through the combination of houses, employment, and social services.[8]

J.J. Cash Ltd. (1858), a ribbon-making factory at West Orchard, owned by two Quaker brothers, constructed 48 three-storey weaver's cottages. John and Joseph Cash were members of the so-called 'Rosehill Circle', a group of social reformers that included Robert Owen, renowned fiction writer George Eliot, wealthy manufacturer Charles Bray and philosopher Herbert Spencer.[9]

6 Robertson A.J. 1971.
7 Fitton & Wadsworth 1958: 224-260.
8 Bell, Colin & Rose 1972.
9 Wikipedia November 2012.

Robert Owen was born in 1771 in Newtown, Wales. He was the son of a saddler and ironmonger. In 1788, he went to Manchester and soon succeeded in becoming manager of a large cotton-spinning mill. After becoming engaged to the daughter of wealthy merchant David Dale, who was the first owner of the cotton factory he founded at New Lanark in 1784 on the banks of the river Clyde, Owen moved to New Lanark in 1800 and stayed there until 1824.

Owen considered New Lanark as an ideal place for social experimentation and for putting into practice his ideas on the improvement of the living and working conditions of the poor and the labouring classes. His policies were a mixture of paternalistic carrot and stick measures. At one point, the workforce consisted of about 2,000 workers, including some 500 pauper children from the age of ten. A 'silent monitor' promoted discipline in the workplace. This was a wooden block, painted in different colours, put on a machine indicating the level of performance of an individual worker. In the factory village, cleanliness was promoted and drunkenness discouraged. On the other hand, Owen's benevolence encompassed a sick fund, medical care, and a public dining room. Additionally, Owen experimented with education. In 1816, he opened the Institute for the Formation of Character with a view to educating his workforce. To him, the character formation implied "the attempt to create a more moral, humane, kind, active, and educated workforce by providing an environment in which such traits could be nourished from childhood onward."[10]

Across time, Owen's ideas became more ambitious. He developed a philosophy encompassing the reform of the whole society. In his famous 'Plan' (1817) he outlined more specifically his social reform philosophy. At its core was solving unemployment caused by mechanization by means of building 'villages of union' of 500 to 1,500 people motivated by 'mutual and combined interest'. These villages, preferably constructed in the form of a large quadrangle or parallelogram with public buildings in the centre and surrounded by private apartments for each family, should be situated in the countryside and make use of 'some machinery' with the goal of being self-sufficient.[11]

In due course, Owen tried to realize his ideal communities in both Britain and the United States. In America, in 1825, he purchased an existing purist Rappite community in Indiana. He subsequently renamed it New Harmony. In Britain, communities inspired by Owen's ideas included Orbiston (1828) near Glasgow and Queenswood (1839) in Hampshire.

10 Claeys 1991.

11 *Ibid.* Bollerey 1977.

Although the majority of his own initiatives or initiatives of his followers did not last a long time, because of internal tensions and conflicts, it is nevertheless relevant to pay greater attention to his American adventure.

In the eighteenth century, the United States was still a sparsely populated agricultural country. In 1790, the country had only five cities with more than 10,000 inhabitants. After becoming formally independent from Britain in1776, America wanted to construct a democratic state based upon Enlightenment values and upon faith in the moral capacity of ordinary people.[12] As Wood argues, "everywhere the boundaries of darkness and ignorance were being pushed back and light and reason were being extended outward."[13] This resulted in the idea of 'American exceptionalism', including a belief in America as a special place and a land of opportunity, social engineering, minimal government, the idea 'that all men are created equal', and, finally, religious freedom and the absence of a divine leader.

Summarizing, it is this extraordinary climate that Owen met in America after arriving there in 1824. In this time period, exceptionalism expressed itself mainly in the form of communitarianism and frontier thinking. Communitarianism can be defined as a method of social reform by means of experimental communities aiming at the pursuit of happiness. It was a sort of new religion and attracted purist sects such as the Shakers and the Rappites. Owen's first initiative in the United States was to visit the Shaker community at Niskeyuna in November 1824. Then, in January 1825, he purchased New Harmony (Indiana). Owen wanted to apply his ideas about an ideal society in both villages, as laid out in his 'Plan' for the reorganization of society (1817) as well as in his 'Report to the County of New Lanark' (1820).[14] In essence, his societal ideal was an agricultural utopia consisting of small self-supporting countryside villages.

This all fitted well with communitarian ideas, as well as frontier thinking or a discussion of space in the United States. As the western parts of the United States were still not served fully by railroad lines, these regions remained worlds apart from the more urbanized Northeast throughout the mid-nineteenth century.

Owen's first and most important stay in America lasted five years, from 1824-1829, but, ultimately, it was not very successful.[15] It also marked his

12 Wood 2011.

13 *Ibid.*: 276.

14 Owen 1991.

15 By the 1840s, Owenism in America had lost its momentum and was overturned by Fourianism (Harrison 1969: 132, 173).

breach with the world of business. After his return to Britain he never went back to New Lanark.[16] Owen increasingly developed himself as a utopian socialist who propagated a new social religion. Therefore, his later thinking can be considered as a "blend of communitarian theory, anti-capitalist thinking and a science of society."[17]

2.3 Jeremy Bentham and the National Charity Company[18]

Utilitarian[19] thinker Jeremy Bentham had a strong influence on Owen's thinking. Bentham even invested money in New Lanark. In a wider context, apart from Bentham, Owen's ideas were very much related those of his contemporaries, such as Helvétius, Godwin, and James Mill.[20]

Bentham is best known for his 'Panopticon', a 'circularly polygonal' designed model prison, based on the principles of permanent observation and control of prisoners. Less known is his companion-plan published a few years later in 1798 as 'Outline of a Work entitled Pauper Management Improved' for the creation of a National Charity Company, organized as a privately-run joint stock company. A national network of 250-500 'industry-houses' or workhouses, spread at equal distance across England and Wales and ultimately covering some ten per cent (one million people) of the whole English population of that time, formed the core of the National Charity Company. The workhouses should operate on the basis of the principle of self-interest and were sold by auction to the highest bidder. Workhouses not only supplied work for the poor seeking relief, but also encompassed housing. Each workhouse contained living and working quarters for 2,000 people, and each room in a workhouse "could be made to accommodate 24 single adults or sixteen married people and thirty-two children."[21] Also foreseen was an infirmary for the sick. The main principle was that the poor had to be productive and should earn their own living. They should not be dependent on charity. Bentham considered the paupers in the workhouses

16 Harrison 1969: 6.
17 *Ibid.*: 47.
18 This section is based on: Bahmueller (1981); Himmelfarb (1985); and Himmelfarb (1986).
19 Utilitarianism is the system of thought that states that the best action or decision in a particular situation is the one that brings most advantage to the most people (*Cambridge Advanced Learner's Dictionary*).
20 Harrison 1969: 83. Harrison argues that Owenism not only fell within the categories of classic Enlightment thought, but was also closely related to Scottish moral philosophy.
21 Himmelfarb 1985: 79; Himmelfarb 1986: 124.

primarily as producers with a certain economic value. Additionally, as in the Panopticon, permanent observation and control of the paupers had to prevail in the workhouses. The architectural design of the workhouses was similar to the Panopticon, "with the inspector's lodge in the middle." Working for the National Charity Company implied an involuntary and totalitarian kind of imprisonment for the paupers concerned. This is implied in Bentham's own words: "undivided authority over the whole body of burdensome poor."[22]

Bentham propagated hard working and refuted idleness. Important in this respect was educating the paupers and the pauper children by remaking them "as models of the secularized Protestantism of work ethics," ready to carry out productive labour.[23] The National Charity Company itself had to work on the basis of the "no idle hand principle."[24]

According to Bentham, "the proper end of education is no other than the proper end of life-well being, not only of the individual to be educated, but also of the parties at whose expense and by whose care he is to be educated-viz. the proposed company."[25]

With his proposal, Bentham tried to put forward a more effective alternative to the inefficient and filthy public workhouses made possible under the poor laws. He also wanted to contribute substantially to the relief of extreme poverty in the country, caused by the famine of 1795.

As has been argued, Bentham was not the first reformist to propose workhouses for the poor. Elizabethan poor law also made it possible in the public sphere. The first local experiment started in Bristol in 1723 and, by 1830, there were more than 4,000 workhouses in Britain. Abroad, too, comparable initiatives were undertaken. Well known is Count Rumford's pauper colony, called 'House of Industry', in Munich. In this case, however, the two functions of working and living were not integrated but separated. Nevertheless, Count Rumford influenced both Bentham and Owen. Owen even referred to Count Rumford in his 'A New View of Society'.[26]

Ultimately, Bentham's National Charity Company never became a reality. Nevertheless, as an expression of Benthamite utopianism based on his rather totalitarian idea of a good society in which paupers were deprived of basic human rights by permanent control and observation, it offers, like the

22 *Ibid.:* 1985: 79.
23 Bahmueller 1981:4.
24 *Ibid.:* 164.
25 Himmelfarb 1986: 132.
26 Owen 1991.

ideas and experiments of Robert Owen, a useful expression of eighteenth-century reformist social engineering. Elements of this would return in the concept of later capitalist paternalistic workingman's paradises in Europe and America. Moreover, as Himmelfarb argues,

> if Bentham was, as is so often said, the father of the New Poor Law, it was neither because of his ideas of poverty and pauperism nor because of his proposal of reform, but because of a rationalistic temper that encouraged a radical break with the past, with traditional ways of thinking about poverty and traditional ways of dealing with the poor.[27]

2.4 French utopian socialism: François Marie Charles Fourier (1772-1837)

As one of the main representatives of French utopian socialism – alongside Proudhon, Saint-Simon, and Cabet – Fourier can be considered as having developed ideas about integrated living and working units, and model cities in which the functions of living and working were integrated. To some extent, Fourier's ideas are similar to the ideas of Owen. Both, for example, lauded the importance of social harmony and the importance of idyllic, mainly agrarian self-sufficient communities. These communities needed to be federalized in a larger societal framework. Both men wanted more than simply to improve the living conditions of the working poor, they also recognized the importance of the mental and moral leverage of these classes. Owen began his social experimentation as a factory owner in his cotton mill in New Lanark. Later, he expanded his social engineering to the community-building level in both Britain and the United States. Fourier, on the other hand, remained a social theoretician. He was unable to realize his ideas in his lifetime. However, he found a strong promulgator in the person of Victor Considérant (1808-1893), who fervently advocated his ideas in writing. Fourier's ideas also got a temporary footing in the United States by 1840. As had earlier been the case with Owenism, in America Fourierism was connected with communitarianism and frontier thinking. Considérant also played a significant role here, by trying to establish Fourierist colonies in Texas.

Born in Besançon in 1772 to a wealthy merchant family, Fourier later worked as a trade agent in Lyon and Paris. He spent almost 40 years of his

27 Himmelfarb 1985: 85.

life, until he died, improving his very detailed system for a perfect society.[28] Fourier published three works in which he explained his principles.[29]

The core of his thinking encompasses a future harmonious world society (world 'phalange', or 'omnarchia'), composed of a great number (2,985,984) of separate small communities ('phalanges' or 'phalanstères').[30]

Each phalanstère consisted of about 1,500-2,000 persons and had to operate primarily as a cooperative agrarian and industrial production and consumption unit. A phalanstère had to be constructed as a sort of baroque castle and furnished with, for example, a dinner room, a study room, a library, an observatory, a meeting room, a ballroom, and a temple. Living quarters varied from one- to four-room houses located in the four storeys that made up the main building. At the back of the phalanstère was a winter garden, designed with permanent green plants. Work itself was carried out in separate but adjacent manufacturing buildings and farmhouses. Work should be inspiring and therefore remain limited to two hours per day. At the same time, a regular change of jobs was part of keeping the workers motivated. Living conditions should be agreeable and resemble living in hotels. All members of the cooperative would receive a wage, dependent on their skills, the utility of their work as well as other factors. At the same time, all members could partake in the capital of the cooperative. Ultimately, each phalange had to guarantee a balance between the interests of the individual and the interests of the collective.[31]

Fourier also designed an ideal model city, the so-called *ville garantiste*. This city consists of three concentric rings. The first (inner) ring was the city centre, which contains a central place or garden. The second (middle) ring consists of the factories. Finally, the third (outer) ring is composed of the suburbs and large avenues. Streets are about eighteen metres wide and are either straight or curved. Contrary to Owen, Fourier's city planning concept rejected the quadrangle or "the monotony of a chessboard."[32]

28 Kolakowski 1980: 227.

29 Théorie des quatres mouvements et des destinées générales (1808); Traité de l'association domestique-agricole (1822); Le nouveau monde industriel et sociétaire (1829).

30 The 'phalange' is the organizational form of the production unit, whereas the 'phalanstère' entails the spatial expression of the phalange (Von Beyme 2012: 74).

31 Bloch 1973: 652; Seng & Saage 2012, in: *L'Architecture Engagée:* 21-22.

32 Bollerey 1977: 102.

2.5 Quakers in England, America, and social reform

The famous German sociologist Max Weber was one of the first scientists who underlined the importance of purist Protestantism for the 'spirit of capitalism'. In his book *Die protestantische Ethik und der Geist des Kapitalismus* (1904 and 1905) he argued that Calvinism, and more specifically its English purist expression, can be considered as the 'father of capitalism' and, subsequently, strongly supported the capitalist spirit of entrepreneurship. Consequently, Quakerism became the tutor of the English middle classes[33, 34, 35].

An essential element of puritanism was the creation of God's Kingdom on earth and the so-called 'Second Coming' of Jesus Christ was predicted in a foreseeable future. At the same time, it implied the possibility of a purer and more stringent form of social morality.[36] Richard Tawney characterizes this as the purist ethic of economic virtues, which expressed itself in tolerance vis-à-vis others and the obligation to support others in need.[37] In its initial form Quakerism was fervently sectarian. One of the first English Quakers, James Nailer, marched on Bristol with a number of 'Children of the Light' or 'Friends of the Truth' in 1656 and re-enacted Christ's triumphal entry into Jerusalem. Nailer wanted to establish the 'New Jerusalem' in England and to remake it in a Godly state.[38] Because of its sectarian nature and deviant doctrine of salvation, Quakers were persecuted and even tortured in the first phase of Quakerism, roughly between 1647 and 1666. Eventually, the doctrine was mitigated by exchanging the Second Coming via a material 'external' coming for a spiritual and illuminating 'internal' coming (known as the 'doctrine of the inner light'). As a consequence, Quakers increasingly became seen as reliable tradesmen in English cities. Their significance also increased in the textile and iron industry. By 1660, London had developed into one of the most important Quaker cities outside of its native ground, the northeast of England. The richest traders of the capital city, such as the Barclays, belonged to the Quakers. Other well-known and, at that time, successful Quaker entrepreneurs were Wedgewood, K shoes, Clarks, Rowntree,

33 Quaker literally means 'trembler'.

34 Tawney 1979: 172.

35 Calvinism in England developed a threefold offspring from the end of the sixteenth century onwards. These were Presbyterianism, Congressionalism and Puritanism. See Tawney 1979, p. 161-162.

36 Claeys 2002: 23.

37 Tawney 1979: 188, 216.

38 MacCulloch 2003: 526-527.

Fry, and Reckitts. From the outset, Quakers organized themselves in the so-called 'Society of Friends'. They rejected the clergy, believing that the Holy Spirit, not the scriptures, is the first and principal leader.[39] They also oppose violence and war.

Quoting Montesqieu, Max Weber argued that, compared to other nations, English entrepreneurs, and in particular Quakers, have achieved the most with respect to pietism, trade, and liberty.[40]

In essence, the Quaker social conscience consists of various elements. These are:

> [A] dislike of exploitation and profit of one man at the expense of another; a traditionally purist view of the stewardship of talents; stressing the value of hard work, lack of waste, the careful organization of resources, and a personal renunciation, all for the service of others; a tradition of egalitarianism and democratic relationships; and an abhorrence of conflict between men.[41]

American Quakerism began in the wake of the religious upheavals of the 1640s and 1650s in Britain. The first English Quakers arrived in America by 1660 and later settled with Quaker immigrant groups in New England, Pennsylvania, and Virginia. As in England, the initial phase of American immigration was characterized by persecutions and purges. Massachusetts, for example, passed harsh anti-Quaker legislation in 1658 with the intention of expelling Quakers. But also in America, Quakers became accepted in due time and developed into admirable members of their communities. The 'Toleration Act' of 1689 legitimized their presence. This also contributed to their prosperity in the commercial area.[42] One of the Founding Fathers of the United States, the English-American Thomas Paine (1737-1809), had a Quaker background. His famous 'Rights of Man' (1791) contains many Quaker ideas.

After the emigration of English Quakers to America, an intensive transatlantic connection remained between the seventeenth and the

39 Jorns & Brown 2003: 27.
40 Weber 2012.
41 Child 1964, 294.
42 Ryan 2009: 42-50.

mid-nineteenth centuries, linked by families and trade. Together, they also constituted a single Society of Friends.[43]

In sum, from the eighteenth century onwards, Quakers were not only in the vanguard of the Industrial Revolution, but also supported social reform. They were against slavery, propagated feminism, peace, and social reforms in education, prisons, and mental health. Like Owen and Fourier, they also dealt with the leverage of the poor living conditions of the lower classes.[44] At the same time, they questioned established authority.[45]

2.6 Conclusion

In this chapter, I engaged with the secular and purist origins of enlightened capitalism. Although the basic principles of secular and purist principles differ fundamentally, there is substantial overlap with thinking about social justice and the practical ways of achieving this. Therefore, the conclusion is justified that, in terms of idealistic motives, later capitalist workingman's paradises and corporate welfare work were strongly influenced by either secular or purist ideas on social justice.

One of the first and most important enlightened capitalist entrepreneurs in this respect was the cotton mills owner Robert Owen of New Lanark in Scotland. He not only provided dwellings for his workers, but also developed a strong paternalistic entrepreneurial social policy. This encompassed, for example, a sickness fund, educational provisions, and a gradual reduction of working hours over time of pauper children employed in his mills. On the other hand, he maintained a strong workers discipline and introduced incentives to increase production. In the living quarters, there was an emphasis on stimulating and maintaining hygienic conditions, as well as preventing drunkenness.

In time, Owen lost his interest in New Lanark and elaborated his ideas into a theory of social transformation and a related practice of social engineering at the community level. After 1824, he and his followers executed various social experiments in America and Britain.

Although Owen can be considered a secular social reformer, he borrowed a substantial part of his ideas from his Quaker friends. Utilitarian contemporaries, such as James Mill and Jeremy Bentham, also influenced him.

43 Burk 2007: 331-332.

44 Ryan 2009: 63; Jorns & Brown 2003: 56-66.

45 MacCulloch 2003: 526.

At the time of his ownership of New Lanark he was interested in more than just improving the output of the mills. Another strong drive was contributing to the physical and mental leverage of the poor. In this respect, Owen was no different from other contemporary reformers discussed in this chapter. Bentham also strived for a leverage of the living and working conditions of the poor in England and Wales, but the way in which he wanted to achieve this differed radically from Owen's ideas. Bentham's National Charity Company was, primarily, a national network of workhouses for paupers based on the same idea as his panopticon prison. That implied tight control of the paupers, as well as permanent observation from a central spatial point. In the end, Bentham's workhouse had more in common with Ledoux's La Saline Royale than with Owen's paternalistic entrepreneurial convictions and ideas of community living. On the other hand, in all three cases the workers or paupers had to earn their own living.

Separate from Owen and the English and Scottish Enlightenment ideas, Fourier developed his social utopia either in the form of a model city (*ville garantiste*) or in the form of a phalanstère. The architecture of the model city and the phalanstère was completely different from the mills in New Lanark and Bentham's workhouse, but had some similarity with Owen's design for the New Harmony colony. At the same time, Fourier and Owen had comparable ideas about provisions for workers, such as agreeable working conditions and working times, education, and relaxation. At one point, Fourier was even more radical than Owen. In his utopia, the workers themselves owned the phalanstère. Both men ultimately strived for a better world in which the negative consequences of the industrializing world were kept at bay and the significance of a sustainable agricultural idyll was stressed.

Finally, Quakers became fervent purist social reformers, mainly because of their doctrine, but also as a consequence of their temporary persecution by the established religious order in Britain and America. They pre-eminently embodied the spirit of capitalism as described by sociologist Max Weber. From the outset they were not only involved in the reform of the English poor law, but also in the social experiments of Richard Owen. A number of years later, an English Quaker architect, Ebenezer Howard, would design the ideal garden city. Another interesting illustration of the social impact of Quaker ideas is Voltaire's curious remark in his *Lettres Philosophiques* (1732). In this book, he said of Quaker life that it formed a new social, religious, and political alternative to traditional modes of authority and belief. According to Voltaire, (American) Quakerism is recommendable because it is a model for a sustainable and virtuous community. In 1754, he went even further by stating that "if the sea did not make me insupportably sick, it is among the Quakers of Pennsylvania that I would finish the remainder of my life."[46]

46 Ryan 2009: 87.

3 Victorian England

From Coketown to Port Sunlight, Bournville and the Garden City Movement

3.1 Introduction

This chapter mainly covers the long Victorian era in the UK, which started with the enthronement of Queen Victoria in 1837 and lasted until her death in 1901. In total, she reigned for more than 63 years. The focus will be on mid- and late Victorian England. This period was preceded by the early Victorian age partly dealt with in the previous chapter. Perhaps the most conspicuous heritage from the early Victorian age was utilitarianism and its most important expression the Benthamite panopticon and Bentham's proposal for a National Charity Company that had to solve the national pauper problem.

By the end of the early Victorian age, about 1845, Manchester, in particular, had become the most important English 'model' factory town. Hundreds of factory chimneys dominated the black-coated city and its skyline. 1845 was also the year in which Friedrich Engels published *The Condition of the Working Class in England*. In this book, Engels denounced the extremely bad living and working conditions of Manchester and the English working class in cities like London, Glasgow, Edinburgh, Birmingham, and Liverpool. In his eyes, workers were reduced to simple 'factory-hands' belonging to a proletariat.

As a centre of the English cotton and wool industry, by the mid-nineteenth century, Manchester had become the so-called Cottonpolis, also immortalized in Charles Dickens's novel *Hard Times* as 'Coketown'. Manchester was an important modern English vanguard city of that time and can be considered as Bentham's Utopia materialized. The utilitarian cash nexus was predominant. Time was money. Everything was measured. Employers showed minimal care for their workers and also the civic architecture of the town was strictly utilitarian.[1]

After a brief section on the Industrial Revolution in England (3.2), I will pay further attention in this chapter to Manchester as a Benthamite factory town and its development towards a more civic Victorian city (3.3). 'Cottonpolis' also provoked a romantic counter reaction in the form of

1 Hunt 2010, chapter 2 Carlyle and Coketown.

labour-utopias directed at changing the nature and circumstances of factory towns in several distinct ways. Most important in this respect is William Morris's mediaevalist-oriented utopia, as described in his well-known novel 'News from Nowhere'. The American writer Edward Bellamy, in his novel *Looking Backward,* designed an opposite to Morris collectivist and industrialized utopia. Bellamy's novel dealt with a fictive twentieth-century Boston. Finally, English Quaker Ebenezer Howard tried to bridge both opposing ends by developing a synthesis between the rural countryside and industrialized towns. He propagated the development of garden cities. This will be the subject of section 3.4. Then, in section 3.5, attention will move towards some of the important English worker paradises of the late Victorian- and early Edwardian age. These are the workingman's garden village Port Sunlight of the Lever brothers near Liverpool, the workingman's garden village Bournville of the Cadbury chocolate factory near Birmingham, and finally some other comparable initiatives, such those of the Fry and Rowntree chocolate factories.

3.2 The Industrial Revolution in England

It is a well-known fact that England gave birth to the first industrial revolution in about 1750. From there it spread to other parts of Europe and the United States. After the development of crucial cost-saving, communication-facilitating infrastructure as well as new technological inventions, agricultural work and local artisan work transformed rapidly into industrial production. Most important in this respect were coal, iron, the steam engine, railways, canals, the steamer, shipping ports, and the telegraph.[2] The Industrial Revolution gave way to a revolutionary increase in productivity and income per head, and moreover generated a strong demand for labour. Initially, factory and mill owners under the new factory system also had to personally take care of their employees and could not fall back on the support of professional managers. In this context, factory owners established a large number of factory villages and factory towns in this period. Economic historian Sidney Pollard has given a noteworthy and detailed overview of the English factory villages during the Industrial Revolution in England. It appeared that, at that time, a commonly accepted social doctrine among employers was still lacking: "Rather, any

2 Briggs 1994; Hobsbawn 1996; Hobsbawn & Wrigley 1999; Landes 1999.

social policies adopted were the results of being driven from expedient to expedient, and from crisis to crisis."

For the most part, the employers believed in utilitarian values. 'Laissez-faire' and the cash nexus were predominant. Workers were considered as 'hands without brains'. This would only change after the implementation of the Factory Acts and other legislation in the early 1830s.

'Enlightened' or liberal employers at the time of the Industrial Revolution had various motives for establishing factory villages. Firstly, it was a way to attract sufficient 'hands'. Secondly, by housing factory workers and their families, both the employer and the 'master of the factory town' could control the labour force and prevent them from striking or rioting; for example, against the introduction of new labour-saving machinery, such as cotton frames, gig mills, and power looms. Thirdly, a factory village or town also provided the employer with an opportunity to prevent or discourage bad behaviour, not only in the factory but also at home after working hours. A final, but important motive was profit. But it is striking, according to Pollard, that this went hand in hand with "attempts to provide continuous employment."

If we look at the welfare work provisions these employers offered their employees, we can conclude that these already had much in common with what will be described hereafter with respect to capitalist workingman's paradises. This implied a variety of the following provisions: the building of cottages that workers could rent for free or against low rents; schools; Sunday schools (also used to teach middle-class morals and obedience); chapels and churches for the same reasons; truck shops; playgrounds; musical lessons and instruments; libraries; cooking and washing facilities; and cafeterias.[3]

3.3 Cottonpolis, Coketown, Manchester

Between 1842 and 1854 several books and reports were published about the then abominable living and working conditions of the working poor in England and, specifically, in factory towns like Manchester.

By 1831, Manchester had 142,000 inhabitants. However, still a relatively small city by current standards, Manchester was considered special because of its size, its industry, its newness, its squalor and, according to the authoritative British social historian Asa Briggs, above all its "unfamiliar

3 Pollard 1964: 513-531. See also Pollard 1968.

and, on occasion, alarming social relationships."[4] This was a city prone to social troubles. In August 1819, the 'Peterloo massacre' took place with more than ten people killed and hundreds injured; and again, in August 1829, social disturbances broke out, making Manchester the capital of discontent.

In 1842, former assistant to Jeremy Bentham, Sir Edwin Chadwick, presented, at his own expense, a *Report on the Sanitary Condition of the Labouring Population of Great Britain* to the House of Lords. The report gave a factual account of the inhumane sanitary living conditions in the fast industrializing British Victorian cities. Frequently there were no paved streets, no drains, no sewers and human and animal excrement and rubbish piled on the streets. As a result, epidemics and high mortality rates were almost a natural phenomenon.[5] In Chadwick's report Manchester statistics were compared with those of Rutland. It turned out that in all discernible professional groups (professional persons, tradesmen, mechanics, labourers and their families) the average age of death in Manchester was significantly lower than the average age of death in Rutland.[6]

Subsequently, in 1845, Friedrich Engels published his book *The Condition of the Working Class in England* in Germany. Although Engels paid attention to other Victorian cities, including London, his description of Manchester is the most vivid. Manchester was the worst industrial Victorian town. The 'shock city of the age'.[7] Together with his female partner of Irish working-class descent, Mary Burns, he systematically visited the poor working-class districts of the city, including 'little Ireland', the over-populated district where the Irish immigrants lived. Engels actually lived twice in Manchester (first between 1842-1844), where his father owned a textile factory. His description of the living conditions of the poor in Manchester and in other British cities, including the capital, is generally in line with Chadwick's observations. Indeed, Engels based his book partly on Chadwick's report. In addition, he had also observed the working conditions for himself.

Engels, like Chadwick, addressed the then strongly emerging social question in England in descriptive empirical terms.

4 Briggs 1986: 89.

5 See also: chapter 26, Anthony S. Wohl, Unfit for Human Habitation; and chapter 27, George Rosen, Disease, Debility, and Death. In: Dyos, H.J. & Michael Wolff (1973), *The Victorian City*. London: Routledge & Kegan Paul, 603-667.

6 Professional persons in Manchester lived, on average, 38 years and in Rutlandshire 52 years. The figures for tradesmen were 20 and 40 years, respectively, and for mechanics and labourers 17 and 38 years, respectively. See: Briggs 1968: 101.

7 Briggs 1968: 88-138. See also Osterhammel 2010: 398-401.

In sum, *The Condition of the English Working Class* can also be read as a time document in the form of a social reportage. Analyzing *The Condition of the English Working Class*, American historian Gertrude Himmelfarb considers Engels's book "a fascinating historical document because it is a picture of the English working classes seen through the eyes of a German radical newly resident in England."[8] Engels himself saw his book as a "bill of indictment" against the English bourgeoisie, containing "descriptions, episodes and statistics culled from parliamentary reports, newspapers, books, and pamphlets, supplemented by Engels's own observations and judgements."

> The effect was a picture of desperate, hopelessly misery: workers dying of starvation or so malnourished and enfeebled as to be on the verge of death [...] Their moral state was no less appalling, as they drowned their sorrows in drink, vented their rage in crime and violence, and lost themselves in the only indulgence left to them, sexual licentiousness.[9]

Also in the memorable year 1845, Prime Minister Benjamin Disraeli published his novel *Sybil, or the Two Nations* in which he described the parallel existence of a poor and a wealthier England. Disraeli's book also referred to Manchester, which, apart from a poor working class, also had a new and increasingly wealthy urban aristocracy consisting of successful businessmen. Furthermore, Disraeli's novel Disraeli describes a rural factory with its own factory village and gardens. This description would inspire Sir Titus Salt to build the factory village Saltaire (1851).[10]

Finally, in 1848 and 1854, respectively, two famous English authors published critical novels about poor working people in Manchester. These were: Elisabeth Gaskell's *Mary Barton. A Tale of Manchester Life*, and Charles Dickens's *Hard Times*. Dickens articulated most conspicuously early industrious Manchester or a smaller equivalent city (most probably Preston in the North of England). Two of his principal characters, schoolmaster Thomas Gradgrind and affluent self-made mill owner Josiah Bounderby, imagined the utilitarian significance of measuring, calculating, and employing rational facts versus suppressive exploitation of poor working people. Dickens also employed the remarkable and well-known metaphors 'Coketown' and 'hands' in his book. However, as English historian Tristram Hunt argues,

8 Himmelfarb 1985: 270-287.

9 *Ibid.*: 275.

10 Albert 1999: 45.

the real architect of Coketown was not Dickens himself, but his friend and influential romanticist philosopher and historian Thomas Carlyle.[11] Carlyle defined the nineteenth century as the 'mechanical age', causing a bleak moral landscape in which despicable cities like 'Coketown' dominated. According to Carlyle, primarily responsible for this bleak moral landscape were the utilitarian ideas of Jeremy Bentham. In this setting, "Mammon, not God, governed industrial society."[12] The centre of Coketown's social life was the factory and its supreme aesthetic achievement was the self-made man in the person of mill-owner Bounderby.[13] It must be kept in mind that, strictly speaking, not all English industrial towns were Coketowns like Manchester and Preston. According Asa Briggs, there were, for example, remarkable differences between Manchester – a city of great capitalists – and Birmingham – a city with a large number of small employers. In its turn, harbour city Liverpool was more mercantile. There were also substantial differences between the smaller industrial towns, such as Oldham, Northampton, Barrow-in-Furness, and Middlesbrough.[14]

In the mid-Victorian age Manchester had an image of being "the city as the cradle of economic wealth and social disorder ". At the same time the city also had a newer, more positive image "as a cradle both of wealth and of new formative social values" Thus, it also expressed the scope of Disraeli's *Two Nations*.[15] The new industrial and administrative city elite fervently posited new, formative social values, partly inspired by romanticist writers such as Thomas Carlyle, John Ruskin, and William Morris. To some extent, this implied a rebirth of romanticist values detrimental to the utilitarian values of Coketown. In fact, the increasingly powerful 'new middle class' in Victorian cities like London, Birmingham, Manchester, Liverpool, and Glasgow gradually succeeded in overcoming the bad image of the utilitarian early Victorian cities. This occurred initially by means of a cultural revival of the Middle Ages, encompassing things like fashion, architecture, politics, literature, and religion, and subsequently by embracing the civic renaissance ideal embodied by the renaissance cities Venice and Florence. Ultimately, in the second half of the nineteenth century, Victorian cities strived to become a 'New Jerusalem'. The ideal of a 'New Jerusalem' expressed the superiority of

11 Dickens dedicated *Hard Times* to Carlyle.
12 Hunt 2010, chapter 2, Carlyle and Coketown.
13 Mumford 1922: 83-84.
14 Briggs 1994: 215.
15 Briggs 1968: 93-94.

the Victorian city with respect to benevolence and philanthropy, reflected in, among other things, its neo-Gothic architecture of town halls, museums, monuments, and trade exchanges.[16]

3.4 The role of labour utopias

Between 1875 and 1905, as a reaction on the economic, political, and social consequences of the Industrial Revolution, about 100 utopian fantasies had been published. At least two of these still attract substantial attention today. These are William Morris's anti-urban utopian fantasy *News from Nowhere* (1875) and its more or less opposite urban industrial utopian fantasy *Looking Backward* (1888) by Bostonian writer Edward Bellamy.[17] Even before that time many utopian fantasies were published but, with one notable exception, their main focus was on pointing out an idealistic static rural society. Well-known examples are Plato's *Republic* and Thomas More's *Utopia*. The exception concerns humanist scholar Johann Valentin Andreae. By 1619, Andreae published his utopian fantasy *Christianopolis*. Christianopolis is a "republic of workers, living in equality, desiring peace, and renouncing riches. The workshop and the worker set the lines upon which the community is developed."[18]

In this context, American sociologist Lewis Mumford made an interesting distinction between two kinds of utopias; that is, 'utopias-of-escape' and 'utopias-of-reconstruction'. Both types can be sub-divided into ideas and practices. Applying Mumford's distinction, Morris's utopian fantasy can be considered as a utopia-of-escape', whilst Bellamy's utopia is rather a utopia-of-reconstruction.[19]

Writer, architect, glassmaker, designer of furniture, wallpaper, and tapestry, William Morris embraced Carlyle's conservative ideas and, in his above-mentioned novel, reversed, in his eyes, despicable industrial Victorian England into a romanticist, albeit non-feudal mediaevalist England. He was also strongly influenced by the ideas of his friend the famous anti-industrial Victorian architect John Ruskin. A key event in Morris's futuristic novel is a civil war in the year 1952. That year turns out to be the factual turning

16 Described in a fascinating way by Hunt 2010.
17 Wheen 2005, in: Wells (1905), Introduction.
18 Mumford 1922: 32.
19 *Ibid.*: 2.

point between industrial England and its transformation towards a more idyllic England. In (fictitious) 1952, the Massacre of Trafalgar Square takes place in London. Morris was referencing 'Bloody Sunday' on 13 November 1886 in London. On this day, the authorities bloodily beat so-called black flag processions of unemployed people.[20] From '1952' onwards, egotism and utilitarianism were banned and replaced by socialism and work based on arts and crafts instead of machine driven work. To Morris, art was not an exclusive affair of social elites, but it should play a significant role in the resolution of the social question in Britain.[21]

Morris was anti-capitalist and against machines. To him machines were like 'hell' By contrast, he lauded craft. His utopian fantasy may be considered as a sort of campaign against mechanization. In Morris's view, mechanized work not only contributed to inhuman work and pauperization, but also to ugliness.[22]

In his utopia there was no room for profit, wages, and money. Capitalism and industrialism are abolished. Factories as such are destroyed. The only way of meaningful and worthy work is craftwork.[23] Morris himself summarizes his utopia as follows:

> This how we stand. England was once a country of clearings amongst the woods and wastes, with a few towns interspersed, which were fortresses for the feudal army, markets for the folk, gathering places for the craftsmen. It then became a country of huge and foul workshops and fouler gambling-dens, surrounded by an ill-kept, poverty stricken farm, pillaged by the masters of the workshops. It is now a garden, where nothing is wasted and nothing is spoilt, with the necessary dwellings, sheds, and workshops scattered up and down the country, all trim and neat and pretty.[24]

In sum, in this transformed England there is no longer a dividing line between country life and town life: "It is a place of communist freedom, where men, women and children are equal, beautiful and healthy; money, prisons, formal education and central government have been abolished, the countryside has been reclaimed from industrial squalor and pollution."[25]

20 MacCarthy 1994: 567-573.
21 Bollerey 2012: 109. In *L'Architecture Engagée*.
22 Bloch 1973: 716-718.
23 *Ibid.*
24 Morris 1891.
25 MacCarthy 1994: 585.

News from Nowhere was subsequently translated into various languages. It also became the bible of British socialists like postwar Prime Minister Clement Attlee and others who became responsible for creating the British postwar welfare state. Moreover, Morris's views led to a significant Morris movement and hundreds of craft communities and workshops between 1890 and 1910 in the United States, in particular in the Boston, New York, Philadelphia, Chicago, and California areas, mainly supported by purist protestants.[26] Abroad, many 'Werkbunds' adopted Morris's ideas as well as architects, such as the Belgian architect Henry van de Velde (1863-1957). Morris also inspired the German social democrats.[27]

Unlike Morris, who created an actual backward-in-time oriented countryside utopia, Edward Bellamy (1850-1898) formulated a future-oriented industrial city utopia in his novel *Looking Backward* (1887).[28] It is a novel about a person, the wealthy Mr Julius West, who fell into a long-lasting magnetic sleep in 1887 in a Bostonian mansion, and awoke in the same mansion not earlier than the year 2000. Meanwhile, the city had changed fundamentally from a traditional nineteenth-century American town into a collectively well-organized industrial city. In this case, the city can be considered as a kind of a corporate state, controlling not only industry and trade, but also social welfare.[29] Every citizen contributes to the 'good life' in the city by means of work or other efforts. There is no unemployment and no poverty; vices such as crime and greed are non-existent. Bellamy's Utopian fantasy is 'Fordist' by nature and although Boston in 2000 is a kind of a socialist society it is very similar to a modern twentieth century industrial town. Because of its structural attention to the well-being of its citizens it is also akin to a large fictive paternalistic company town. As in Morris's *News from Nowhere*, private property in Boston in 2000 is abolished, as well as money. Goods and vouchers reward labour. Social competition on behalf of the city is the most important civic drive. Spatially seen, Boston in 2000 was a city far removed from a rural Arcadia. On the contrary, it was an industrial, technologically highly developed city with large 'Hausmannesque' boulevards, parklands, and a civic architecture.[30]

As has been argued, English town planner Ebenezer Howard (1850-1928) tried to bridge and integrate the two opposite country and town perspectives

26 Ibid: 603-604.
27 Bollerey 2012: 116.
28 On Bellamy's thoughts and ideas, see Haber 2002, pp. 417-440.
29 Wheen 2005, in: Wells (1905), Introduction.
30 Bloch 1973: 715-716; Hunt 2009, chapter 10, Garden Cities and the Triumph of Utopia.

of Morris and Bellamy, respectively.[31] Howard, a Quaker, was born in London as the son of a shopkeeper. When he was 21 he went to America, first as a farmer to Nebraska and later as a court and newspaper reporter to Chicago. He became good friends with the famous American poets Walt Whitman and Ralph Waldo Emerson. In 1876 he returned to England.

In his book *Garden Cities of Tomorrow* (1902; 1st ed. 1898) he suggested combining the best aspects of two worlds. Apart from Morris and Bellamy, Howard was inspired by the ideas of the economist Henry George and his then famous book *Progress and Poverty* (1879) and also by utopian writer James Silk Buckingham and his book *National Evils and Practical Remedies* (1849) about model city 'Victoria'. But his American experiences in the garden city Chicago were also important. Henry George pleaded for nationalization of land ownership in order to be able to solve the poverty problem. James Buckingham's model city served as the basis for the development of Howard's Garden city. Additionally, one other important source of Howard was Benjamin Ward Richardson's *Hygeia, or a city of Health* (1876). Richardson, a then famous physician, propagated the construction of noiseless, clean, and durable cities of about 100,000 inhabitants with two large boulevards (north-south and east-west) and 20,000 houses.[32]

Generally, Howard was dissatisfied with the development of the English industrial cities in the second half of the nineteenth century. He particularly disliked London, earlier in nineteenth century stigmatized by Cobbet as 'the Great Wen.' The British capital had grown out of human proportion and with his ideas Howard hoped to reverse the, at that time, strong immigration trend to this city.

Briefly summarized, Howard discerned three different magnets representing country, town, and town-and-country, respectively. He regarded the combination of country life and town life as the perfect one. Subsequently, he constructed an illustrative circular diagram of the three magnets, which also made the main advantages and disadvantages of each magnet visible. The town-and-country magnet supposedly neutralized the disadvantages of the two other magnets, while simultaneously capitalizing their advantages: "The two magnets must be made one. As man and woman by their varied gifts and faculties supplement each other, so should town and country."

Howard's garden city has a circular plan and, idealistically, has no more than 30,000 inhabitants in the city itself and an additional 2,000 in the agricultural estate. In the central part there is a 'Crystal Palace', which

31 This section is mainly based on Howard 1902.

32 Bollerey 2012: 91; also, Ward 1876.

serves as a shopping centre, but additionally as a winter garden. The outer ring of the town consisted of factories, warehouses, dairies, markets, coal yards, timber yards, etc. The central city is connected by a number of smaller satellite cities and forms a network with a maximum of 250,000 inhabitants.

A 'Board of Management', consisting of a 'Central Council' and various executive 'Departments', governs the garden city. For example, the 'Social and Educational Department' is responsible for education, libraries, wash-houses, and recreation.

The garden city also possesses a number of 'pro-municipal' institutions, such as philanthropic and charitable institutions, banks, building societies, religious societies, and 'educational agencies of various kind'.

Finally, industrial life in the garden city should be organized in semi-municipal enterprises. These are neither fully private, nor fully public.

Buckingham, too, proposed combining country and town. In fact, Howard's model town is almost identical to that of Buckingham's except that Howard's was laid out in a circular fashion, while Buckingham's Victoria was laid out as a square. There was, however, one major difference in Howard's eyes:

> The inhabitants of Garden city enjoying the fullest rights of free association, and exhibiting the most varied forms of residual and co-operative work, and endeavour, the members of Buckingham's city being held together by the bonds of a rigid cast-iron organization, from which there could be no escape but by leaving the association, or by breaking it up into various sections.[33]

By the end of the nineteenth century, in 1899, the English Garden City Movement was founded and soon after also the first two garden cities were built in England, Letchworth (1904) and Welwyn Garden City (1919). In fact, it was enlightened philanthropic entrepreneurs, such as Cadbury, Lever and Rowntree, who first copied Howard's views. Moreover, George Cadbury, one of the two Cadbury brothers, also played a prominent role in this movement.[34]

33 Howard 1902.

34 Bollerey 2012: 124. Bollerey also cites the formal definition of garden cities as applied by the Garden City and Town Planning Association in 1919: "A Garden City is a town designed for healthy living and industry; of a size that makes possible a full measure of social life, but not larger; surrounded by a rural belt; the whole of the land being in public ownership or held in trust for the community". In this definition Howard's views are easily recognized.

All in all, it can be concluded that the three important utopias described here contributed significantly to transforming the early Victorian utilitarian Coketowns into more civilized mid- and late Victorian cities, both in a material and a moral way. It is also remarkable that Howard, in his synthesising of utopia, had some difficulties in accepting the consequences of industrialism. He related this mainly to the disadvantages of large-scale labour immigration into London. Also significant is the influence of Carlyle's views. Carlyle had not only had a strong influence on Dickens, but also on Morris. The common denominator among Carlyle, Dickens, Morris, and also Ruskin was their dislike or even hatred of mechanizsation and its consequences for human labour. However, unlike Morris, Carlyle did not want to return to the pre-industrial Middle Ages. To him, the solution of the labour problem and its related social question lay in the hands of the captains of industry. Therefore, according to German philosopher Ernst Bloch, Carlyle can be considered as the first person who propagated the possible benefits of industrial neo-feudalism.[35].

3.5 Industrial garden cities and welfare capitalism in Britain

The examples of the early English factory villages and Owen's New Lanark establish that preliminary forms of welfare capitalism already developed from the outset of the Industrial Revolution in England in the eighteenth century. However, its scale was rather limited; it was the exception rather than the rule. A majority of employers still imposed vicious conditions on their workers.[36]

After Owen's New Lanark, only the newly designed factory town Saltaire, near Bradford, constructed between 1851-1871 by textile mill owner and philanthropist Sir Titus Salt, can really be considered a significant and successful mid-Victorian example of welfare capitalism in Britain. There were, however, two less substantial initiatives in the 1840s and 1850s. The first one was Bessbrook in Ireland. Bessbrook encompassed linen mills, which employed 2,500 workers who were provided accommodation in a number of adjacent four-roomed cottages. The owners, Messrs' Richardson, also provided schools, churches, a meeting hall, and a library. The second

35 Bloch 1973: 718-720; also Carlyle 1843.
36 See also Pollard 1974: 513-531.

initiative was Bromborough in England, a small village built for the workers of Price's candle factory.[37]

Saltaire[38] in West Yorkshire outperformed these initiatives by far. All the houses in Saltaire had water, gas, sewerage and lavatories. Sir Titus Salt was a wealthy Victorian self-made entrepreneur and he ultimately employed 3,000 workers in Saltaire. On 21 September 1853, the *Manchester Guardian* cited Salt's ideas, which he would go on to achieve in the next 20 years:

> Wide streets, spacious squares, with gardens attached, ground for recreation, a large dining hall and kitchens, baths and wash-houses, a covered market, schools and a church; each combining every improvement that modern art and science have brought to light, are ordered to be proceeded with by the gentleman who has originated this undertaking.[39]

Salt also completed a Congregational church in Saltaire (1859) as well as a Wesleyan Chapel, factory schools, a hospital, a community centre and a park. Ultimately, Saltaire consisted of 800 houses inhabited by 3,000 people.

From the end of the nineteenth century until the beginning of the twentieth century welfare capitalism got a broader and more intensive momentum in Britain. The most topical examples in this respect are William Hesketh Lever's garden village Port Sunlight and Cadbury's garden village Bournville. Subsequently, particularly Bournville and/or its welfare capitalism were more or less copied in New Earswick by Joseph Rowntree in Yorkshire as well as by Fry in Bristol and by Reckitt for his Hull Garden Suburb. Other notable examples of industrial garden villages are Foyers Estate at the head of Loch Ness, Woodlands Colliery Village near Doncaster, Brodsworth Main Colliery Co., and the new waterworks of the Birmingham Corporation.[40]

After the turn of the century, the creation of industrial garden villages in Britain became supplanted by the creation of non-company related garden cities, such as Letchworth Garden City and Welwyn Garden City. Finally, nineteenth- century capitalism resulted in the spread of a new kind of suburb near old centres.[41]

37 Ashworth 1954: 126.

38 The factory operated from 1853 and started on the fiftieth birthday of the owner. Ashworth 1954: 126.

39 Ashworth 1954: 127.

40 Also Gaskell 1979: 437-458.

41 Cit. in Ashworth 1954: 146.

Port Sunlight

William Hesketh Lever (1851-1925), the co-founder of soap manufacturer Lever Brothers, constructed Port Sunlight, named after the well-known brand 'Sunlight Soap', on the river Mersey near Bebington in Cheshire as of 1889.[42] In the beginning, Port Sunlight entailed 52 acres and was extended later to 500 acres. It contained a model industrial colony,[43] the factory and a park. The semi-detached houses in the village, which increased from 28 houses in 1890 to 720 houses in 1909, had a picturesque Old English style with a garden in the front and at the back. In 1907, Port Sunlight had 3,000 inhabitants, whereas in total 3,000 workers worked in the factory at Port Sunlight, also coming from elsewhere.

Part of Lever's inspiration for his housing project came from the model village Agnetapark in Delft, realized by the Dutch entrepreneur Van Marken. Lever visited Delft several times. All the houses in Port Sunlight were different. Architect William Owen and some 30 other architects, like Lever's former classmate and personal friend Jonathan Simpson, designed them. Two houses, for example, resembled Shakespeare's birthplace in Stratford-upon-Avon. Other houses had a recognizable Tudor-style or had an Old Dutch or Flemish appearance. The streets were wide. The houses had two basic designs: the smaller 'kitchen type', with one large living room downstairs and two bedrooms upstairs, and the larger 'parlour type' with an extra bedroom. In the middle of the village a 'pastiche-medieval' gothic church, the Congregational 'Christ Church' (1902) was constructed. In addition, there were: dining halls supplying inexpensive meals; shops; two schools; a technical institute; a hospital; a post office; tennis courts; a bowling green; a football and a cricket field; a swimming pool; a gymnasium; a pub; an auditorium; a library; and a museum (the 'Lady Lever Art Gallery'). Every employee could opt for a dwelling in the colony. The rents, which were not particularly low, were deducted from wages.

Lever's philosophy was to bind his employees to the company and into one big 'Sunlight' family. To this end, all kinds of social clubs were also promoted. At one point there was a 'Port Sunlight Prize Band', a 'Horticultural Society', a 'Philharmonic Society', an 'Old English Choir', etc. In sum, Port Sunlight was

42 This section is mainly based on the following sources: Ashworth 1954: 118-146; Jeremy 1991; McQueen 2004; Oxford DNB 23 January 2013; Wilson 1970, Vol. 1: 142-158.

43 Ashworth argues that in 1908, twenty years after its foundation, in Port Sunlight only half of the families of the firm's employees could be housed. Ashworth 1954: 134.

> a strange little fiefdom that made its own rules, as self-contained and inward looking as any medieval city-state. Its borders were rigidly defined: the factory dominated the south, while the New Chester toll road sliced dead straight through the countryside; the London and North-West Railway line marked the western limits just as clearly.[44]

It is noteworthy that, because of the relatively better living conditions in Port Sunlight, the mortality rate was below national average: in 1909 nine in 1,000 in Port Sunlight and more than 20 in 1,000 in Liverpool across the river. Infant mortality in Port Sunlight was half that of Liverpool.[45]

Each working day started at 8.30 am. Female workers arrived ten minutes before the male workers and left half an hour earlier. Children worked from the age of thirteen, but had to spend part of their working time on free in-company education. William Lever had his own space in the 'General Office'. It was glass walled, so he could watch directly the hundreds of clerks and vice versa. Instead of the widespread twelve-hour working day, Port Sunlight's employees worked eight hours per day six days a week. The remuneration was rather generous and working conditions includedalso sick benefits and healthcare belonged to the working conditions. Pensions were introduced in 1905 and a collective profit sharing regulation, which was transformed in 1909 into a so-called 'co-partnership scheme'. This implied a dividend for al co-partners in years with profit. In 1912, there were 2,000 official co-partners company wide. In Lever's view, only the ideal worker could become a co-partner. His ideal worker was the worker who "didn't drink, didn't gamble, who also went to church and kept his garden tidy."

The factory also boasted a safety inspector, a company doctor, a voluntary ambulance corps and a fire brigade.

Over time, a growing proportion of the workers lived outside Port Sunlight. This weakened the sustainability of Port Sunlight's culture and institutions.

Apart from being a benefactor and a paternalistic employer, William Lever was also rather progressive in the context of his time.[46] He allowed unions in his enterprise and accepted collective agreements. Politically, he was a radical liberal and for a while, between 1906-1909, he also acted as a Member of Parliament. To some extent, his entrepreneurial social policy can be considered a precursor of the later British welfare state.

44 McQueen 2004: 72.

45 *Ibid.*: 73.

46 Jeremy describes him as "that most agile and ingenious of paternalists." Jeremy 1970: 59.

In sum, William Lever's reform policy was, largely, a combination of 'better housing' policy (Port Sunlight) and what he called 'prosperity sharing'. Prosperity sharing went one step further than profit sharing, in the sense that company profits had to be reinvested in the company to the benefit of all the workers in the collective.

After the death of his devoted wife Elisabeth in 1913, and after the Great War in which many of the 700 volunteering Sunlighters ('the Port Sunlight Pals') were killed, Lever Brothers entered more difficult waters. This was reinforced by the large unemployment situation and financial crisis in Britain directly after the war. Yet, in July 1914, the first congress of the 'International Garden Cities and Town Planning Association' took place at Port Sunlight. High inflation and souring markets for raw materials urged Lever Brothers to dismiss 3,000 employees at Port Sunlight between 1918-1923. As a consequence, they also forfeited their homes and other social privileges. In 1923 William Lever lost his absolute power in the company and henceforth had to share it with the former company accountant Francis D'Arcy Cooper. William Hesketh Lever died as the first Viscount Leverhulme in 1926. In 1930, the company merged with the Dutch margarine company Van den Bergh & Jurgens and the new multinational company Unilever was established.

With hindsight, William Lever can be considered an autocratic and moralistic benefactor. For example, in 1919, the Secretary of the Bolton Branch of the Engineers' Union wrote very critically: "No man of an independent turn of mind can breathe for long the atmosphere of Port Sunlight [...] The profit sharing system not only enslaves and degrades the workers, it tends to make them servile and sycophant, it lowers them to the level of machines tending machines."[47] Church life in the village also contributed to paternalistic moralism of the entrepreneur. Apart from the Congressionalist Church, three other religious organizations were encouraged at Port Sunlight that contributed to Lever's paternalist and moralist ideas. These were the Boy's Brigade, the Sunday school and a masonic lodge. He even appointed a minister as a social director of the company.[48]

The working and living conditions in Port Sunlight were rather revolutionary. There were only two strikes in the company before 1926; one in 1911 and another, bigger one, which lasted 23 days, in 1920. In the village, William Lever succeeded in creating a "strong sense of community, high standards of health and morality and good social relations." However, "the

47 Cit. in Wilson 1970: 150.

48 Jeremy 1991: 58-81.

Image 1 House at Port Sunlight, England, built for the workers

Photo by Stephen Cosh (original work, Creative Commons CC-BY), via Flickr

whole village was dominated by the spirit of soap", also because all the villagers worked in the factory.

Prosperity sharing and co-partnership were based on strong moral ideas. Not everyone could become a co-partner and co-partnership was not limited to the workers at the Port Sunlight site. 'To qualify as a co-partner, an employee of either sex had to be not less than twenty-five years old, and to have completed five years' service with the company. There were four classes of co-partners: "Director, Management, Salesmen, and Staff, and in each class the total issued certificates were not to exceed one quarter of the whole."'[49]

Bournville, 'the Factory in a Garden'[50]

Richard and George, sons of Cadbury's founder John Cadbury, erected the industrial garden village Bournville adjacent to their chocolate factory at

49 Wilson 1970: 153.

50 This section is mainly based on the following sources: Albert 1999, Ashworth 1954, Cadbury 2010, Bryson & Lowe 2002, Dellheim 1982, Rowlinson 1988, Rowlinson & Hassard 1993,

Bournbrook, near Birmingham, between 1895-1915. They were Quakers and, much more explicitly than in the case of William Hesketh Lever, their religion played an important role in the creation of both the garden village and the company's culture and social policy. Richard and George Cadbury shared the Quaker vision of social justice and reform: "a new world, in which the poor and needy would be lifted from the ruin of deprivation."[51]

The early death of Richard in 1899 meant that almost all the credit for the development of Bournville went to George Cadbury, who, for reasons of continuity established the 'Bournville Trust' (BVT) in 1900. Its aim was "the amelioration of the conditions of the working class and labouring population."

The Bournville Trust ultimately transformed the village into a site with more than 1,000 cottages. The 'Bournville Building Estate' (1895-1900) preceded the BVT. The Estate constructed sixteen semi-detached red brick cottages "with rough-cast and half-timbered walls, green slates and red tiles"[52] and with front and back gardens for the higher Cadbury staff and management. It was only after establishing the BVT that Bournville developed into a model garden village, adding a substantial number of more modest, low-rent houses for the factory workers and other interested lower-middle-class people.

George Cadbury was also one of the important co-founders of the British Garden City Movement in 1899. Its first conference was organized in September 1901 at Bournville and, certainly, Bournville can be considered an important example in the development of the garden city movement. Bryson & Lowe argue in this respect that the garden city movement in Britain has been a "complex movement" consisting of "three types of planned settlement: model villages, such as Port Sunlight; garden suburbs, such as Hampstead Garden Suburb and garden cities, such as Letchworth."[53]

The chocolate company Cadbury, in need of more space, relocated its factory in 1879 to a rural green site just outside Birmingham. In 1895, the company acquired 120 acres and Cadbury started developing the garden village Bournville next to the factory. In 1900, Cadbury owned 330 acres on which it built 300 cottages. Its three respective architects were George Gadd, Alfred Walker, and William Alexander Harvey. Harvey, in particular, was responsible for the typical Bourneville style, which resembled the architectural Arts-and-Crafts style of William Morris. Over time, they also

51 Cadbury 2010: 39.
52 Albert 1999: 47 (cit.).
53 Bryson & Low 1992: 37.

built churches (Quaker Meeting House in 1905, Church Hall in 1913, Anglican Church in 1925), a library, schools (elementary school in 1906, infants school 1909), and shops (1908).

The Bournville Trust operated as an independent institution taking over all financial responsibility for the further development of Bournville from Cadbury. Profits made by the Trust had to be reinvested in the garden village.

The cottages at Bournville were not built exclusively for Cadbury employees and their families; about half of the houses were occupied by working people employed in or near Birmingham. All of the houses had large gardens. Roads were tree lined. About ten percent of the area was intended for parks and recreational grounds.

Initially, George Cadbury personally financed Bournville. He also planned in detail the houses, roads, and parks of the village. His ideas on designing the village as well as on the social policy of his firm were strongly influenced by his Quaker background. This implied the 'pursuit of happiness' for all his workers by creating a sort of 'Society of Friends' or 'brotherhood' at the company level, initially also with collective daily prayers at the start of the working day. Labour was seen as more than a commodity. The Cadbury brothers felt personally responsible for the well-being and educational development of their workers and treated them, both men and women, as equally as possible. The working and living conditions contrasted significantly, in a positive sense, with neighbouring industrial Birmingham. As in the case of Port Sunlight, the Cadbury employees lived longer on average and were less prone to illnesses. Also, infant mortality was significantly lower in Bournville than in Birmingham.[54]

The business philosophy of the Cadbury firm was a combination of non-authoritarian entrepreneurial benevolence and efficiency. Commitment to so-called 'associated control' by means of realizing, firstly, cooperation and consensus was a cornerstone of its internal industrial relations. This did not take away from the fact that Cadbury, like some other large British enterprises in that period, experimented, at least to some extent, with 'scientific management' methods as developed by American engineer and Quaker Frederick Winslow Taylor. This gained weight in time with the advent of the next generation of Cadbury's, alongside George Sr. (d. 1922) after 1899. In particular, George's sons Edward and George Jr. played an important role in the process of making the firm more efficient.[55] The firm

54 Bournville Works Magazine 1919: 36 (cit. by Bryson and Lowe 1992: 42).

55 Cadbury 1912; Rowlinson 1988.

can be considered as an early adopter in Britain of a modified form of scientific management. The core of this was the introduction and dissemination within the company of a piece rate system, as well as the introduction of time-and-motion studies. Contrary to Taylor's scientific management, Cadbury's version remained in combination with welfare work measures. Other aspects of the more moderate form of Cadbury's scientific management were the acceptance of trade unions in the firm and a rejection of the differential bonus schemes and the related task idea. The problem with the latter was the risk of reinforcing the extent of monotonous work in the factory. One of the main measures to combat this was introducing shorter working hours as well as encouraging, in particular, younger workers to utilize educational provisions in the company.

Furthermore, the quality of the Cadbury products had always been an important element in the business philosophy, an aspect related to the Quaker ethic: "The goods Quakers produced or sold had to be fairly priced and socially useful,"[56]; or, in the words of a Cadbury salesman in 1912: "The mission of Cadbury is to provide high-quality products and good value to the consumer, and the advancement of the social, moral, and, physical well-being of all connected with Bournville."[57]

In addition to the, at that time, rather generous wages, the company introduced dining rooms for workers and, more importantly, various welfare schemes, such as a sickness benefit (1903), free medical- and dental care, a pension system in 1906 for male workers and in 1911 for female workers, as well as a system of profit sharing in the 1920s.[58] In 1919, the work week for men was reduced from 48 hours (since 1911) to 44 hours. Women had already been working 42.5 hours per week since 1911. The firm also offered various educational programmes, including commercial, technical, and physical training. Worker participation or industrial democracy was institutionalized by means of a suggestion box (1902), a 'Cardbox Shop Committee' (1910) discussing the changes of the payment system in the card box department, and a works council, functioning as an umbrella for group committees and shop committees (1918). The main purpose of worker participation was "to encourage and establish good relations between workers and management and to maintain a spirit of co-operation, and in this way to promote the welfare and prosperity of the Bournville community."[59]

56 Dellheim 1987: 16.
57 *Ibid.*: 26.
58 In the case of factory workers paid on basis of piecework. Dellheim 1987: 29.
59 Dellheim 1987 cit.: 38.

Finally, an important complementary welfare provision was the publishing of the 'Bournville Works Magazine' as of 1902. The magazine reflected the spirit of the company and, more in particular, of Bournville.

In sum, Cadbury was a harmonious model factory, without any significant labour disputes until 1926, when Cadbury workers joined the national General Strike. Apart from this, the only notable exception was the resistance of mainly skilled workers to piecework. Regarding this, Dellheim argues that the firm was not so much a paternalistic company, but a firm that primarily intentionally empowered its employees by "establishing works councils, supporting trade unions, and providing education". "Welfare work was a vital part of factory organization."[60]

As I have argued, the Cadbury culture and social policy were, at least up to the turn of the century, largely determined by religious (Quaker) origins than was the case with that of the Lever Brothers.[61] However, historians Rawlinson & Hassard put this into some perspective by contending that in its labour-management institutions Cadbury primarily responded to contemporary social movements rather than to Quaker inspiration. They discern five specific Cadbury labour-management institutions:

- The Bournville village. According to both authors, the development of Bournville was more influenced by the Garden City Movement, Ebenezer Howard's book *Garden Cities of To-morrow* (1902), and early town planning in Britain than by Quaker ideas.
- The welfare work of the company was motivated particularly by the removal of the company from Birmingham to Bournville as well as by increasing competition with other competitors in an expanding market.
- The rigid gender division in the firm, including the 'marriage bar' (not allowing married women to work in the company and dismissing pregnant women) was not a unique Cadbury policy at that time.
- The type of scientific management the company applied was not a direct Quaker policy.
- The establishment of a works council scheme also reflected the gender division of labour in the factory. There were separate councils for men and women.[62]

Bournville, then, was Cadbury's model garden village. Compared to Port Sunlight it was not a pure company village. Moreover, non-Cadbury

60 *Ibid.:* 42 & cit. 44.

61 See also in this respect Child 1964: 293-315.

62 Rowlinson & Hassard 1993: 313.

Image 2 The shops in Bournville, Birmingham, England

Photo by Gavin Warrins (original work, public domain) via Wikimedia Commons

employees were also allowed to live there. Nevertheless, the culture of living in the model village, on the one hand, and the factory culture and social policy on, the other hand, were firmly interwoven. Likewise, the 'human relations' oriented approach of the industrial relations in the firm was based on Quaker principles. In this respect, Cadbury was not the only Quaker firm in England. There was a rather large group of Quaker led firms. They were united from 1918 onwards in the 'Conference of Quaker Employers', which met four times until 1948, and thereafter in a new series of 'Conferences for Friends in Industry'. The Quaker employers formed a rather dense network of employers, including a number of personal friendships, for example between George Cadbury and Joseph Rowntree and between George Cadbury and the Frys. In 1918, the Fry chocolate works merged with Cadbury. The Quaker employers discussed industrial relations and worker participation in their firms. They also influenced the broader acceptance of their ideas in British managerial thought.[63]

63 Child 1964: 308; Child 1969.

Other Quaker industrial garden villages in England

One of the earliest examples of a Quaker garden village was the factory villages Nent Head and Middleton, created by the 'London Lead Company' in the first third of the nineteenth century. The company provided shelter and additional social services to almost 4,000 miners and the villages were amply provisioned with vegetable and flower gardens. A horticultural society stimulated gardening among the employees.[64]

A number of decades later, comparable initiatives to Bournville were undertaken by chocolate companies Fry in Bristol and Rowntree in York. Also, Reckitts household goods copied Bournville with its garden suburb, close to its four factories in east Hull, with nearly 500 houses for 3,300 workers.

Even though Fry had no free space available at its premises to construct a garden village like Cadbury's, the company introduced a strong welfare work programme for its employees, including rather generous wages. Fry also built libraries, schools, a community centre, playgrounds, a hostel, and organized dramatic societies. This resulted in the 'Fry Spirit', "built on centuries of Quaker values."[65]

Chocolate manufacturer Joseph Rowntree built the picturesque garden village New Earswick, which included different types of cottages and houses, schools, playgrounds, and a village hall. Architects Raymond Unwin and Barry Parker designed the houses. In almost all facets, New Earswick was a copy of Bournville. This implies, apart from the many amenities for the workers, open accessibility of the village to different types of external workers. Like Cadbury, Rowntree wanted to contribute to the amelioration of the bad housing conditions of industrial workers.

In 1904, Rowntree handed over the village to the 'Joseph Rowntree Village Trust' and, at the same moment, established two other trusts, the 'Joseph Rowntree Charitable Trust' and the 'Social Services Trust', aimed at investigating social and religious matters. He donated half of his wealth to the three trusts.[66]

In 1954, New Earswick had almost 500 three-bedroomed houses, and 90 cottages as well as flats with one or two bedrooms.[67] Welfare work was also well developed at Rowntree. There was a pension scheme, a works council,

64 Gaskell 1980: 482.
65 Cadbury 2010: 114.
66 *Ibid.*: 185-186.
67 Vernon 1958: 149.

a free Saturday (1919) and a week of paid holiday every year (1918). Finally, departments got a say in the appointment of their foreman.[68]

The Garden City Movement

The Garden City Movement was the institutional outcome of a long discussion in England about the ideal town. In the context of this discussion, backward-looking rural and forward-looking industrial utopias were formulated, like the model cities Victoria and Hygeia. There were also the practical experiences of Robert Owen with New Lanark, of Titus Salt with Saltaire, and some others philanthropic entrepreneurs. Ultimately, Ebenezer Howard's book, *Garden Cities of To-Morrow* played a significant synthesizing role. Howard influenced both enlightened entrepreneurs and city planners. At the same time, his book was a clear manifestation of the mid- and late Victorian values that followed on from early Victorian utilitarianism, such as the value of public spirit alongside to a laissez-faire approach and self-responsibility. In his book, Howard tried to bridge the contradiction between 'country' and 'town'. By doing this, Howard attempted to neutralize the darker side of living conditions for masses of workers, often Irish immigrants in industrial towns, and simultaneously to revive rural life. Like Edward Bellamy, he believed in cooperation between men and equality in the emancipatory benefits of technological advance.[69]

At the onset of the Garden City Movement, industrial garden villages were paramount, also because entrepreneurs felt responsible for contributing to the solution of the major housing problem in Victorian cities and towns. This changed after the turn of the century, when responsibility for living conditions and welfare work was factually decoupled. As a consequence, the existing industrial garden villages remained, but almost no new ones were built in England after 1900. Instead, the broader concept of a garden city steadily gained momentum and burgeoned. As a first result, the Garden City at Letchworth in Hertfordshire was established in 1904. Subsequently, from then on, at the firm level, welfare work without providing workman's housing became predominant in enlightened British companies.

Architects Raymond Unwin and Barry Parker, who designed New Earswick, also drew plans for Letchworth. Letchworth was to be a substantially larger version of Bournville or New Earswick and it was predicted that 30,000 inhabitants would live there. This garden city, however, was not

68 Ibid.: 187-188.
69 Albert 1999: 61

built adjacent to an existing factory; rather, it was planned that the factories would arrive later. The original plan of the city contained a central square, sites for a public hall, municipal buildings, places of worship, schools, hotels, a post office, open spaces, and parks. In conformity with Howard's ideas, surrounding rural and industrial belts were envisaged. The city cottages were very similar to those in New Earswick.[70]

Apart from the increasing popularity of the idea of a garden city, entrepreneurs had various other reasons not to invest in new industrial garden villages. Ashworth gives the example of the colliery villages in South Wales and elsewhere. The mining companies simply did not have enough money to invest in attractive but expensive industrial garden villages. Other companies preferred to settle in the midst of large towns because it was easier to keep " [...] contact with their customers, suppliers, and competitors. They gained access to a convenient reserve pool of labour; they obtained for a relatively low charge the advantage of such public services as existed and thus conserved their capital for direct use of their own businesses.'[71]

3.6 Conclusion

In this chapter, I have described the development of welfare capitalism in Britain from the onset of the industrial revolution until the first part of the twentieth century. The focus was on the long Victorian age between the 1830s and the turn of the new century. This period can be subdivided into three successive parts: the utilitarian period, the romanticist period, and a period that I characterize as the period of enlightened capitalism. In some sense, this last period is a synthesis of the two preceding sub-periods.

Employer initiatives with respect to welfare work originate as far back as the time of the Industrial Revolution, from about 1750. Apart the many notorious vicious manufacturers, there were also a number of employers who introduced welfare measures for their employees, including building houses for them. However, a concise social doctrine was still lacking. Utilitarianism was dominant. This was translated into a laissez-faire attitude, stressing self-responsibility, exerting worker control and administering the measurement of workers' output. In the middle of the nineteenth century, the fictive industrial city Coketown was a simulacrum of this attitude. On the other hand, financial profit was not the only motive of quite a

70 *Ibid.*: 66.
71 Ashworth 1954: 145-146.

large number of employers; indeed, for some, maintaining or safeguarding employment was a strong motive.

The abuses of the early Victorian age with respect to bad living and working conditions caused a romanticist counter reaction. In this context, Dickens, but also Engels, Morris, Ruskin, and, particularly, Carlyle played a decisive role. In this case, it was not the labouring class that protested against the advance of machinery, but the new English Victorian middle class. Some, like Morris, wanted a return to the idyllic and rural Middle Ages. Others, like Carlyle, wanted the captains of industry to take a leading role in solving the social problems. Finally, some, like Engels, propagated a social revolution.

In the last sub-period, various and sometimes even contradictory lines converged into the birth of the industrial garden villages of Port Sunlight, Bournville, New Earswick, and some others, as well as the birth of the broader idea of the garden city. The architecture of the worker garden villages, and also the architecture of Letchworth Garden City, was strongly inspired by the romanticist ideas of William Morris and the Arts-and-Crafts movement. The strong paternalistic, and sometimes autocratic, nature of the entrepreneurs involved conformed with the ideas of Carlyle. Even the adoption of the garden city concept was not accidental. It was part of a long English tradition of searching for the ideal town that combined the benefits of the countryside and the town. For that reason, the proposals put forward by Ebenezer Howard gained, after initial hesitation, rapid momentum in England shortly after the turn of the century. This caused a split in welfare capitalism in England. From then on, almost no new worker garden villages were built, but welfare capitalism continued inside companies as welfare work or personnel policies. To a large extent, from the outset, welfare capitalism in Britain was strongly influenced by Quaker principles. This was already the case with non-Quaker entrepreneur Robert Owen and, later, more distinctly with Quaker chocolate manufacturers Cadbury, Fry, and Rowntree.

In sum, English welfare capitalism in the Victorian age contained elements of both a utopia-of-escape and a utopia-of-reconstruction.

4 'The American Way'

Factory system, mass production, welfare capitalism, and company towns in the US

4.1 Introduction

In his novel *Riven Rock* (1999), American author T.C. Boyle refers several times to the enlightened capitalism of the former McCormick reaper factory in Chicago. Established in 1847 by Cyrus McCormick, this company (later International Harvester) introduced at an early stage various remarkable forms of welfare capitalism, such as worker participation. Particularly important in this respect were Cyrus's sons, Cyrus Jr. and Stanley. Boyle also refers to the fact that the McCormick's motives were both economic and idealistic.[1] Boyle is not the first American novelist to pay attention to welfare capitalism in fiction. John Dos Passos (1933) pointed in his *U.S.A.* trilogy towards welfare capitalism in American labour relations. He mentions the important, from a historical perspective, strike in 1894 at the Pullman Palace Car Company near Chicago. The strike broke out after a 28 per cent reduction of wages following the economic panic in 1893.[2]

Compared to the other countries in this book, the United States deviate significantly with respect to the number of company towns, usually owned by a single enterprise, as well as in terms of the size and nature of welfare capitalist initiatives.[3] More than 2,000 company towns were built over time and welfare capitalism expressed itself in manifold forms from about 1880 onwards.[4] This raises an interesting question about whether this development can be considered as an expression of "American exceptionalism" or "an America conceived as a historical whole."[5] Put into perspective, this is not the case, if compared, for example, with the German *Sonderweg* and other commonly used national characterizations. According to historian

1 Boyle, T.C. (1999). On welfare work of McCormick and International Harvester see also Marchand 1998.

2 Dos Passos (1966): 38-39.

3 Crawford cites the useful definition of company towns given in the Encyclopedia of Social Sciences: "a community inhabited chiefly by the employees of a single company or group of companies which also owns a substantial part of the real estate and houses." Crawford 1995: 1.

4 Green 2010; Brandes 1976.

5 Rodgers 2004: 22.

Daniel T. Rodgers, American exceptionalism is not a valid empirical concept in itself and appeals mostly to conservative forces in the United States. In his opinion, a more appropriate concept is the 'American way'. This concept mainly considers the United States as a closed, a-historic nation driven by a particular universal mission. The validity of the concept ultimately boils down to the important question, why has a viable form of socialism or Marxism, similar to socialism in European countries in the first half of the twentieth century, not developed in the United States?[6]

Comparative research shows that, from a historic viewpoint, there have been many parallel reform efforts on both continents, albeit with a different outcome. For example, as in many European countries, during the so-called 'Progressive Era', covering the period 1880-1920, there was also a substantial and influential group of social reformers in the United States. Many of them interacted and actively exchanged views with their European homologues. However, the most outstanding result of their efforts in the United States was not a European-style welfare state, but alternative paternalistic welfare work or welfare capitalism at the company level, combined with a mixed welfare state or interaction between private and public forms of social welfare. The main explanation for this is not primarily the existence of American exceptionalism, but significant differences in the set-up of political institutions and preparation of legislation in both the United States and European countries, as well as the timing of capitalist development. For example, from the onset of American capitalism, the influence of employer interests on decision-making in the American Congress has been remarkably stronger than in Europe. In this respect, the commerce clause in the American Constitution, guaranteeing full freedom of commerce and owner prerogative, played a key role. This also sustained anti-union practices in American industry. At the same time, it blocked a timely development of federal labour law and collective labour relations until Franklin Delano Roosevelt's New Deal in the 1930s.[7] Additionally, as important for the explanation of the vast quantity of company towns constructed in the United States between 1880 and 1920, was the ample availability of empty space and land mass, the rapid growth of the American population in the nineteenth century, as well as a rapid economic growth, based, to a large degree, on the immigration of foreign workers and, subsequently, internal migration of workers.

6 *Ibid.*

7 Rodgers 1998; Kloppenberg 1986.

Looking at the construction of company towns and welfare capitalism, American employers often combined various 'negative' and 'positive' motives to embrace this practice on a rather large scale. Taken together, the most important 'negative' motives were: retaining workers and limiting excessive labour turnover; avoiding labour conflicts; keeping trade unions out; and, from the 1920s, Americanizing the big waves of foreign immigrant workers to the United States. On the positive side, also idealistic or value-driven motives played a role, sometimes based on the religious background of the employer and his family. In a number of cases, additional aesthetic motives with respect to the design of factory buildings and company towns by renowned architects were also important, such as Albert Kahn in the case of Henry Ford's new Highland Park and River Rouge factory buildings (see 4.4). Likewise, improvement of work satisfaction remained an employer motive in a mechanized industrial world. One of its most outspoken protagonists was labour relations expert and Harvard President, Charles W. Elliott. Until his death in 1926, he not only pleaded against labour monotony and its negative consequences for joy in work (alienation), but also propagated industrial democracy, pensions, factory betterment, and profit sharing in order to make work more attractive to workers.[8]

4.2 Labour utopias in the US

'Socialist' or 'communistic' experimenting between 1820 and 1850 preceded the heyday of paternalistic capitalism in America. Subsequently, the 'Back-to-the Land movement in the 1920s and in the 1930s, at the time of the Great Depression, succeeded the golden age of capitalism.

The utopic experiments can be divided into Owenist or Fourierist experiments, on the one hand, and revivalist or purist experiments, on the other hand. The Back-to-the-Land movement was mainly directed at relocating unemployed workers and their families from industrialized city environments to rural settings.

Utopic experimentation considered America as the land of the new beginning of western society, with European immigrants at its heart. For the experimenters, the so-called 'pastoral ideal' defining 'the meaning of America', the ideal of self-proprietorship and the image of yeoman farming played an important role. To some extent, this was also the case for the Back-to-the-Land movement more than half a century later. At its core, the

8 Rodgers 1978: 233-242.

pastoral ideal implied that the New World was, from the outset, an unspoiled territory or "the dream of a retreat to an oasis of harmony."[9]

In sum, socialist or communistic experimentation in the nineteenth century encompassed about 100,000 'communards' in hundreds of experiments all across the US. Ultimately, most of these were unsuccessful. In chapter 2, I already pointed briefly to the failed Owenite settlements at New Harmony and Niskeyuna. Here, I would like to focus on the revivalist and secular experiments carried out by the Shakers and the Fourierists. I will also deal briefly with the Inspirationists and the socialist initiative in Llano del Rio, California.[10]

The Shakers, originating from England, formed an important purist and economically successful group.[11] Like other communistic groups, they considered the New World as a potential paradise. Their main centre was at Hancock, Massachusetts. They constructed there their model town with the purpose of neutralizing problems created by the Industrial Revolution in Europe and the, at that time, also industrializing American cities and towns.

The Shakers called their society, marked with a strong feminist accent and inspired by the Holy Bible, a 'living building'. Self-sufficiency, based on agriculture and industry, had to make this possible. Additionally, this system created an ideal balance between 'country' and 'city'. If compared, for example, to 'hellish' and unhealthy industrial Manchester, England, Hancock was their natural 'City of Peace'. The Shakers established a total of 25 villages in the United States.

At one point, the Hancock community possessed 3,500 acres of land, large barns, a garden house for drying and packing seeds and herbs, a dairy, a sawmill, shops, and small factories. The town as a whole, like other Shaker villages, was a close network of several families of believers consisting of 30-100 persons, living and working in mainly wooden buildings. In addition to their dwellings, each family had other buildings. For example, Hancock's Church, East, Second and West families had a meetinghouse, a schoolhouse,

9 Marx 1967.

10 Hayden 1976; Noyes 1870; Nordhoff 1875.

11 The next part of this section is mainly based on Hayden 1976. In this splendid work Dolores Hayden carefully describes various American utopias between 1790-1975 with respect to seven groups and seven sites. The seven groups are Shakers, Mormons, Fourierists, Perfectionists, Inspirationists, Union Colonists, and Llano Colonists. The seven sites are Hancock, Massachusetts; Nauvoo, Illinois; Phalanx, New Jersey; Oneida, New York; Amana, Iowa; Greeley, Colorado; and Llano del Rio, California. Four communities were religious and three non-religious. According to Hayden, these seven groups give a fair representation of the communitarian movement and its geographical spread in America between 1790 and 1938.

woollen mills, an iron mine, a clock- and a chair factory. Dwellings were aligned along the main road.

The Shakers saw God as the 'Great Architect', and considered themselves as 'master builders'. Architecture and design of landscape, buildings, furniture, and crafts were highly functional and, in hindsight, might also be considered as precursors of twentieth century 'New Objectivity' architecture and design (Bauhaus).

The Shaker villages in America formed a closed and disciplined system. They were also highly successful as agrarian communities until the outbreak of the Civil War.

There were also a substantial number (30-40) of Fourierist experiments in the United States between 1843 and 1858, mainly on the East Coast, where, at the time, unemployment and poverty resulting from the industrialization process were increasing significantly. Contrary to the Shakers, their inspiration was not religious but secular; but, as was the case with the Shakers, the Civil War caused the definite decline of Fourierism in America. Leading American Fourierist propagandists were Albert Brisbane, William H. Channing, and Horace Greeley. They belonged to the intellectual 'Brook Farm Circle' that propagated the social experiments.

The most important and also largest expression of Fourierism in the United States was the North American Phalanx, constructed in New Jersey on 673 acres with a number of farm buildings south of New York. Its 60 founders, among them a number of merchants, a shoe store owner, a hat maker and the owner of a small steamship line, considered the phalanx as a means for sustainable collective living by agriculture and industry. After completion, there were 100-120 people (families and single persons) living and working at the phalanx. Several new buildings were constructed between 1843 and 1856, such as the new phalanstery, a communal dwelling, a carpenter shop, and a mill.

Another significant initiative was the Wisconsin Phalanx founded by Warren Chase. Also remarkable is the short-lived initiative to found a phalanx in Texas by Frenchman Victor Considérant, the most important disciple of Fourier. After travelling through Texas in 1853, he purchased a piece of land near Dallas with the intention of developing a European-American agricultural Fourierist colony, to be called Réunion. The colony was founded in 1855, but had already dissolved, due to internal strife, by 1856.[12]

12 Also, Blokker 2012.

In short, the mostly limited Fourierist experiments in the United States each included some 24 to 500 persons and lasted from a few months to 18 years.[13] The intention of the experiments was to establish a sort of utopian socialist Eden in the United States, in order to be able to improve living and working conditions of the mostly poor communards and European immigrants in the case of Réunion.

Between 1843 and 1862 the Inspirationist or the 'True Inspiration Congregations of Amana', a group of former German immigrants, established 13 communities in the United States. Some of these survived until 1932. Their main establishment was Amana, Iowa, encompassing seven communities. All communities combined agriculture with complementary crafts and industrial activities, such as a blacksmith's shop, a cabinetmaker's shop or furniture factory, a bakery and other stores, a dairy, and, in Amana and Middle Amana, also woollen mills and spaces for dyeing cotton cloth. Compared to other utopic groups, the Inspirationists were remarkable builders in a quantitative sense. Apart from villages, they constructed churches, schools, kindergartens, kitchen houses, communal houses without kitchens, as well as single-family houses.

Llano del Rio, California 1914-1917, subsequently succeeded by Newllano, Louisiana (1917-1938), was not inspired by religious motives but, initially, by Ebenezer Howard's *Garden Cities of To-morrow,* Edward Bellamy's *Looking Backward* and William Morris's Arts and Crafts ideas (see chapter 3). Job Harriman took the initiative for the foundation of this 'Socialist City' after he was defeated as the Socialist Party and Labor Party candidate for mayor of Los Angeles. In practice, the community was led by architect Alice Constance Austin and based on the following four criteria: beauty; illustration of the solidarity of the community; illustration of equal opportunities for all; and employment of labour-saving devices. First, a model garden city was designed. Then, various buildings were constructed, such as single-family homes, a dormitory and hotel, and industries. In addition, a separate governmental structure, including a Board of Commissioners, a General Assembly and a Board of Directors, was created. By 1917, the community encompassed some 900 members as well as: a shoe shop; laundry; cannery; garage; machine shop; blacksmith shop; rug works; planing mill; paint shop; lime kiln; sawmill; dairy; cabinet shop; brickyard; flour mill; bakery; fish hatchery; barber shop; commissary; print shop; cleaning and dyeing plant; nursery; rabbitry; poultry yards; hog raising; vinegar works; drafting studios; and art studio. After moving to Louisiana, because of financial

13 Bollerey 1977: 140-141.

constraints, Newllano's members were urged to jettison their idealism. The town survived until 1938, reaching a maximum of 500 members in 1930.

To some extent comparable with the utopian communistic experiments is the so-called Back-to-the Land movement in the 1920s and 1930s. However, with some exceptions, it was not religious or socialist groups that took the initiative, but the federal government. A common theme in the US is the enduring pastoral ideal; that is to say, the idea of balancing city and country life more equally in an industrialized world. The Back-to-the-Land movement got its momentum in particular after The First World War and at the time of the Great Depression. Many demobilized soldiers had to be resettled. Private property or cooperative farming offered relief instead of, or was complementary to industrial re-employment. Something comparable occurred during the Great Depression. Resettlement of unemployed workers from cities and towns to rural regions solved the unemployment problem to a certain extent. It became an important part of the social New Deal policies of President F.D. Roosevelt. Based on former experiences, the 'Resettlement Administration' (in 1937 succeeded by the 'Farm Security Administration') was established. This administration had constructed 58 farm colonies by 1937 with 4,441 farmers, mainly in the South. Plans existed for resettlement of half a million persons. Usually, a colony consisted of a community of households and a number of functional cooperative associations running stores, warehouses, repair shops, mills, a healthcare centre, a community centre, and a local government.[14]

Two remarkable examples of cooperative communities were Penn-Craft, near Pittsburgh and Norvelt in the Southern Alleghenies, both in Pennsylvania.[15] The Society of Friends (Quakers) took the initiative for Penn-Craft (1937). It was a relatively small colony with initially no more than fifty houses and a small sweater factory. By contrast, substantially larger Norvelt (1935) was a government initiative. It survived as a farmers' colony until 1944. Its cooperative store shut down in 1950 and its small cooperative garment factory, with some 150 workers, was turned over to private hands.

4.3 The Industrial Revolution, the development of the factory system, and mass production in America

Compared to England, the United States remained an economically backward country until at least the mid-nineteenth century. The economy

14 Rodgers 1998: 318-366.
15 Hoagland & Mulrooney 1991.

remained predominantly agrarian. This was caused by the fact that the United States only reached political independence from imperial Britain at the end of the eighteenth century (1776). The American colonies were completely economically dependent on imports from, and exports to Britain of mainly agricultural goods. Both the War of Independence and the later war of 1812 with Britain triggered economic growth, primarily based on the construction and merchandise of weaponry, textiles, and other goods.[16] Later, in particular the development of rail transport, but also the Civil War, and the First World added significantly to a strong industrial economic growth in the United States.

After gaining independence from Britain, until the middle of the nineteenth century, there was a significant controversy between federalist and republican factions in the American Congress with respect to the most desirable character of the American economy. Republicans, like founding father Thomas Jefferson, supported the continued dominance of a pre-industrial agricultural country, whereas federalists, like Alexander Hamilton, promoted industrial development and centralized government. In 1791, Hamilton established the 'Society for Establishing Useful Manufacturers' (SUM), later renamed Paterson, New Jersey. Paterson was the first industrial factory town in the United States where, initially, cotton, paper, revolvers, silk, and subsequently steam-powered locomotives were produced. Until the second half of the twentieth century, Paterson was "a dynamic center of enterprise and innovation that brought together investors, inventors, engineers, merchants, and a large competent workforce."[17]

By 1815, the American economy was still based on relatively primitive agricultural methods, but there was also a strong undercurrent of innovation and ambition. This finally made possible a transition of rural America towards an industrializing and capitalist America between1815-1860. The main drivers of this development were a revolution in water and railroads transportation (steamboats, canals, and railroads), and a revolution of communication with the invention of electric telegraphy.[18] For example, in 1825, the important Erie Canal, connecting New York with the Great Lakes, was completed. In the 1850s, the total trackage of railroads in the whole country increased from 9,000-30,000 miles. Becoming the first big

16 Morris 2012.

17 Lind 2012, chapter 1.

18 Howe 2007, chapter 1. Also: Chandler 1977.

business in the United States, railroads "knit[ted] together a vast continent of island communities into a single national market."[19]

Thus, it was in this period that the first industrial revolution took off in America, particularly on the North Atlantic seaboard and in Chicago.[20] The steam engine was introduced on a wide scale as a source for powering mills. In addition, there was an almost endless supply of resources in the form of water, timber, coal, cotton, ores, etc. As a result, by the 1870s, the United States had become the biggest economic power in the world.

The first industrial revolution in the United States was succeeded by a second industrial revolution between 1870-1920. This second industrial revolution was based on electricity, the automobile and science-based chemical industries. In this context, from 1900 onwards, the steam engine was replaced by the electric motor. Subsequently, productivity increased significantly and large manufacturing enterprises and retail chains arose.[21]

In sum, since becoming independent from Britain, the United States developed from a mainly agricultural country in the eighteenth century into a powerful industrial country in the nineteenth century. The industrial revolution in its first phase was initiated by steam and rail, and in the second phase by the electric motor. Large companies only emerged from the end of the nineteenth century, mainly in the textile industry, railroads, metals, and machinery. Alongside big railroad companies, one of the first big industrial companies was also the McCormick reaper factory in Chicago. We can assume that by 1870, this company, with about 500 workers, was the largest in the United Sates.

At the same time, the organization of production evolved from small-scale manufacturing in the eighteenth century and early nineteenth century to the factory system – the so-called American System – in the nineteenth century, and eventually to Fordism or the system of mass production and mass consumption in the 1920s.[22]

With a focus on the period 1880-1930, important aspects of this evolution were the introduction of: the foreman; the drive system; professional engineers and managers; scientific management; Fordism; and welfare capitalism, respectively.

19 Berke 1994: 3.

20 Cronon 1991: 68. The southern economy remained largely dependent on the British economy by exporting cotton to the textile mills of the Midlands. See Argument in *The age of Steam*. Lind 2012.

21 Lind 2012. See also Chandler 1977.

22 The next section is based on Brody (1993), Chandler (1977), Hounshell (1985), Jacoby (2004), and Nelson (1985).

Until the First World War, the foreman played a dominant role in many companies. In a literal sense, company management was not present at the shop floor level; authority was delegated to the foreman. As a result, the foreman was the first person responsible for reaching productivity goals, as well as for production costs, quality of production, supervising workers, wages, and hiring and firing workers, mostly on the basis of an informal system of labour recruitment. In many cases, the foreman also operated as an intermediary contract regulator. As a worker incentive, the foreman frequently applied the coercive and arbitrary drive system. This system consisted of psychological pressures on workers, close supervision, as well as a number of financial incentives forcing workers to work harder. An example of a financial incentive is performance remuneration. At one point, production became lesser artisan and technologically more complicated; consequently, companies needed professionally trained engineers. These employees became the first professional managers on the shop floor and caused the gradual erosion of the dominant role of the foreman. This ultimately resulted in the American System. This is a set of manufacturing methods that made extensive use of interchangeable parts as well as of mechanization. Before spreading across the United States, the American System was first developed in the armouries industries at Springfield.

By the end of the nineteenth century, engineer Frederick W. Taylor developed what is called scientific management or 'Taylorism'. In subsequent decades, many companies introduced scientific management on a broad scale, often in combination with welfare work programmes.

Scientific management differed from earlier forms of shop floor management and work organization with its focus on time and motion studies, and rate setting. In this context, welfare work compensated for the possible demotivating consequences of scientific management by introducing, for example, profit sharing plans and other provisions to the benefit of the workers. A pioneering company in this respect was Heinz of Pittsburgh.

By 1920, the American System had evolved into a system of mass production and mass consumption ('Fordism') in which the organization of production and consumption for the first time were considered to be two sides of the same coin. The most illustrative example in this respect was the Ford Motor Company in Detroit. On the basis of his welfare work oriented reform programme, and alongside the introduction of a Sociological Department and the elimination of the former foreman's empire, Henry Ford introduced the assembly line in 1913-1914. This was followed by the introduction of the five-dollar day in order to keep employees, who now faced an incredibly intense workload. Eventually, this translated into a shorter workday, provided that productivity kept pace. The assembly line not only increased productivity in a revolutionary sense, but also lowered production costs significantly. As a result, car sale prices went down. The five-dollar day, a rather high wage at the time in comparison with the wage that workers earned in other companies, allowed Ford workers to buy Model T-Fords produced by themselves. Thus, the system of mass production and mass consumption was born. Fordism can be considered as an important building block of business and also of American welfare capitalism from 1913/1914 onwards, if the need to sustain high levels of production is taken into account.[23]

4.4 Welfare capitalism and model company towns

Introduction

As pointed out, a large number of worker colonies and company towns were constructed in the United States, compared to other countries.[24] With respect to welfare capitalism in a more narrow sense – that is, the introduction of progressive social worker policies without constructing a company town or worker garden city per se – it is impossible ignore the enormous significance of welfare capitalism introduced by Henry Ford in his company[25] and others, such as John D. Rockefeller Jr., Procter & Gamble, as well as large New England department stores, particularly Filene's founded by William Filene, and subsequently owned by his sons Edward and Lincoln Filene. Based on the distinction of 'old' versus 'new' company towns, which were designed by independent professionals, the chronological development of company towns – as well as the introduction of welfare capitalism without constructing a company town per se – I will pay more specific attention to the following model company towns: Lowell, Massachusetts; Pullman, Illinois; Vandergrift, Pennsylvania; Gary, Indiana; Fairfield, Alabama; Indian Hill, Massachusetts; Hershey, Pennsylvania; and the ill-fated Fordlandia, Brazil.

23 Also, Neye 2013.
24 See for example: Carlson 2003; Crawford 1995; Dinius & Vergara 2010; Garner 1992; Green 2009; Meakin 1905; Taylor 1970.
25 Brinkley 2004.

Historical development of welfare work

American welfare work prospered between 1880-1930, an era in which Americans witnessed the most incredible surge in business growth. Before 1880 there were companies that introduced one or more forms of welfare capitalism and although the economic crisis of the 1930s put an end to many welfare work initiatives it never completely vanished after that period.[26]

American welfare work can be defined as a momentous new management philosophy in a time of incredible stand-offs between workers and employers, in particular in the railroads, coal, and steel industries. At its core, it was strongly paternalistic and directed at overcoming what had become a war between classes. It was employers, rather than trade unions or workers themselves, that initiated welfare work. As has been pointed out, the reasons for introducing welfare work were based on a mixture of economic and idealistic motives, such as: preventing labour unrest; keeping the trade unions out; limiting excessive labour turnover; being more attractive as an employer for workers; making work less alienating; motivating workers; and taking part in the redistribution of material wealth created by the company. Until President F.D. Roosevelt's New Deal in the 1930s, several presidents, such as William McKinley, Theodore Roosevelt, William Taft, Woodrow Wilson, and Herbert Hoover as well as the federal government, had supported the introduction of corporate welfare work. Moreover, a number of well-known social reformers, such as philosopher John Dewey and management theorist Mary Parker Follett as well as various social reform movements, strongly encouraged welfare work.

Based on his 'science of participation', pragmatist John Dewey believed in the blessings of welfare capitalism with respect to industrial democracy as well as economic efficiency. This was equally the case with Mary Follett, but she also based her ideas on the 'new psychology' of industry.[27]

The 'League for Social Service' (later renamed in the 'American Institute of Social Service'), founded in 1898 and headed by protestant minister Josiah Strong and its 'Director of Social Betterment' William Howe Tolman, made it a point of principal to get welfare work introduced in industrial companies. This was also the case with the 'National Civic Federation' (NCF, 1901).[28] The NCF had its own 'Welfare Department', steered by former McCormick-International Harvester employee and renowned welfare work

26 Jacoby 1997.

27 *Ibid.*: 17-19.

28 Also Weinstein 1968: 3-39.

proponent Gertrude Beeks. The NCF also created a committee on welfare work. This committee organized national conferences and meetings on welfare capitalism and had a membership of more than 500 employers and government representatives. Previously, the Young Men's Christian Association (YMCA) had played a significant role, for example by setting up meeting points and work houses where workers could meet and relax after work time and attend bible classes. Also supporting the idea of welfare work was the social-Christian 'Social Gospel Movement'. Important proponents in this case were reformers Richard T. Ely, Jane Addams, and Graham Romeyn Taylor. Worth mentioning, finally, is the 'Taylor Society', which brought many of these individuals together in one reform-oriented institution. The Taylor Society propagated welfare capitalism and, more in particular, worker participation, as complementary to scientific management and industrial efficiency.[29]

By 1916, the government defined welfare work as: "anything for the comfort and improvement, intellectual and social, of the employees, over and above wages paid, which is not a necessity of the industry nor required by law."[30] Apart from workingman's housing, welfare work usually encompassed one or more of the following provisions: education; recreation; profit sharing; stock ownership plans; medical care; sickness payments; pensions; social work; grievance procedures; and worker participation.

Though the first welfare capitalist initiatives in the United States originate from the eighteenth century, the heyday of American welfare capitalism was concentrated in the period between 1915 and 1929, when a growing number of large companies started to introduce welfare work, to right former wrongs. Particularly in the 1920s, welfare capitalism was shored up by a new management philosophy, containing a mix of two, until then, rather seldom combined arguments; namely, the paternalistic-idealistic argument that cooperation between management and labour would benefit the well-being of workers, and the argument that the well-being of workers would also increase efficiency and production.[31]

29 *Ibid.*: 17. On the Taylor Society and 'the little band of taylorites' see also Haber 1964: 31-50.
30 Crawford 1995: 48; Brandes 1957: 5. Another (older) definition of welfare work was formulated by the NCF in 1904. Welfare work "involves special consideration for physical comfort wherever labor is performed; opportunities for recreation; educational advantages; and the providing of suitable sanitary homes [...] plans for saving ad lending money, and provisions for insurance and pensions." Nelson 1995: 99. The year 1916 is also incredibly important due to the release of the Commission on Industrial Relations (Walsh Commission). This concerned an eleven volumes report on the poor conditions facing workers in US industries.
31 Brody 1993: 50 and 52.

This happened after a time of nationwide antagonism between labour and capital, culminating in the bloody 'Ludlow massacre' in Colorado in 1913. However, the thirteen victims changed mine owner John D. Rockefeller Jr.'s attitude towards his workers in a positive way.

Generally, the strategy of a large part of the organized American employers was anti-unionist and from 1921 also formally based on the 'American Plan'. This plan contained a number of far-reaching measures, such as strikebreaking, policing and spying on workers, directed against access and organization of trade unions in their companies.

John D. Rockefeller Jr. was the first influential major entrepreneur to propagate the importance of harmony of interests between management and workers. His 'Colorado-' or 'Rockefeller Plan' (1915) underlined the importance of the collaboration of capital and workers at the company level. It contained some constitutional rights for workers in terms of representation and participation as well as welfare work measures with respect to wages, working hours, medical care, profit sharing, life insurance, housing, schools and recreation. Because of its broader impact on national industrial relations, the Rockefeller Plan can also be considered as the beginning of the human relations- or personnel management movement in the United States. From that moment, other companies, including Rockefeller's Jersey Standard, Procter & Gamble and Eastman Kodak, changed policies and institutionalized personnel departments in their companies and defined welfare plans as well. At the same time, the anti-trade union American Plan-movement gradually lost significance. As a result, by the end of the 1920s, welfare work plans covered more than 1.5 million American workers, compared to 600,000 in 1922.[32] Moreover, a larger number of workers, at the minimum four million, participated in one or more company welfare work practices.[33]

In America, welfare capitalism started in New England in the 1790s and subsequently spread across the country. Samuel Slater, cotton mill-owner, is generally seen as the pioneer having initiated a Sunday school and thus providing his young workforce an opportunity to learn one day a week. Slater was also involved in the Merrimack Manufacturing Company in Lowell, Massachusetts. After Paterson, Lowell was the first nineteenth-century company town in the United States. There, a school, a hospital, an Episcopal church, and boarding houses for the farm girls who worked in the

32 Bernstein 1960: 144-189.
33 Brandes 1976: 28.

mills were constructed. The Ludlow Manufacturing Company of Ludlow, Massachusetts went a step further by making "investments in the town's community services" and constructing "streets, a sewage system, water works, gas works, a church school and a masonic hall."[34] This example shows that welfare capitalism, in many cases, started in rural areas, where there was an abundance of space and water. In those cases it was usually a question of pure necessity for the employer to build a whole company town, not only to supply the necessary dwellings for workers, but also to supply a combination of non-existing basic public services and other provisions and facilities like schools, libraries, churches, and gardens.[35]

A subsequent development occurred in the railroad industry, so important to the US economy. By 1880-1881, manufacturer George M. Pullman designed the Pullman Palace Car Company near Chicago and adjacent to that the quasi-utopic company town of Pullman. For some time, Pullman would become one of the national and international showcases of American enlightened capitalism. It encompassed a new factory, employee housing, shops, a library, a theatre, a church, and a hotel. Also available were a company doctor, an accident insurance plan, a school system, a savings and loan association, an athletic club, a company band, and social clubs.

Manufacturer of plumbing fixtures, N.O. Nelson, imitated Pullman's initiative on a smaller scale by building 'Leclair' near Edwardsville, Illinois.[36]

Another significant example in this period was Heinz of Pittsburgh. As an urban employer in the 1890s, Heinz provided a recreation room, a relief association, annual outings, and acted as counsellor. In addition, exclusively for female workers Heinz provided dressing rooms, washroom, lockers, and a roof garden for lunch-hour strolls.[37]Before and briefly after the turn of the century other existing and newly organized companies undertook welfare work initiatives, like the Solvay Process Industry (including the construction of a clubhouse and an auditorium), the National Cash Register (NCR), soap maker Procter & Gamble, Standard Oil of New Jersey, United States Steel and International Harvester.

NCR (Dayton, Texas), and more in particular its president John H. Patterson, built a new and clean factory, lauded by a journalist as "a sermon in steel and glass," and "a temple of work."[38] By 1900, NCR had introduced a

34 *Ibid.*: 11.
35 Nelson 1995: 91.
36 Garner 1971: 219-227.
37 Nelson 1995: 100.
38 Marchand 1998.

lavish welfare programme encompassing: suggestion boxes; prizes for the most efficient departments; health and sanitary measures; a relief association; medical services; baths for the employees; a dining area; free cooking lessons; an eight-hour working day for women; a library; a kindergarten; a reading room; organized gardening programmes; Sunday schools; choral societies; musical groups, etc. NCR also built the 'NCR house' (a clubhouse and model worker's home) and a model town. Finally, the corporation possessed a personnel department, the first modern one in the United States.[39] A pamphlet entitled *The Human Side of Industry* defined welfare work at NCR as "the heart of this business."[40]

Also good at welfare work were hotels and large department stores. An important reason for this was their great public visibility.[41] Mass retailers like Macy's in New York, Filene's in Boston, Marshall Field's in Chicago, and Wanamaker's in Philadelphia and New York probably introduced the earliest and most elaborate welfare work programmes in the United States, with a view to preventing or dispelling negative ideas among the public about their employment policies. Another motive was that welfare work "ensured popularity" and contributed to "the larger purpose of meeting consumer needs".[42]

Macy's welfare system encompassed a hospital, a compulsory mutual aid association, a private school, and a welfare department.

Filene's Department Store in Boston pioneered welfare work extensively from the 1890s, and added the idea of a credit union for employees and the cooperative to American corporate welfare capitalism. Filene also introduced employee representation associations in 1902. Until 1928, when Edward Filene had to drop his managerial authority in favour of his younger brother Lincoln, the store operated as a 'cooperative association', intending, ultimately, to transfer store ownership to Filene employees. Apart from the credit union supplying savings and loan programmes, Filene's welfare work encompassed a works council, welfare benefits and programmes for education, recreation, hygiene, bonus, and mutual insurance.[43]

Wanamaker's had about 15,000 employees by 1915 and was considered 'a very good store to work in'. Since 1886, the store had a profit-sharing scheme and, later: employee restaurants; medical clinics; public libraries; a Sunday

39 Nelson 1995: 105-107.
40 Marchand 1998.
41 Leach 1993: 118.
42 *Ibid:* 121.
43 McQuaid 1976: 77-94.

school; a hotel for women employees; pension plans; clubs for language instruction; a large open-air gymnasium on the roof of the Philadelphia store; other sports facilities; paid vacations in store camps on the New Jersey seashore and in the Pennsylvania countryside; and a state-accredited 'American University of Trade and Commerce' in the Philadelphia store.[44]

The First World War gave new impetus to welfare capitalism and an increasing involvement of the federal government. Under the auspices of the new Council of National Defence (1916) and its executive Advisory Commission, a Committee on Welfare Work consisting of representatives of active welfare work companies was created. This committee's tasks included improvements to sanitary facilities in factories, improvement of sanitary practices in workers' homes, improvement of workers' housing and encouragement of recreational activities for workers. The Housing Corporation, created by the War Department, built homes for workers. Renowned American architect Frederick Law Olmsted took part in the planning activities and designed "a whole series of company towns during World War I."[45]

As argued, the 1920s are considered the heyday of American welfare capitalism. The majority of the company welfare work plans in this period was directed at preventing or combatting the hazards of industrial life by introducing saving plans, stock ownership, house ownership, compensating the costs of illness, disability, work accidents, old age and death, and, most of all, providing some sort of employee representation (company unions or works councils). In labour historian David Brody's opinion, employee representation, or the introduction of industrial democracy, was "the most celebrated experiment of the decade" and the "capstone of welfare capitalism."[46] One step ahead is labour historian Sanford Jacoby, who argues that, in combination with company unions and corporate efficiency, American welfare capitalism in the 1920s was a distinctively American response to 'the labour question', which can be characterized as intense workers distress and activism. It even came to be seen as America's future by a substantial part of the American business establishment, united since 1919 in the 'Special Conference Committee' (SCC). The SCC encompassed ten leading American companies, such as Jersey Standard, Bethlehem Steel, Du Pont, General Electric, General Motors, and International Harvester.[47]

44 *Ibid.:* 118-122.
45 Brandes 1976: 26.
46 Brody 1993: 55-56, 58.
47 Jacoby 1997: 20-21.

An interesting and somewhat deeper insight into the matter offers a case study on industrial workers in Chicago in the period 1919-1939 conducted by Lizabeth Cohen.[48] She not only considered five big Chicagoan firms with respect to motives, organization, and introduction of welfare work plans, but also the reactions of their workers to the employers initiatives.[49] The five companies were Western Electric (Hawthorne Works), International Harvester (McCormick Works and Wisconsin Steel), Swift and Company, Armour and Company, and US Steel (South and Gary Works). All five companies introduced comprehensive welfare work programmes during the 1920s, which involved the following five parts: "restructuring interpersonal relationships at the plant, rewarding workers through wages, and promotions, experimenting with industrial democracy, instituting welfare programs, and an assuming community responsibilities." The employers concerned were motivated to take these initiatives in order to end the outbreak of worker militancy during the First World War and directly after the war in 1919. This would eradicate the problem of extreme labour turnover, which, at times, was more than 100 per cent per year, and would take back control in the form of private action over wartime public policies mandating wages, working conditions, hours, etc. Employers wanted to keep the state out of welfare and social legislation and did not like any kind of 'European parasitism' in America. In short, they wished to keep welfare capitalist initiatives to themselves. It was also important for the employers to restrain the key position of the foreman and the linked drive system. Finally, as the workforce consisted of many nationalities with different ethnic backgrounds, there was a tendency among the workers on the shop floor to form into groups with people of their own country or ethnic group. Thus, national or ethnic solidarity was more important than solidarity with the firm. This caused 'unproductive' tensions between various parts of the workforce. By introducing, for example, individualized wage incentives, individualized promotions, establishing building and loan associations (Western Electric), introducing life insurance plans, and organizing joint sports and leisure activities employers tried to neutralize these tensions and, at the same time, build corporate loyalty. This was also the era of 'Americanization' campaigns directed at Americanizing immigrant workers. The workers were sensitive to these initiatives, albeit not uncritically. They accepted the new welfare work programmes and used

48 Cohen 1990, chapter 4: 159-211.

49 See also Roethlisberger & Dickson 1950.

them primarily for their own personal or familial purposes.[50] Considerable gaps remained between employers' intentions on paper and employers' practices. For example, there was still a lot of dissatisfaction among workers with various parts of welfare work with respect to recurring lay-offs during economic downturns and persistent bad working conditions. However, in the workers' perception some of the five companies scored better than others as welfare capitalists.

This important period of welfare capitalism ended provisionally with the onset of the Great Depression. The slump heralded a steep and rapid decline in American welfare capitalism. During the first years of the Great Depression, several attempts were made, to no avail, to soften the serious consequences of the economic downturn by applying new forms of welfare capitalism focused on stabilizing employment. Examples include: guaranteeing employment security for a pre-fixed time; introducing work sharing; and, at a broader societal level, organizing employment security and workers' income insurance ('Swope Plan').[51] Ultimately, welfare capitalism only underwent a serious revival after the Second World War, but in a very different context of labour-friendly labour law and formally recognized trade unions.[52]

All things considered, after some early pioneering initiatives, American welfare capitalism evolved between 1880 and 1930. It frequently started with the construction of company towns in rural areas; but big firms in urban areas also introduced welfare capitalism. In the early phases of welfare capitalism housing was one of the most important issues, followed by financial and income provisions. In the 1920s, the most important welfare work issue was worker participation, very often linked with efficiency thinking. Not all small and large firms introduced welfare work plans, but, eventually, a majority of big companies did so to a larger or lesser extent. In the 1920s, welfare capitalism appeared to be accepted by many firms, but also by its workers. However, in the 1930s, as a consequence of the Great Depression, welfare capitalism at the firm level declined significantly. After the Second World War welfare capitalism revived in a completely changed context in which labour protection law and statutory recognized trade unions competed as alternatives.[53]

50 See also: Zahavi 1983: 602-620.

51 Gerald Swope of General Electric proposed his plan in 1931. Swope proposed industry regulation by trade associations under supervision of the federal government. The Swope Plan received nationwide interest but was overhauled by the increasing seriousness of the economic crisis. Brody 1993: 70-71.

52 Jacoby 1997.

53 De Gier 2010; 2011. See also Cohen 1990, chapter 4: 159-211.

A closer examination of some exemplary model towns

After reviewing the historical development of welfare capitalism in the United States, I will now deal in more detail with a few exemplary cases of model company towns. The term company town was minted in the United States and implies a settlement built and operated by a single enterprise.[54] Additionally, a 'model' company town is a settlement of exceptional interest. Because of the enormous quantity and variety of company towns, it is impossible to be comprehensive. Over the course of a century, Margaret Crawford diagnosed the following historical succession of types of company towns in America: the mill village; the corporation city; the lumber camp; the mining town; the industrial suburb; and the satellite city.[55]

Historically seen, the most important were the New England textile factory villages and factory towns. I have already referred to Lowell, Massachusetts; also worth mentioning is Willimantic, Connecticut with its Willimantic Linen Company. Willimantic, part of a group of New England textile factory villages that not only offered welfare work to the workers, such as libraries, hospitals and profit sharing, but also nice dwellings set in attractive rural New England landscapes, has been immortalized in Julian Alden Weir's paintings 'Willimantic Thread Factory' (1893) and 'The Factory Village' (1897).[56]

Next, railroad towns, steel towns and other model towns developed, often as satellites to big cities such as Chicago (Pullman, Gary, US Steel), St. Louis (Leclair), Birmingham (Fairfield), and Cincinnati (Proctor & Gamble, Ludlow, Norwood). Finally, after the turn of the century, the so-called 'new' company town was born. In terms of the design and planning of new company towns the role of professionals, such as architects, welfare secretaries in companies, and social reformers is more prominent than in the case of the company towns constructed in the nineteenth century. The most important period in which the new company towns flourished was between 1913 and 1925. Examples were Indian Hill (Norton Company) and the mining town of Tyrone.[57]

54 Garner 1992: 3.
55 Crawford 1995: 6.
56 Rosenbaum 2006: 78-111; Crawford 1995: 33-34.
57 Crawford 1995: 1-7.

A vanguard textile corporation town

Lowell, Massachusetts, is generally considered as an exemplary model of a company town in the United States. Because Lowell encompassed not one single enterprise, but a group of interlocking independent corporations, the town can also be labelled as a 'corporation city'. Only the hydropower development in Lowell was centralized in a single corporation.[58] In 1810, Francis Cabot Lowell founded the Boston Manufacturing Company. Francis Lowell and a number of associated investors searched for a suitable site where they could set up an industrial town, with access to enough water to generate ample energy to run a number of mills all year round. They chose a site on the Merrimack River, where a canal had been built around a waterfall. The town was named after Francis Lowell who died in 1817. Initially, the involved entrepreneurs employed young, unmarried New England farm girls. From the mid-1820s until the Civil War, Lowell would become a leading centre of the large-scale mechanized cotton industry in the United States and also experimented with rudimentary forms of welfare capitalism.[59]

Kirk Boott, agent and treasurer of the Lowell project, planned and developed the town according to the ideal of Francis Lowell with a view to creating a manufacturing town to be organized as an ideal architectural and social community. This community should consist of a group of well-built factories and a settlement of well-arranged houses, schools, churches, a railroad station, and shops.[60] Boott hired the construction workers, laid out the streets, and designed the first standardized five-storey high mills, as well as the more diverse housing for executives and houses for skilled and unskilled mill workers. The mills were constructed first. Then, the town was built on the remaining space. The formal development of the town was in the hands of the 'Locks and Canals Company', a subsidiary of the Boston Manufacturing Company. By 1850, Lowell had 40 redbrick mill buildings run by several textile corporations, such as Merrimack Co., Hamilton Corp, the Appleton and Lowell corporations, the Middlesex Corp., the Boott Corp., and the Massachusetts Corp. In the 1830s, the mills employed some 10,000 workers mostly living in boarding houses close to the mills. Indeed, the workers lived closest to the mills; executives were housed further away

58 Candee, in Garner 1992: 3.

59 Chandler 1977: 58-59; Lind 2012: chapter 4.

60 The next part on Lowell is based on Green 2010: 13-26; Crawford 1995: 23-27, and Coolidge 1993.

from the factory premises. The basic foursquare house type could be used either as a boarding house or as a family house.

By 1850, the town had 33,000 inhabitants and also possessed areas of middle-class housing, shops, a number of schools, churches, but also shanties. 'New Dublin' was the poorest part of town, consisting of shanties inhabited by Irish immigrants.

From the viewpoint of paternalism and welfare work, the years between 1820 and 1850 were the most significant. During this period, the workforce consisted of young farmwomen originating from nearby farms and villages, who, on average, spent only three years of their lives as factory workers, before returning home or getting married. From the 1850s onwards, the nature of the workforce changed fundamentally and was gradually replaced by immigrants from Ireland, Canada, other countries, as well as children. At the same time, welfare work became rather marginal and no new company housing was built. If the first twenty years of Lowell had been an era of profitable paternalism, the succeeding period, by contrast, was one of nepotism and mismanagement.[61]

In the first period, when Lowell was still a sort of utopian community based on the ideals of Francis Cabott Lowell, welfare work at Lowell can be summarized as follows: The factory girls were rather well paid in cash. There was no compulsory truck system; thus, the girls could spend their wages freely. The girls lived in boarding houses constructed by the mill owners, closely supervised by housekeepers. Good food was served twice a day. Twenty-five women were boarded in each house, six per bedroom. As the girls had to work and live together permanently, there was almost no privacy. Not only the level of the wages contributed to the attractiveness of living and working in Lowell, but also the supply of cultural assets such as pianos and libraries. The girls used these facilities extensively. They even had their own literary periodical, the 'Lowell Offering', containing essays, poems, and stories of the mills.

After the turn of the century, Lowell gradually declined as a company town. The last mills closed in the 1950s. In 1978, the mill district at Lowell became an urban national park.

A unique 'showcase' company town

In the historical evolution of American (model) company towns at that time Pullman, Illinois is an indisputable showcase comparable to Saltaire

61 Coolidge 1993: 105.

in England, Margarethenhöhe (Krupp, Essen) in Germany, and the Familistère (Godin, Guise) in Northern France.[62] There is evidence that in the period before Pullman some fifteen planned industrial communities were constructed in the United States.[63]

George Mortimer Pullman (1831-1897), founder of the Pullman Palace Car Company (1867) and maker of the famous beautiful and luxury Pullman railway sleeping cars, moved his main factory in 1881 some thirteen miles south of Chicago to the western shore of Lake Calumet. Inspired by the English model town Saltaire and the social paternalism of its proprietor Sir Titus Salt (see Chapter 3), in 1880 Pullman commissioned architect Solon Spenser Beman (who would later design Grand Central Station in Chicago) and landscape architect Nathan F. Barrett to design, on 4,000 acres of prairie land, the new factory and, bordering it, a brick town and parks. Pullman town had to be functional as well as beautiful, based on Pullman's aesthetic conviction about the commercial value of beauty. It was laid out as a geometric iron grid. The town was separated from the factory by the main Florence Boulevard and provided with greens, and a public park with a lake vista. Housing consisted of family tenement buildings in rows and semi-detached blockhouses for the unskilled, as well as single-family homes for skilled workers and the management. All were located in pleasant green settings. The public buildings encompassed the church, the hotel Florence, the multipurpose Arcade building (community centre, shops, library, bank, post office, and theatre), a large central stable and the Market building (shops). The Market building, located on a market square, burned down in 1892 and was rebuilt on the same site in 1893. The architectural style of the town was eclectic and contained Gothic as well as Queen Anne style elements. In 1885, the town encompassed over 1,500 buildings, increasing to 1,800 units in 1894.[64]

A closer look at George Pullman's ideas about welfare work shows that he believed in the contribution of worker well-being and good health to the productivity of his enterprise. In his eyes, this would prevent labour conflicts and labour unrest. Therefore, according to Pullman, the cooperation between employer and workers turns out to be beneficial for both. However, Pullman workers had to behave fully in line with the paternalistic ideas of their employer with respect to good manners, and (middle-class) values

62 The following part on Pullman is based on Buder 1975; Crawford 1995: 37-43; Ely 1885; Green 2010: 27-33; Lindsey 1971: 1-89; Taylor 1915: 28-90.

63 Meakin (1905): 382-414.

64 Lillibridge 1953: 17-22.

Image 3 The town of Pullman, Illinois, USA, East View from Top of the Arcade Building, 19th century

Courtesy of the Pullman State Historic Site, Paul Petraitis Collection

such as respectability, morality, frugality, and industry. This was based on the Victorian philosophy of self-help and self-improvement. Expressions of these values included: the accentuation of private and public hygienic conditions in a model town and factory; the presence of a school and a large number of social organizations in town (a military band, an athletic club, a women's union, a chess and whist club, a choir, etc.); the lack of saloons and brothels in the model town (there was only one bar in the hotel); and the need to pay a fee for the usage of various worker amenities (such as for the membership of the town library). George Pullman considered the new factory and town primarily as an economic investment that, in the long run, had to generate an annual return on investment of six per cent. Houses were only for rent and remained property of the enterprise. The company itself took care of the necessary public utilities (delivery of gas and water, organizing the sewerage system). The town was run as a private company and not as a political and administrative entity. There was no local government, but instead there were six 'town agents' directly responsible to George Pullman himself.

The factory at Pullman consisted of three divisions: passenger car production, freight car production, and car repair. In the mid-1890s, it employed 5,500 mostly skilled or semi-skilled workers.[65] About ten per cent of the workforce was of Dutch descent, originating from nearby Dutch settlement Roseland. Another big worker contingent was of Swedish and German descent. Wages were average and did not differ significantly from wages in other neighbouring companies. Temporary sick workers received full pay. Pullman provided suitable employment in the company for disabled workers. Pullman also had its own company doctor. The company did not have, or introduce a formal system of worker participation. In this respect, George Pullman's authority was formally absolute. He considered strikes and individual initiatives of workers as sinful. His so-called 'Pullman system' was paramount. By combining the roles of landlord and employer he hoped to introduce a decent and obedient "superior type of American workingman."[66]

The number of inhabitants of Pullman town increased from four in January 1881, to 8,603 in 1885 and to 12,600 in 1893.

In 1894, Pullman was hit by a big strike, lasting for several months. In this strike the American Railway Union (ARU), led by renowned trade

65 The company as a whole employed by the end of 1893 more than 14,000 workers and belonged, at that time, to the giant corporations of American industry.

66 Foglesong 1986: 191-192.

union leader Eugene V. Debs, played a crucial role. The catalyst for the strike was a substantial cut in wages in the context of an economic depression at the onset of the 1890s, coupled with the company's refusal to lower the housing rent. George Pullman considered wages and rents as two separate, unrelated entities. The strike had huge consequences. From then on, it made many employers hesitant about imitating Pullman's example. Moreover, public opinion became more negative with respect to too much one-sided economic power in the hands of factory owners. As a consequence, the Illinois Supreme Court decided in 1894 that Pullman had to sell its model town and to concentrate its activities in the factory. A federal government commission, examining the causes of the strike, debated the overly paternalism of Pullman as 'un-American'. This turned out to be the beginning of the end of Pullman's workingman's paradise. The town was dismantled and sold in the following years. Today, a big part of the original complex has been demolished, including the 195-foot water tower that once dominated the town, and the great interior space of the Arcade. Still preserved are the Hotel Florence, the Greenstone Church, and a substantial number of the 1,400 row residences in the iron grid.[67]

To conclude, it is worthwhile briefly considering the findings of two important American social reformers who both visited and assessed the Pullman experiment at two different moments in time. The first is economist Richard T. Ely, who went to Pullman in 1884-1885 and subsequently published in 1885 a spectacular article in Harper's Magazine, entitled 'Pullman as a Social Experiment'. The second is Chicagoan economist and journalist Graham Romeyn Taylor, who went to Pullman in 1915 for research on his book *Satellite Cities.*

After initial enthusiasm about and endorsement of Pullman's experiment, Ely gradually became more critical. In his study, Ely tried to answer the following four questions: "Is Pullman a success from a social standpoint? Is it worthy of imitation? Is it likely to inaugurate a new era in society? If only a partial success, what are its bright features and what its dark features?"

In particular, the lack of freedom of the workers to decide about their own living conditions and the intensity of the control and lack of democracy on the shop floor brought him to the "unavoidable conclusion" that Pullman was "benevolent well-wishing feudalism, which desires the happiness of the people, but in such a way as shall please the authorities," and that "the idea of Pullman is un-American."

67 Schulze & Harrington 1993: 245-246.

In *Satellite Cities*, Graham Romeyn Taylor regarded Pullman's model town as a satellite or industrial suburb of, and economically at least partially dependent on, Chicago. By 1915, Pullman was already absorbed by an expanding Chicago. Like Ely, Taylor considered the lack of land and home ownership as a clear risk for the ultimate success and continuity of Pullman. Another cardinal risk factor, in his eyes, was the autocratic personal power of George Pullman with respect to the government of both town and factory: "beneath this attractive picture of the model town was the spirit of substance and paternalism." In an additional chapter on Pullman in Taylor's book, social reformer Jane Addams compared George Pullman with Shakespeare's King Lear, calling him "a modern Lear," who not only "socialized the factory, but also the form in which his workmen were living."

Overall, Ely and Taylor, but also Addams and some government observers, pointed to the need for professional architects and designers to have a larger role in conceptualizing and planning new company towns. Such professionals could act as buffers between capital and labour and thus enhance chances of success for future company towns.[68]

Despite Pullman's failure and, in the short term, a degree of aversion to following his example, there were, nevertheless, several new and to some extent comparable employer initiatives to construct model company towns. Three notable examples are Leclair, Illinois (N.O. Nelson Manufacturing Company), Vandergrift, Pennsylvania (Apollo Steel), and its copied larger version Gary, Indiana (US Steel).

As pointed out, Leclair, a painting and plumbing company, was the only actual comparable imitation of Pullman.[69]. N.O. Nelson, the president of the N.O. Nelson Manufacturing Company (St. Louis, Missouri, 1877), founded Leclair in 1890 near Edwardsville and at short distance from St. Louis. It existed as a company town until 1934. The overt paternalism of Pullman was absent in Leclair. Nelson, inspired by European examples such as Godin's Familistère at Guise, France (see chapter 6), funded his welfare capitalism on the principle of a well-balanced cooperation between employer and factory workers. Ultimately, the workers should cooperatively own the factories and the town. Therefore, Nelson gave his workers an annual dividend, to be paid in company stock. Thus, he was one of the first entrepreneurs in the United States to introduce profit sharing.

68 Crawford 1995: 45.
69 Based on Garner 1971: 219-227.

Leclair was constructed on 125 acres of farmland. On it, designed by architect C.A. Cameron, Nelson built the new one-storey factory buildings, a number of detached houses, a cooperative company store, a clubhouse, and community facilities. The factory buildings were lighted, heated, and ventilated with fresh air. The houses consisted of four-, six-, and eight-room houses, including sitting room, kitchen, bathroom, and one or two bedrooms. Inhabitants who left Leclair had the right to resell their house to the corporation. This prevented eventual speculation.[70] All rules of conduct in the town and the factory had to be mutually agreed by the employer and his employees.

In 1911, the town had 700 inhabitants who lived in 150 brick houses. The town had: paved streets; sidewalks; two railway stations; a public hall (lyceum); a library; a kindergarten; a clubhouse; an academy for training in the vocational arts; a village green and a lake; a dance pavilion; and a cooperative store. Additionally, the company took care of water, electric lights, and fire protection. The company also had its own music band. Ultimately, by 1934, the town had 2,000 inhabitants.

In sum, in the American context, Leclair was more than the usual model company town. It was "a unique community that offered its workers a program for social harmony and cultural uplift," without sacrifice of independent decision-making or even property ownership.[71]

Steel company towns

In 1895, the Apollo Iron and Steel Company (AI&S), and in particular its chief executive George Gibson McMurtry (1838-1915), commissioned the firm of renowned landscape architect Frederick Law Olmsted Sr. to design the new model town Vandergrift on 640 acres in a bend of Kiskiminetas River.[72] The location was about one mile from Apollo and 40 miles north-east of Pittsburgh. The town was named after AI&S's founder and main investor Jacob J. Vandergrift. After a trip to Europe, McMurtry had been inspired by European welfare capitalist initiatives, such as in English factory villages, and by Krupp in Essen, Germany, and Schneider at Le Creusot, France.

70 Foglesong 1986: 196.

71 Garner 1971: 226.

72 The following part on Vandergrift is mainly based on Mosher 1995; Mosher 2004; and Mosher & Holdsworth 1992.

The Olmsted firm planned a picturesque pattern of long meandering curvilinear boulevards, streets, and surrounding green settings.[73] The town would also be equipped with paved roads, a modern sanitary infrastructure, gas, water, and electricity. After the realization of the model town, and contrary to Pullman, Apollo Steel sold the rather expensive homes in Vandergrift to workers with low-interest loans, albeit only to skilled, and white-collar workers. Later, in 1896, Vandergrift was expanded; first with the less expensive Vandergrift Heights (a thirteen-block grid-iron street plan, not designed by the Olmsted firm), mostly inhabited by Italian immigrants; and subsequently with the much less attractive Morning Sun ('East Vandergrift'). Morning Sun, a residence without paved streets and without the infrastructure of the main borough, became a sort of 'hunkeytown', mainly for unskilled immigrant workers from Eastern Europe.[74]

The residents themselves governed Vandergrift via a burgess and a council. The majority of the town government consisted of mill workers.

McMurtry took the initiative to build the new model town after the 1894 Apollo strike and lock out of unionized workers. Vandergrift was destined to become a non-unionized steel factory and model town and only non-unionized workers were allowed to live in the model town. McMurtry wanted Vandergrift to be "something better than the best". For this reason, he combined urban design with social reform, good infrastructure and private home ownership. McMurtrey expected that, as in the European model towns of Krupp and Schneider, homeownership would contribute to a sustainable emotional as well as financial commitment of its inhabitants to Vandergrift. In combination with healthy and good working conditions in the new mill this would also transform the workers and their families into better citizens and Christians. The core of McMurtrey's approach was a dual strategy of environmentalism and home ownership to ensure a loyal workforce.[75] Moreover, "good homes make good workers," as renowned muckraker Ida M. Tarbell remarked on Vandergrift in her 1916 book *New Ideals in Business.*[76]

The model town consisted of: single-family detached, front-street and alley houses; a village square; a village green; a train station; schools; hotels; stores; churches; a courthouse; and office buildings. The mill was adjacent to this settlement.

73 Mosher 1995: 82.
74 Green 2010: 116-118.
75 Mosher 1995: 92.
76 Tarbell 1916: 134-162.

Between 1895 and 1910, the population of Vandergrift, inclusive of its later two extensions, increased from zero to over 9,000 inhabitants.

In 1901, Vandergrift merged with other steel companies and became part of the newly formed steel giant US Steel Corporation.

As the 1901 steel strike showed, McMurtrey's approach of 'cordial collaboration' between capital and labour turned out to be successful at Vandergrift. The Vandergrift workers did not join the strike, because they "received good wages, steady employment, and everybody is entirely satisfied, no friction or discontent [...]."[77] Organized labour remained absent at the mill.

Some fifteen years later, Tarbell also confirmed Vandergrift's success as a model town by contending: "It would be difficult in the United States to-day to find a prettier town, greener, trimmer, cleaner, and more influential than this town of Vandergrift [...]." However, "The difficulty with such towns as Vandergrift and [...] indeed most of our industrial cities is that they meet the needs of only the highly paid workmen."[78]

In 1906, US Steel founded the model company town Gary, Indiana. US Steel, created in 1901, was a merger of over 200 former independent corporations. The new town and mills were named after Elbert H. Gary, chairman of US Steel. From the beginning, Gary was intended as a much larger version of Vandergrift. Gary (nicknamed the 'Magic City', because of its lofty ambitions to be the most spectacular model town of the century) would, in time, become the largest company town in the United States. It was laid out on 9,000 acres alongside the Indiana shore of Lake Michigan. The Grant Calumet River separated the town from the mills. By 1909, the town had 12,000 inhabitants and only three years later, in 1914, no less than 50,000 inhabitants. At this time, the model town also had: two banks; six hotels; three newspapers; two schools; ten church dominations; a multitude of shops; and two parks.[79] The mills employed almost 12,000 workers in 1917. At least half of them were foreign-born encompassing over 20 different nationalities.[80] This made Gary a largely immigrant company town. The number of immigrants had increased in the 1920s to almost 80 per cent and the number of nationalities to over 50. The majority of the immigrants originated from Southern- and Eastern Europe and, after the First World War, also from Mexico. Moreover, after the First World War, national black

77 Mosher 1995: 101.

78 Tarbell 1916: 134-162.

79 Green 2010: 122.

80 *Ibid.*: 109-110; 122 and 128.

migration from the South to the North of the United States contributed significantly to Gary's workforce. By 1930, the population of the town surpassed 100,000.[81]

As at Vandergrift, to prevent overly Pullman-like paternalism – encompassing total control of the employee – houses in Gary were sold from the outset to Gary mill workers as well as to others. Design and planning of the new model town remained in the hands of the company itself and was not contracted out to external professional architects. 'Rule of thumb' planning was its maxim. This resulted in a functional rectangular but simultaneously monotonous grid-iron lay out of the town, with different types of houses for skilled workers, unskilled workers, clerical workers, foremen, and other managers. Two boulevards bisect the grid, one running east-west (Fifth Avenue) and another running north-south, to and from the mill entrance (Broadway). Although the company took care of the essential infrastructure (public utilities, parks, and recreation facilities), the residents themselves became primarily responsible for building the necessary community buildings, such as schools, libraries, hospitals, and churches, usually funded by donations. For example, steel magnate Andrew Carnegie donated the public library and Elbert H. Gary the YMCA building. This explicit division of responsibilities was based on the principle of 'self-help', previously propagated by Vandergrift's McMurtry. Other important Vandergrift hallmarks were copied in Gary, such as construction of single-family detached houses, and introduction of welfare work in its plant, including a pension plan.[82]

The for-profit Gary Land Company, a subsidiary of the corporation, developed Gary. It also constructed, sold or rented the houses. For example, the first 506 houses built by the Gary Land Company encompassed fifty different four-room frame houses, 94 five- and six-room frame houses, 100 six-room frame houses and 266 brick, cement, and timber houses with five to ten rooms.[83] Because house prices and rents were relatively high, immigrants and low-paid workers could not afford buying or renting a house in the original town. They were abandoned to other, cheaper and significantly less attractive extensions of the originally laid out town, such as the 'Patch' and 'South Side'. There, the company, in collaboration with private real estate speculators, constructed cheaper boarding houses, barracks, and shacks with a minimum of public utilities and provisions. As

81 Mohl & Betten 1972: 361-376.

82 Crawford 1995: 43-44 and 84; Mosher 1995: 102.

83 Taylor 1915: 184.

Graham Taylor described in 1915, living conditions of worker families and boarders in the poorer parts of Gary were extremely bad if compared with the living conditions in the better parts of the model town. To some extent, bad living conditions were compensated with the presence of an excessive number of 238 saloons in Gary in 1911 when the population mounted to 21,000 inhabitants.[84]

Ultimately, Gary did not result in an 'industrial utopia'. On the contrary, according to Mohl & Betten, the corporation primarily built the town to attract and house the, at the time, rapidly increasing number of workers in the new steel mills, rather than with the intention of providing a model of industrial planning. In their opinion, Gary proved to be a failure for the perspective of planning.[85]. Instead of a model workingman's paradise, Gary developed into the first "made-to-order city" as well as into a "spectacular civic by-product of the new industrialism" in America. The model town stood out "as the greatest single manifestation of industrial power to be found in America."[86]

'New' company towns

As remarked, the last step in the evolution of company towns in the United States before 1930 was the rise of the so-called 'new' company town.[87] Between 1910 and 1930, more than forty 'new' company towns were designed. On behalf of industrialists, these towns were designed and planned by professional and independent architects, landscape architects, and planners, such as Grosvenor Atterbury, Bertram Goodhue, John Nolen, and Earle S. Draper. Characteristic of new company towns was the physical separation of the community and the factory or mine, as well as the avoidance of the monotonous grid-iron layout of many earlier company towns. There was also greater diversity in house design. Application of new, inexpensive materials, such as concrete, and standardization of the building process decreased construction costs substantially. Three company towns, built between 1909 and 1913, can be considered as the precursors of the later range of new company towns. These were: Fairfield, Alabama; Torrance, California; and Goodyear Heights, Ohio.[88] Characteristic of these company

84 *Ibid.*: 207.
85 Mohl & Betten 1972b: 203-214.
86 Taylor 1915: 165 and 227.
87 Crawford 1995. The part on new company towns is based on her book, the only recent overview study of new American company towns so far. See also Crawford 1999: 48-57.
88 Crawford 1995: 78-98.

towns is that, apart from the architects, the workers also played a 'decisive' role in the design and planning. The employers considered the workers not only as employees, but also as consumers. Therefore, the housing had to anticipate the taste and preferences of the workers with respect to style, prices, and diversity. To achieve this, the architects involved processed experiences in the United Kingdom with model company towns like Bournville and Port Sunlight, as well as with the English garden city movement. To achieve both housing reform and industrial betterment, they tried to synthesize the principles of 'environmental determinism' with 'functionalism'.[89]

For example, according to Graham Taylor, Fairfield (1910, US Steel), was the "first well-planned industrial town in the South," built as a company town exclusively for skilled workers.[90] The town combined a grid of small blocks with curvilinear streets, a central square with a fountain, a park, and public and small-business buildings. A landscaped parkway was laid out as a spine through the centre of the town. Town and plant were spatially separated. The houses, other buildings, and landscapes were designed by New York architect William Leslie Welton and Boston landscape architect George H. Miller. They applied three planning styles in three different zones of the town. The residential area was styled according to the 'craftsman style', with a pattern of partial curvilinear streets, four- and five-room one-storey bungalows and two-storey duplex houses. The architectural style in the central public area was 'Beaux Arts', and 'functional' in the peripheral commercial area.[91]

Grosvenor Atterbury designed the first real 'new' company town in 1915. This was Norton Grinding Company's Indian Hill at Worcester, Massachusetts. At Worcester, where the corporation manufactured machine tools, Norton employed 3,500 workers by 1914. Norton, a company in the vanguard of American welfare capitalism, already possessed an extensive welfare work programme, encompassing: a company hospital; factory safety and sanitation programmes; worker dining rooms and cafeterias; paid vacations; pensions; educational and recreational facilities; and a mutual benefit society. Like Fairfield, Indian Hill was destined for skilled and supervising employees. According to Crawford, Atterbury invented a newly Americanized, albeit eclectic, company town image, characterized by specific site planning techniques, urban design, and architecture. He

89 *Ibid.*: 89.
90 Taylor 1970: 247.
91 Crawford 1995: 84-86.

was influenced by already existing New England company towns, colonial cottages, as well as by English and German garden cities.[92] The result was a romantic and picturesque Dutch colonial styled town with single-family houses in six sub-types and with five, six or seven rooms, and shops surrounding a town square.[93]

Another illustrative example of a 'new' company town was Hershey, Pennsylvania, established by the chocolate manufacturer of the same name. Hershey was very similar to Cadbury's Bournville in England.

In 1903, Milton Snavely Hershey, known as the 'King of Caramel', purchased 1,200 acres at Derry Church, Pennsylvania to construct an American Bournville. Quaker and Mennonite principles influenced Milton Hershey's philanthropic ideas. With the help of a local architect, C. Emlen Urban, he built Hershey in 1904. There was: a public library; parks; a zoo; a swimming pool; a golf course; free schools; a dance and skating hall; a medical clinic; shops; and a trolley system. By 1930, a community centre, a theatre, sports venues and a large hotel in a traditional Italianate and Spanish style were added. The town had two main thoroughfares, Chocolate Avenue and Cocoa Avenue. Noteworthy is the Hershey Industrial School, founded in 1909 by Milton Hershey and his wife Kitty. This school was a residential institution for orphan boys. The varying attractive dwellings, all with electricity, central heating, running water, and a garden, and were offered for sale to the workers. The limestone factory buildings were separated from the town. By 1911, the company provided employment to 1,700 workers. Hershey's paternalism was comparable to the paternalism of George Pullman. He acted simultaneously as employer and town mayor. He and Kitty lived in the middle of his 'chocolate utopia' in a big mansion, called 'High Point'. Hershey died in 1945. The company still exists today and the model town has become an amusement park, attracting many tourists.[94]

A third, but rather extravagant, example of a 'new' company town is Fordlandia.[95]

Henry Ford and his son Edsel founded Fordlandia in 1928 in the Brazilian Amazon, on the eastern side of the Tapajos River in the state of Pará, at the point where the Tapajos ends in the Amazon River, some 600 miles from the Atlantic. The land purchased by Ford covered 2,5 million acres,

92 *Ibid.:* 110.
93 *Ibid.:* 114-115.
94 Green 2010: 35-41; Cadbury 2010: 164, 200-201, 210-211.
95 The part on Fordlandia is based on Grandin 2009, and Esch 2011: 91-110.

Image 4 Fordlandia Dance Hall, Boa Vista, Brazil, circa 1933

Courtesy of the Collections of the Henry Ford, Beson Ford Research Center, Dearborn, Michigan, USA (THF 115496-64.167.74.10)

about the size of Connecticut. The main motive was Ford's conviction that the Ford Motor Company needed to control the whole production process to prevent dependency on one or more external suppliers. This is called 'vertical integration' of the production process. By establishing a rubber plantation in Brazil, Ford wished to exclude or diminish his, till then, full external dependency on rubber as well his lack of control of the, at the time, sharply increasing rubber prices.

Ford was not the only American entrepreneur who built a company town in Latin- or Central America after the First World War. The above-mentioned 'King of Caramel', Milton Hershey, did it in 1917 when he founded a company town with American-style bungalows, luxurious houses for staff, schools, a hospital, sports facilities, movie theatres, and a sugar mill, called Hershey, in Cuba near Santa Cruz.

In Fordlandia, Henry Ford constructed a complete new town from scratch, with: Cape Cod styled houses; modern wooden houses for the American staff; palm-fringed paved streets; sewerage; a town square; a water tower; a power house; a sawmill; a dining hall; schools; recreational and sports facilities; a hotel; an open-air dance hall; shops; and a hundred-bed hospital. Architect Albert Kahn, who also designed Ford's Highland Park and River

Rouge plants in Detroit, designed the hospital. Outside the official town cafes, bars and brothels sprang up.

By the end of 1930, Fordlandia employed some 4,000 workers. The majority of them originated from poor northeast states of Brazil. Initially, the town only housed the workers and not their families.

In the end, Fordlandia was anything but a success. Mismanagement, hubris, and institutional racism, labour riots against the highly controlled living and working conditions on the plantation, and, not least, a failing rubber production, contributed to its complete demise. During the Second World War, to support the war effort, the American government nationalized both Fordlandia and the later-built smaller company town and plantation Belterra, constructed some eighty miles away. After the war, in 1945, the Ford Motor Company ended its Amazonian adventure. The plantations were turned over to the Brazilian government.

4.5 Conclusion

In this chapter, I dealt with the extensive history and evolution of American welfare capitalism and company towns. With respect to company towns, I limited myself to model company towns and did not pay attention to the also extensive incidence in America of 'soulless corporations' or even 'satanic mills, mines and company towns'. Compared to England, France, and Germany, America in the nineteenth- and twentieth centuries, seemed to be a land of unlimited possibilities and opportunities. At least, in the vast and still empty United States, the mistakes and negative effects of the Industrial Revolution in England could be avoided. This explains the many socialist and communistic experiments in America in the first half of the nineteenth century. The initially often-European immigrant initiatives stressed the significance of the pastoral ideal or strived for an equivalent balance between land and city life. These early socialist and communistic experiments had much in common with the company towns initiated by enlightened employers in the second half of the nineteenth- and beginning of the twentieth centuries, such as new settlements designed or not designed from scratch, the organization of all kinds of necessary and supportive collective provisions, overly or strong paternalism by a sectarian leadership or the company leadership, and, not least, the significance of self-help and personal responsibility.

Nevertheless, it should be kept in mind that the economic, social, and demographic background conditions changed fundamentally over time. In the second half of the nineteenth century, the United States developed rapidly and, in a relatively brief time period, transformed from a predominant rural country to the most important industrialized economy of the world. The outcome, Fordism – or mass production and mass consumption – set the frame for a blossoming period of American welfare capitalism and the rise of 'new' company towns between 1900 and 1930. In hindsight, and in a certain sense, Pullman implied a turning point. Pullman mirrored, to some extent, past experience with the idyllic factory villages in New England and Europe. At the same time, Pullman anticipated later, less overly paternalistic welfare capitalist initiatives and 'new' company towns. He also united, at an early stage, idealistic, materialistic, and aesthetic principles, while also demanding ultimate control of assets.

In the course of time, the voice of the general public, factory workers, and external 'brokers' such as architects, designers, planners, and social reformers got more weight. This caused a further extension of welfare work programmes with, for example, the introduction of industrial democracy in large companies, increasing influence of professionals on the development of welfare work programmes and design of factory buildings and company towns, and, finally, the employer's conviction that welfare work is also functional with respect to productivity.

In sum, it is no exaggeration to contend that, with respect to the period 1900-1930, there was talk of an evolving 'new' corporate ideal in the then dominant liberal state. In the opinion of James Weinstein, more specifically, "the ideal of a liberal corporate social order was formulated and developed under the aegis and supervision of those who [...] enjoyed ideological and political hegemony in the Unites States: the more sophisticated leaders of America's largest corporations and financial institutions."[96] The new corporate ideal not only included attention to welfare work, professional architecture of factory building and company towns, but also encompassed attention to the relationship between art and industry, or the design of mass-manufactured consumption goods. In the new 'arts-in-industry movement' or 'good-design movement' art museums and art schools played a significant role. For example, in 1912, John Cotto Dana of the Newark Museum organized an exposition of the work of the Deutsche Werkbund, the German industrial design organization (see next chapter). Stewart Culin of the Brooklyn Museum made his museum a centre for 'artistic industries'. However, most influential in this respect was to become the Metropolitan Museum of Art in Manhattan. In 1914, the Metropolitan

96 Weinstein 1968: Introduction ix. See also: Wiebe 1967.

created a new position, associate in industrial art, and established narrow ties with manufacturers and designers. The Metropolitan organized its first big industrial arts exhibition in 1917.[97]

97 Leach 1993: 156, 166-173.

5 Worker colonies and settlements, joy in work, and enlightened entrepreneurs in Germany

5.1 Introduction

Germany was becoming the most important industrialized country in Europe during the Wilhelmine era and the subsequent Weimar Republic. The industrial revolution in Germany took off relatively late in time, during the second half of the nineteenth century, resulting in a heavy concentration of mining and steel industry in the Ruhr region in the west of the country. Later, other important regional industrial agglomerations developed, such as coal mining in Upper Silesia and the Saar region, chemical industry in the Rhine-Main region (Bayer in Leverkusen, BASF in Ludwigshafen) and, not least, in Berlin where, machine manufacturing (Borsig, Schwartzkopff) and electrical industries became predominant (AEG, Siemens).

After first briefly examining the nature and development of the industrial revolution in Germany, I will subsequently shift my attention to early factory architecture and the origin of worker colonies (*Arbeiterkolonien*) and worker settlements (*Arbeitersiedlungen*), mainly in the Ruhr region. In this context, prior to coal mining corporations like Gelsenkircher Bergwerks-AG (GBAG), steel and arms company Krupp played a key role. Krupp also acted as a national forerunner in terms of the size of corporate welfare work and workingman's housing.

From about the turn of the century, social reform movements, such as the 'Verein für Sozialpolitik' (VfS), the Heimatschutz movement ('Bund Heimatschutz'), and the 'Deutsche Werkbund' (DWB) co-determined, to a large extent, the rather specific nature and further development of corporate welfare capitalism in Germany after 1900. In particular, the Deutsche Werkbund succeeded in successfully linking large, mostly manufacturing firms to renowned industry architects and industrial designers, such as Peter Behrens, Walter Gropius, Hermann Muthesius, and Hans Poelzig. Consequently, more than elsewhere, applied arts became a central element of German corporate welfare capitalism, notably between 1907 and 1930. Moreover, the Deutsche Werkbund and its pre-eminent foreman and politician Friedrich Naumann also introduced and propagated an influential new key welfare-work-concept, quality work (*Qualitätsarbeit*). On the other hand, compared to the United States, the establishment of worker model towns remained rather limited in Germany in a quantitative sense. However, the Krupp worker model town Margarethenhöhe at Essen, built between 1909 and 1918, became world-renowned. The worker garden city Hellerau, near Dresden also gained prominence. It was constructed in 1909 by another eminent DWB-member, furniture manufacturer Karl Schmidt-Hellerau, in collaboration with the architects Richard Riemerschmid, Heinrich Tessenow, and Hermann Muthesius.

With respect to welfare capitalism in a stricter sense, other important firms after 1900 included the biscuit company Bahlsen in Hanover, Fagus-Werk (shoe-lasts) in Alfeld an der Leine, and the Bosch electrical repair and manufacturing company in Stuttgart. Alongside Siemens AG, Bosch was also one of the first corporations in Germany to introduce scientific management as an essential part of its welfare work policies. Finally, as regards New Objectivity (*Neue Sachlichkeit*) avant-garde factory architecture in the second half of the 1920s, without any doubt, Shaft 12, then belonging to the time GBAG-mining complex and cokes factory Zeche Zollverein in Essen, is exemplary. Architects Fritz Schupp and Martin Kremmer designed this shaft, forming the central part of Zeche Zollverein.[1]

As in England and America, labour utopias also played a role in Germany as an inspirational source for ideas about the construction of workingman's housing and living. Examples are the eighteenth-century utopia of Franz Heinrich Ziegenhagen, conceived as the ideal anti-urban settlement community (1788), Theodor Fritsch' s 'city of the future' (1896), and Victor Aimé Huber's proposals about housing reform (1848).

Ziegenhagen, merchant and freemason, pleaded for a new society composed of a network of productive agricultural settlements, without private property, and without city noise. He tried to achieve his utopia on a newly acquired estate, conceptualized as an ideal combination of agriculture and the art of gardening.[2]

Fritsch also propagated an ideal combination of city and land, but, contrary to Ebenezer Howard's garden city, Fritsch's city was segregated and the wealthy lived in nice villas in the city centre. Worker settlements and the factories were banished to the periphery of the city.[3]

Huber, a reformist professor of philology in Berlin and adversary of the, in his eyes, unrealistic labour utopias of Owen, Fourier, and Cabet, advocated

1 Busch & Scheer 2002.
2 De Bruyn 2012: 40-51.
3 Hartmann 1976: 33.

instead the creation of self-help organizations or 'latent associations', each consisting of a central building and surrounding cottages. Public utilities had to be organized from the centre. A self-help organization should have a number of collective provisions, such as a school, a library, a dancing and music hall, and a kindergarten. Ultimately, Huber's ideas would be applied in the French *cité ouvrière* in Mulhouse (see chapter 6).[4] Subsequently, the Mulhouse *cité ouvrière* was copied by German employers such as BASF, Farbwerk Höchst, the Bochumer Verein, and other Ruhr coalmining companies.[5]

After the turn of the century, the ideas and experiences of the English garden city movement (Ebenezer Howard, Cadbury, Port Sunlight, New Earswick) got a firm footing in Germany, in particular with respect to the choice of the cottage as an attractive form of a workingman's dwelling, instead of rental barracks. A German garden city movement ('Deutsche Gartenstadt Gesellschaft') was founded in 1902.

5.2 The German industrial revolution

The industrial development of Germany started in the first half of the nineteenth century. Until then, Germany was a predominantly agrarian country. An important incentive in this respect was the constitution in 1834 of the so-called Zollverein, a free-trade customs union between the various German Länder and free cities under the aegis of Prussia. Only from 1871 was the 'German Kaiserreich' unified politically and economically in one country the, until then, separate German 'Länder' already partly collaborating in the German Bund and its successor the 'North German Bund'.[6] The Zollverein eased and stimulated further intra-German economic cooperation and economic growth. As in the United States, countrywide railway construction became, for a while, the leading sector in the industrialization process. Contrary to Great Britain, the not unimportant textile industry did not become a key industry in Germany. On the one hand, railway construction required extensive coal mining and iron and steel works; on the other hand, it demanded the manufacture of steam engines and locomotives. Coalmines and iron and steel works were concentrated in a

4 *Ibid.:* 22. See also: Bullock & Read 1985: 25-28.

5 Honhart 1990: 7.

6 The German Mark was introduced in 1871 as a national currency. The Reichsbank, the national bank, was founded in 1876.

few regions. Most important were the Ruhr, the Saar, and Upper Silesia. Notable companies in this respect were, for example, Krupp in Essen, the Gutehoffnungshütte in Oberhausen, and the Gelsenkirchner Bergwerke AG (GBAG) in Gelsenkirchen. Machine manufacturing mostly took off in bigger cities such as Berlin, where August Borsig became a leading machine and locomotive manufacturing company.

The real take off of the German industrial revolution occurred in the 1850s and lasted until the outbreak of the First World War in 1914. In Germany, this period is usually divided into the so-called *Gründerjahre* (formation years) between 1850-1871 and the period of the *Hochindustrialisierung* (high level industrialization), in the years thereafter. Despite several temporary economic downturns in between, overall, the time period between 1850 and 1914 is generally considered as a long period of economic growth and increased economic prosperity. During these decades, Germany became one of the three leading economic countries of the world, even surpassing Great Britain. Next to mining and steel works and machine manufacturing new leading industries emerged in the electrical industry (for example, Siemens, AEG, Bosch) and the chemical industry (for example, BASF, Bayer, Agfa). These companies recruited mainly high skilled workers. Also in this period, the German population increased substantially to more than 62 million in 1925. At the same time, there was a substantive intra-German migration from the east to the west, and from the countryside to the cities, towards *Kleinstädte* as well as *Großstädte.* Many low-skilled Polish workers also migrated to the Ruhr region.

Two more specific features played a significant role in the time of the *Hochindustrialisierung* and resulted in a remarkable form of cooperative managerial capitalism in Germany. These were the leading role of the banks and the formation of horizontal and vertical price and production cartels, as well as other forms of interfirm collaboration between companies, mostly in heavy industries. By 1913, almost two-thirds of the 200 largest industrial companies were clustered in metals, chemicals, and electrical and other machinery.[7] Banks were mainly private and were crucial for financial investments in the railways and other companies. Likewise, many bankers took roles on supervisory boards. Cartels contributed to narrow interfirm collaboration and to the creation of joint ventures, such as Telefunken, a joint venture of Siemens and AEG. An example of an important cartel is the creation of the so-called *Dreiverband,* consisting of three big chemical

7 Chandler, Jr. 1990: 394.

companies, BASF, Bayer, and Agfa, and also constituting the core of the giant company IG Farben, created in 1925.[8]

5.3 Early welfare work: Worker colonies and settlements and Krupp's welfare work policy

In fact, welfare work in Germany started as early as the sixteenth century, when wealthy banker and merchant Jakob Fugger founded the 'Fuggerei' in Augsburg (Bavaria) in 1521. The Fuggerei, built for needy hand workers and day labourers, consisted of 67 row houses with 140 dwellings. For the first time in German history the functions of living and working were separated in the Fuggerei.[9]

In Germany, from the beginning, the industrial revolution encompassed the establishment of worker colonies and worker settlements. The difference between the two categories is that settlements were more comprehensive than colonies with respect to additional facilities, such as schools, churches, and company shops. The pace was also set by the Prussian state, which provided simple utilitarian housing for miners in Prussian mines in the Ruhr, the Saar, and Upper Silesia, and later also by other German states and the German empire for railway and other state workers. Examples are worker housing at the main railway depot at Laienhausen near Hamburg, and worker housing at the Imperial Torpedo Factory at Friedrichsort near Kiel.[10]

The oldest industrial worker colony dates back to the eighteenth century and was built by textile factory Cromford at Ratingen. The oldest worker settlement in Germany was the colony Eisenheim in Osterfeld, near Oberhausen in the Ruhr region. It was built in several phases from 1844 by the largest employer of the Ruhr at that time, the company that would later become the Gutehoffnungshütte (GHH), owned by important steel-entrepreneurial family Haniel. Eventually, the Eisenheim settlement consisted of 51 houses, a school, and a children's home. By the mid-1850s, the Gutehoffnungshütte employed more than 3,000 workers. The brick houses in Eisenheim, some of which are still lived in today, all had two storeys and were aligned along a few straight streets. By 1910-1911, the Gutehoffnungshütte also constructed

8 This section is based on: Pierenkemper & Tilly 2004, Tilly 1990, and Chandler, Jr. 1990.

9 Until that time living and working was combined in the larger household. See Hartmann 1976: 34.

10 Bullock & Read 1985: 116-118.

a then avant-gardist white collar and managerial technical staff colony in Oberhausen, designed by renowned Berlin architect Bruno Möhring. This park-like settlement 'Am Grafenbusch' covered 12,5 hectares, with 21 houses containing 35 dwellings for 180 people.[11]

It is important to keep in mind that workingman's housing was implemented in several big waves in Germany. The first real housing boom took off at the beginning of the 1870s and lasted until the economic slump of 1873-1874. This resulted in several thousand apartments being constructed by the Ruhr mining company, Krupp as well as by machine manufacturer Cramer-Klett in Nuremberg. The second wave started in the 1890s and lasted until the First World War. Also in this period, thousands of dwellings (very often including complementary facilities such as schools, churches, shops) were built not only by the Ruhr coalmining companies, but also by the coalmining and steel companies in Upper Silesia, steel factories Krupp and Gutehoffnunghütte, and also by Cramer-Klett. For example, the Gutehoffnungshütte built fourteen new colonies between 1898 and 1914. Other significant examples were BASF, Farbwerk Meister, Lucius & Brüning, and Villeroy & Boch. The third and last wave occurred during the 1920s and the beginning of the 1930s, the years of the Weimar Republic.

During the various waves, the role and involvement of employers changed from direct to indirect involvement. At the time of the first and second waves company-owned housing was predominant. During the third wave, direct involvement of employers reduced throughout Germany and company-supported, municipal, or social intermediary building societies took the lead in planning and constructing workingman's housing.[12] Illustrative examples of the third wave are the employee housing projects in Berlin with the involvement of local employers such as AEG and Siemens, as well as the municipal workingman's districts the Neue Frankfurt by architect Ernst May in Frankfurt, and the Hufeisensiedlung at Berlin-Britz by architects Bruno Taut and Martin Wagner.[13]

In accordance with the development of the industrial revolution in Germany, the first worker colonies were built by textile manufacturers (for example, Cromford) and succeeded in time by steel producers (for example, Haniel, Krupp), coal mines (Ruhr, Upper Silesia, Saar), machine industry

11 Günter & Herzog 1975: 158-211.

12 New tenant protection legislation in the Weimar Republic prohibited coupling of labour contracts and house rental contracts and so made a definitive end to company-owned housing in Germany in favour of municipal and social building organizations. See Neuymeyer 1978: 132.

13 Honhart 1990: 9-12; Bullock & Read 1985: 211; Eisen 2012: 252-277.

(for example, Borsig, Cramer-Klett), process industry (for example, BASF, Bayer), and other remaining industries. The most comprehensively planned settlements were built after 1900. These were Krupp's Margarethenhöhe in Essen, MAN's Werderau near Nuremberg, Salzmann AG's Salzmannshausen near Kassel, Gmindersdorf of Spinnerei Gminder in Reutlingen, Hüttenau near Hattingen an-der-Ruhr of the Heinrichshütte, and garden city Hellerau near Dresden.[14]

In the remaining part of this section, I will focus on worker colonies and settlements in the Ruhr region and, in particular, on the Krupp settlements built before and after the turn of the century as well as on Krupp's welfare work policy codified in the so-called *General Regulativ* (company constitution) of 1872, and the coal mine colonies in Upper Silesia, and worker settlements and worker *Mietshäuser* or *Mietskasernen* (rental barracks) in Berlin (Borsig, AEG, and Siemens).

'Mythus Krupp': Krupp settlements and Krupp's welfare work policy

The Krupp Corporation, founded by Friedrich Krupp in 1811, grew rapidly, enabled by important technological innovations during the founding years of the firm with respect to the production of high quality crucible steel as well as by a steep increase in demand. Initially, this was caused by a boom in railway construction in Germany, and subsequently by arms production as a consequence of the Franco-Prussian War in 1870. To meet increasing demands, Krupp needed huge supplies of workers. To attract workers to Krupp's home base, the then small town of Essen in the Ruhr, the company paid rather high wages for the required skilled workers.[15] As adequate municipal housing was not available, Friedrich's son and successor Alfred Krupp decided to build worker colonies and settlements. This started in the 1860s, with the first dwellings built for foremen and workers, and continued in the period after the economic downturn at the beginning of the 1870s. Krupp was not the first entrepreneur building worker colonies, but he outpaced other in terms of the number of colonies and the general quality of the dwellings and available facilities, particularly after 1890. Moreover, the Krupp Corporation soon became the nationwide model-builder of worker colonies for the coalmines, steel producers, and other companies. Alfred Krupp even made housing initiatives a central element

14 Honhart 1990: 19.

15 In 1800, Essen had 3,860 inhabitants. A century later, the number of inhabitants had increased to 182,178. Günter 1980: 470.

of the firm's marketing strategy by organizing company tours for an ever-increasing stream of curious national and international visitors as well as by showing physical displays at international trade exhibitions.[16] One remarkable foreign visitor was Harper's New Monthly Magazine. Its author, Moncure D. Conway, published a positive article about Krupp in the spring of 1886, reporting on the living conditions of the worker families in the then existing colonies. He wrote that "The women living in the 'flats' which I visited seemed cheerful, and said they found their dwellings healthy and comfortable."[17]

Between 1870 and 1873 the number of Krupp dwellings increased explosively from 154 in 1870 to 2,680 in 1873. In the same period, the number of workers at the main Krupp site, the Guβstahlfabrik in Essen, increased from 7,337 in 1870 to 11,867 in 1873. By 1914, about a twenty per cent of all Essen Krupp workers (10,000) lived in a Krupp colony or settlement in or near Essen.[18] In total, the firm built some 20,000 dwellings.

From the 1860s until the First World War, Krupp successfully built the following worker colonies and settlements: a small number of foreman's dwellings at Hügelstrasse (1861-1862); Alt-Westend (1863); Neu-Westend (1871); Nordhof (1871); Schederhof (1872-1873); Baumhof (1872-1890); Cronenberg (1872-1874 and 1887-1892); Altenhof I (1890-1893) and II (1899-1907); Alfredshof (1894-99); Friedrichshof (1899-1900); Brandenbusch (1895-1897); Margarethenhof (1902); Beisenkamp/Emscher-Lippe (1907); Dahlhauser Heide (1907); Heimaterde (from 1918); and the most prestigious settlement of all, Margarethenhöhe (1911). Until 1900, the largest settlements were Cronenberg with 1,500 families or 8,000 people, and after 1900, the extended settlement Alfredshof and Margaretenhöhe had up to 16,000 inhabitants.[19]

Schederhof and Baumhof were the first non-temporary colonies and the houses were built henceforth of brick instead of wood. With the exception of Altenhof I and II, Alfredshof, Margarethenhöhe and some others, the early Krupp colonies and settlements were built adjacent to the factory premises of the Guβstahlfabrik. Most of them had at least a school, a grocery shop, a beer hall, and green spaces. Margarethenhöhe had a comparatively complete city infrastructure consisting of a central marketplace, churches,

16 Bolz 2010: 90-116.

17 Conway 1886: 516.

18 Günter 1980: 474. The number of blue- and white-collar workers in Essen (Guβstahlfabrik) increased from 109 in 1849 to 41,179 in 1914. The corporation in its entirety employed in 1882, 109 workers and in 1914, 79,671. See: Tenfelde 1994: 20.

19 On Krupp's settlement policies see also: Schlandt 1970, and Stemmrich 1981.

schools, shops, a butcher, a baker, a hotel, and a park.[20] Overall, the diversity in housing in the colonies and settlements was rather broad. For example, Westend located adjacent to the factory – with 219 worker and white-collar dwellings having two-to-five rooms, a grocery shop and a beer hall – consisted of wooden barracks without a garden, whereas the later settlements, built by Alfred's only son and successor Friedrich Alfred Krupp – Altenhof, Alfredshof, and Margaretenhöhe – were small worker garden settlements with cottage-style dwellings, with private gardens.

Friedrichshof, constructed in a more urban environment, had three-storey housing blocks with inner courts serving as communal gardens, and children's playgrounds. All dwellings had a scullery, which also served as living- and a dining room.

Cronenberg, also adjacent to the factory premises, had the appearance of a workers model village. Here, the streets were tree-lined and the houses had a garden. The village also had a market place, a small park, schools, a grocery, and a beer hall. Finally, in the direct neighbourhood bathing facilities and a swimming pool were available.

Brandenbusch, adjacent to the private home of the Krupp family, the Villa Hügel, was designed by Krupp architect Marx and especially built for the home service staff of the villa. The houses, with one or two storeys, were ornamented and featured a cellar. Although the architectural style of the village was not completely comparable to the later Margaretenhöhe, Brandenbusch contained some garden city elements.

Altenhof I and Altenhof II had 607 dwellings with small gardens, a Catholic and evangelical church, a lending library, two groceries, bathing facilities, and a basket weaving shop for retired workers who still wanted to do some light work. These two adjacent worker settlements were located at a substantial distance from the factory and were especially intended for Krupp's old age, disabled workers, and also some single workers. Disabled workers were exempted from paying housing rent. Altenhof I was designed in cottage style by the head of Krupp's company building office, Robert Schmohl. The houses with bay windows were ornamented and some had small towers. Altenhof II, also designed by Schmohl, contained more diverse, albeit simpler, housing.

The architectural layout of Alfredshof was still conventional with a rigid geometry of linear streets, whereas both Altenhof II and Margarethenhöhe had curving streets and were more picturesque.

20 Günter 1980: 482.

Alfredshof, designed by Robert Schmohl and his colleagues, ultimately had 1,695 dwellings. It started with cottages and resulted in a number of one- to four-room family houses. Streets were wide and lined with trees. Alfredshof also had a park, a marketplace, a grocery, a beer hall, and was an exemplary settlement when it was built.

Margarethenhöhe, like Heimaterde, was not exclusively intended for Krupp workers and their families. Other citizens of Essen, ultimately about 50 per cent of the settlement's population, were allowed to rent a house in this remarkable worker garden city. The population was mainly white-collar and middle class. The Margarethe Krupp Foundation ('Stiftung für Wohnungsfürsorge für minderbemittelte Klassen'), chaired by Friedrich Alfred Krupp's spouse, Margarethe Freiin von Ende, founded Margaretenhöhe. Independent Werkbund-architect Georg Metzendorf designed it in a romantic South-German small city style. I return to Margarethenhöhe in more detail in a subsequent section.

Finally, Heimaterde was founded by a new intermediary Krupp-related settlement society and designed by architect Theodor Suhnel. This settlement consisted of non-detached and semi-detached family houses provided with a kitchen, which also served as a living room, three bedrooms, a stable, and a garden.

In sum, until 1905, the planning and construction of Krupp-owned worker colonies and settlements was in the hands of the Krupp building office. After 1905, Krupp initiated separate intermediary building companies. However, these were still narrowly linked with the firm, such as: the 'Bauverein Kruppscher Beambten' (1905), the 'Siedlungsgenossenschaft Heimaterde' (1916), and the 'Kleinwohnungsbau Gesellschaft' (1919).[21]

Krupp's settlement policy was embedded in Krupp's remarkably extensive welfare work policy.[22] This policy was strictly paternalistic and framed by a mixture of utilitarian and ideal motives. Alfred Krupp, who became general director of the company in 1848, was the main architect and founder of Krupp's welfare work programme. It consisted of various building blocks. Apart from the workingman's settlements, welfare work at Krupp ultimately encompassed: secure employment; high wages; sickness insurance; industrial accidents insurance; old-age pensions; and a number of general welfare provisions, such as a large lending library,

21 Bolz 2010: 93-94; Bullock & Read 1985: 119-125, 139; Krueger 1999.

22 See McCreary 1968: 24-49; Reif 1986: 51-91; Tenfelde 1994: 24-32; Grütter 2012: 316-354; James 2012: 72-78.

two hospitals, social institutions, and later a number of recreational facilities. Also important was the so-called 'Konsumanstalt' or company grocery store.

It is important to understand that, at the time, Krupp was not unique in introducing welfare work in Germany. As has been pointed out, other companies also built worker colonies and settlements. And also other welfare work measures were taken elsewhere, often for cases of sickness or work accidents. At the start of the nineteenth century, for example, so-called 'Knappschaften' were established in the coal mining industry. This was a sort of sickness savings system based on self-help for labourers. Another example is the 'Unterstützungskasse', a special support fund for steelworkers in case of sickness, initiated for its workers by the Gutehoffnungshütte in 1832.

The Krupp Company started its first voluntary sickness fund in 1836. In the decades thereafter this idea was further developed into an extensive company-wide system of worker insurance, ultimately covering and protecting all workers from the cradle to the grave. This system not only encompassed sickness insurance, disability and old-age pensions, but also a supportive aid fund for workers' family members, survivors pension, several medical clinics, a hospital, and subsidized life insurance. Besides, the Krupp Company founded complementary social provisions for its workers and their family members. I have already mentioned the Altenhof settlement for retired and disabled workers and the hospital. The hospital started in 1870-1871 as a sick-barrack for wounded Krupp workers in the French-German War, which, after that time, developed rapidly as a fully equipped hospital with more than 600 beds in the 1920s. Other relevant provisions were: a hostel for single workers; the workers recovery home 'Kaiserin Auguste Victoria'; the women and children's home 'Arnoldhaus' – a home for childbearing women – bathing facilities inside and outside the factory; schools; company schools; a girls household school; savings banks; churches of different denominations; a casino in a large park setting; and donations for cultural activities after Alfred Krupp's death by his successor Friedrich Alfred.

The lending library, founded in 1899 by Friedrich Alfred Krupp, had 70,000 books, making it the second largest library in Germany at that time.

The company store started in 1858 as an internal factory bakery and after the company adopted a consumer union in 1865 it continued as the 'Konsumanstalt' in 1868. The 'Konsumanstalt' had a central building and from 1874 every Krupp settlement had a separate shop offering a broad supply of goods that went beyond daily fresh dairy products, clothing and groceries.[23] As part of Krupp's welfare work system, the 'Konsumanstalt' provided workers and their families with economical shopping.

In short, for Krupp there were some obvious reasons to construct such an extensive welfare work system. Firstly, the Krupp firm expanded rapidly in its founding years and needed many workers in a short time. Steel production also required skilled workers. Therefore, the company had to pay high wages, and had to invest in training and internal company schools. Important for Krupp in this context was making its workers loyal to the company, and to prevent extensive turnover of workers. The coupling of a labour contract and a house-renting contract as well as offering company insurance and complimentary social provisions turned out to be very successful and made long-term working for Krupp very attractive for many workers. As a result, labour unrest at Krupp was limited. Strikes rarely broke out before the First World War.

Another important reason was the high risks of steel working in heavy and dangerous working conditions. In this case, company insurance could contribute to a better and more attractive work climate.

Welfare work was embedded in a progressive company philosophy, formulated by Alfred Krupp and most comprehensively described in his *General Regulativ* or company constitution, published in 1872.[24] In addition to the main principles of company management and its caring duties, the General Regulativ defined the special relationship between the group of high-skilled core labourers, the so-called *Stammarbeiter,* in the Gußstahlfabrik with the firm. The General Regulativ comprehensively expressed the paternalism of Alfred Krupp and his attitude regarding the work ethic by contending that "The purpose of work should be the common good, then work is a blessing, work is a prayer." On the other hand, Alfred Krupp did not like trade unions or any kind of political activity by his workers.[25]

From the 1890s, the Regulativ also contributed to the creation of the so-called 'Kruppianer system'. This was the extensive Krupp cradle-to-grave welfare work programme combined with the company's ambition to produce high quality steel products, and the company culture defining rights and duties as well as special privileges of all Krupp workers. This

23 By 1900, the Konsumanstalt had 55 shops and also beer halls, a bakery, a mill, a slaughterhouse, a coffee roaster company, a hotel, etc. See Tenfelde 1994: 29.

24 The General Regulativ also contained an organizational structure for the company. In total, it encompassed 72 sections on Krupp's welfare work programme, warnings with respect to "unfaithfulness and betrayal" by workers and the functions of the company's central management board, the so-called 'Prokura'. See Grütter 2012: 349.

25 James 2012: 75.

resulted in the establishment of a large and, for the external world, mythical 'Krupp community', based upon "gratitude for material security and pride in an elite status."[26]

Non-Krupp worker colonies and settlements

As has been argued, Krupp was not unique in building worker colonies and settlements and, equally, this was not the case with respect to welfare work. What was unique, however, was the scale and size of Krupp's initiatives, as well as, after 1870, its quality. Some textile-, steel-, machine- and coalmining companies preceded Krupp. Active players in this respect were companies such as the steel company Gutehoffnunghütte in Oberhausen and the coalmining company Gelsenkirchener Bergwerks-AG. After workers colony Eisenheim (1844) was established by Gutehoffnunghütte, the next colony in the Ruhr was built in Hörde (Dortmund) in 1853 by Hörder Bergwerks- und Hüttenverein, followed, in 1858, by the Siedlung Stahlhausen in Bochum by the Bochumer Verein, and in 1861 the Siedlung Loh by the Heinrichshütte. The first coalmining settlements were the Knappenviertel by Zeche Oberhausen in 1858, and a Thyssen coalmining colony at Hamborn (Duisburg), succeeded by a first boom of miners' worker settlements in the Ruhr in the 1890s.[27]

Outside the Ruhr region, machine manufacturer Cramer-Klett in Nuremberg started building workingman's housing in the 1870s and the 1890s.

Also in the 1890s, coalmining companies and steel mills in Upper Silesia built large numbers of company owned houses and dormitories.[28] Their paternalism was not as intrusive as Krupp's and some other Ruhr companies. Like Krupp, Upper Silesian entrepreneurs, at least formally, embraced the idea of *Stammarbeiterschaft,* but realised that, in their case, this would not be sufficient to bind workers and their families in the long run. Their welfare work policies were mainly instrumental and driven by actual product- and labour market conditions in the region, rather than by paternalistic or idealistic motives. Motivated by a substantial shortage of available workingman's housing, the core of their welfare work efforts was offering rental company housing to workers. Initially, in the 1870s, government-owned companies leased small parcels of land to workers for ploughing, and a number of private employers rented small farms to workers. But by the late

26 McCreary 1968: 47.
27 Günter 1980: 468.
28 Schofer 1975: 78-101.

1880s, because of the increasing scarcity and high costs of land, employers turned to building company-owned workingman's housing. In general, this housing consisted of two types, dormitories for single workers and small family houses. The quality of the Upper Silesian company housing was substantially less than in the Ruhr; indeed, the dwellings were simple and usually smaller. One worker colony in Upper Silesia was built in the 1870s by the Berlin firm A. Borsig, on behalf of its blue- and white-collar steel mill workers. Another more exemplary worker colony in Upper Silesia was Gieschewald, built in 1906 by Giesche's Erbe. Gieschewald housed 642 families in individual family houses "in traditional Upper Silesian peasant style, including a garden and good water supplies for each house."[29] As in the Ruhr, many mining companies and steel mills also offered additional welfare work provisions, frequently in the form of payments in kind, such as the delivery of free coal and cheap meals in company restaurants. This was also necessary because the wages were low.

A pace setter in this respect was the Donnersmarckhütte in Zabre. The additional welfare work programme of the Donnersmarckhütte was rather extensive and encompassed, for example: old-age pensions; supplementary work accident insurance; retirement homes; unpaid vacations; libraries; company schools; kindergartens; parks; and bathing facilities.[30]

Third-party company housing, for example, supported by BASF, as well as by other large industrial companies elsewhere in Germany, started to boom in Berlin after the First World War.[31] From a historical perspective, compared to, for example, Essen, Berlin had a relatively small number of company-owned workingman's houses. Only machine manufacturing company Borsig at Borsigwalde, machine manufacturing company Schwartzkopff at Wildau, painting shop W. Spindler in Berlin-Köpenick, and mortar factory Guthmann at Königswusterhausen built a limited number of company-owned workingman's homes, usually on factory land.

In the 1870s, only Spindler built one, albeit partially realized, worker colony in Berlin, Spindlerfeld, after moving the company from the city centre to Köpenick. From 1870 onwards, the *Mietskaserne* (rental barrack) became the usual and only affordable form of workingman's housing in Berlin.[32] After 1900, mostly large companies in Berlin stimulated and also financially supported intermediary building organizations to construct

29 *Ibid.*: 87; Neumeyer 1978: 51.

30 Schofer 1975: 92.

31 Honhart 1990: 3-21.

32 Neumeyer 1978: 95 & 110.

workingman's housing in the form of rental barracks on the periphery of the expanding city. Building worker colonies turned out to be too expensive for employers in densely populated, big city areas with high land prices. Another significant factor was that Berlin was not like the Ruhr, the centre of the first industrial revolution in Germany. Instead, it became the nucleus of the second industrial revolution (*Hochindustrialisierung*) in which the heavy industry of the Ruhr and other more traditional industrial regions were usurped by the manufacturing and chemical industries in large cities and big-city regions like Berlin, Mannheim, and Ludwigshafen. These new industries needed high-skilled workers, who, as a rule, were more emancipated and less inclined to live in company-owned workingman's housing.

In sum, after the turn of the century until the mid-1920s, about eleven larger industrial companies, mostly machine manufacturing and electric industries, in Berlin were involved in the construction of third-party worker settlements as close as possible to their new factory settlement on the fringes of Berlin. These were: Siemens AG; Bosch; Chemical Factory Riedel de Haen; Borsig; Schwartzkopff; AEG; Osram; Schering AG; Flohr-Otis; F. Werner; and F. Seiffert & Co.[33] Borsig, for example, built worker settlement Borsigwalde in Berlin-Tegel, with mostly two- and three-storey apartment houses in blocks and rows. Schwartzkopff realized worker settlement Wildau at Königswusterhausen, with 164 two- and three-storey houses in rows, containing 820 apartments. In the 1920s, Siemens built Siemensstadt, adjacent to its Werner Werk M, designed by in-company architect Hans Hertlein (1881-1963), Walther Gropius, and other DWB-architects. Siemensstadt would encompass several hundred apartment houses with a maximum of four storeys at Spandau and Nonnendamm. Finally, AEG created settlements in Hennigsdorf and Oberschöneweide with two-, three- and four-storey apartment houses in rows and connected blocks. Since 1907, AEG's advisory in-company architect, Peter Behrens, also eminent member of the Deutsche Werkbund, designed two AEG settlements. The first AEG workingman's housing was built in 1910-1911 on the Rathenaustrasse in Hennigsdorf. Apartments were semi-standard and were part of three-storey housing blocks with a courtyard at the centre and gardens front and back. Rows of two-storey one-family houses were built in 1914-1915 in larger settlement Oberschöneweide. Finally, in 1918-1919,

33 *Ibid.*: 11 & 23.

Behrens returned to Hennigsdorf to build single and double units on Paul Jordanstrasse as part of cluster housing.[34]

In sum, the architectural style of the houses in Siemensstadt, Hennigsdorf, and Oberschöneweide was functional and adapted to the changed living habits of workingman's families. The still relatively small apartments had smaller parlours, but more kitchen or bedroom space, and also contained built-in furniture as well as time-saving appliances.[35]

5.4 Social reform movements, factory architecture, and worker Gartenstädte

Utopian thinking, but also reform movements, played a role in the development of worker colonies and worker settlements in the Wilhelmine era and the Weimar Republic. Influential in this respect were, in particular, the *Gartenstadtgesellschaft* (garden city movement), the *Bund Heimatschutz* (Heimatschutz movement), and the Deutsche Werkbund. This resulted in a few 'model' worker colonies, such as Krupp's Margarethenhöhe in Essen, the Hellerau garden city near Dresden, and the previously mentioned Peter Behrens worker settlements in Berlin. Put succinctly, this development was characterized by the intensive connection between art and industry in Germany, from the end of the eighteenth century until the resolution of the Weimar Republic at the beginning of the 1930s. The main purpose of this connection was the improvement of the overall quality of German products, including the design and the way in which products were manufactured by means of 'quality production'.

The reform movement started in the 1890s and was aimed at ethical and cultural *Lebensreform* or life reform. The movement encompassed not only the three movements mentioned above, but also a broader spectrum of other organizations, such as utopian socialists, liberal reformists, and conservative nationalists.[36]

The Gartenstadtgesellschaft was founded in 1902, following the example of the British garden city movement, by a group of social reformers consisting of the brothers Kampffmeyer, Hart, and some others. The organization was primarily a propaganda organization directed at disseminating and propagating the idea of garden cities as a solution to the land question and

34 Anderson 2000: 174, 237; Neumeyer in Buddensieg & Rogge 1979: 127-140.

35 Neumeyer 1978: 166-257; Honhart 1990: 19-20.

36 Jefferies 1995: 51-52.

related housing problem in Germany at this time. In this capacity, it also exerted influence on the conception of the future worker garden cities Margarethenhöhe (1909) in Essen and Hellerau (1909) near Dresden.

The Heimatschutz movement was the first important nationwide reform organization orienting itself around the reform of architecture and, in particular, industrial architecture. It had close links with the local and national authorities. The organization, founded in 1904 and chaired by renowned German architect Paul Schultze-Naumburg (1869-1949), attacked dominant historicist industrial architecture and propagated instead honest, simple, and solid architecture. Model examples of the historicist industrial architecture after 1900 were neo-gothic Gelsenkirchner Bergwerks-AG's Zeche Zollern and adjacent company housing in Dortmund, built in 1901-1903 by architects Paul Knobbe (1867-1956), Bruno Möhring (1863-1929) and Reinhold Krohn (1852-1932), and the neo-Baroque styled Zeche Jacobi of the Gutehoffnungshüte, designed and built in 1912-1914 by Carl Weigle (1849-1932).[37]

Historian Matthew Jefferies characterized and summarized the Heimatschutz movement's view of industrial architecture in three broad areas as follows:

> Firstly, that industrial and technical buildings should be built in the established tradition of indigenous architectural forms, using local materials wherever possible. Secondly, that industrial and technical buildings should be >honest< in reflecting their practical function, without over-emphasising >naked< engineering. And thirdly, that such buildings should not be sited in sensitive locations, but that where their existence was unavoidable every effort should be made for the building to blend with the local landscape.[38]

Prime examples of Heimatschutz industrial architecture were the new red-brick factory of the North German Net Company at Itzehoe (Holstein), designed by Heimatschutz architect Fritz Höger (1877-1949), and the factory designed and built in 1909 by Richard Riemerschmid (1868-1957) for the Deutsche Werkstätten für Handwerkskunst at Hellerau, near Dresden. According to Jefferies, the Heimatschutz movement primarily attempted to find practical solutions and genuine answers in the context of rapid industrialization in Germany. In hindsight, the movement turned out to

37 *Ibid.:* 31-39.
38 *Ibid:* 65.

be more pragmatic than idealistic, more active than passive, and more optimistic than pessimistic.[39]

The Deutsche Werkbund (DWB) was founded in 1907 in Munich and soon became more important than the Heimatschutz movement.[40] Thirteen renowned architects, and political and intellectual reformers such as Peter Behrens, Hermann Muthesius, Richard Riemerschmid, Friedrich Naumann, Karl Schmidt as well as ten craft firms, including the Deutsche Werkstätten für Handwerkskunst, founded the DWB. The objectives of the DWB largely overlapped with those of the Heimatschutz movement, but were more modernistic. Also, more explicitly than the Heimatschutz movement, the DWB intended to link art and industrial production to improving the, until then, comparatively rather poor quality of German products on the world market. The objective was to produce henceforth products of 'exceptionally high quality', which, according to Protestant politician Naumann "could only be economically achieved by an artistically cultivated people, oriented towards machine production."[41]

Soon, many industrial enterprises felt attracted to the objectives of the new organization and joined the Deutsche Werkbund, including AEG, Siemens, BASF, Bayer, Bahlsen, Kaffee HAG, MAN, and a number of smaller companies. Henceforth, these companies would involve DWB architects in the design of their products and new factory buildings. One of the most emblematic factory buildings designed by DWB-architect, Peter Behrens (1868-1940), was the eclectic-functionalist turbine factory building of AEG in Berlin-Moabit (1909). This building, at that time the largest steel and glass factory in Berlin, employed some 4,400 workers in 1914. Other exemplary DWB projects were the design and construction of the new Fagus shoe-last factory in Alfeld an der Leine by Walter Gropius (1883-1969) between 1911-1914, and the model H. Bahlsen biscuit factory in Hannover. The main building of the new Fagus Werke, completed in 1911 and owned by Carl Benscheidt, was flat roofed, had a steel structure and also had a glass facade. Inside the building, glass curtain walls were applied instead of brick stonewalls to separate the various office and production rooms, as well as the offices of Benscheidt and his son. In principle, this made working transparent and removed a clear division between administrative and productive work. Benscheidt was a progressive entrepreneur and organized

39 *Ibid.*: 65, 81, 100.

40 About the history of the Deutsche Werkbund see: Campbell 1989; and Müller 1974.

41 Frampton 1980: 110.

his workforce of about 500 workers as a *Betriebsgemeinschaft,* the so-called Fagus Family, built on devotion and trust. Benscheidt paid rather high wages and introduced an eight-hour working day at a relatively early stage in Germany.[42]

Bahlsen, founded in 1889 by enlightened entrepreneur Hermann Bahlsen (1859-1919), introduced progressive industrial relations in his factory, like the introduction of company health insurance in 1899, and combined these with technical and organizational innovations originating from the United States, such as the assembly line. Architect Karl Siebrecht (1875-1952) designed between 1909-1911 the modernistic, steel-framed Bahlsen factory building as well as the more conventional office building. The new factory complex and its 1,700 workers were provided with a roof garden, a music room, a library, restaurants, bathing facilities, and a company shop. On the walls hung paintings by Hodler, Heckel, and Modersohn. There were also frescoes and other objets d' art, on show, such as sculptures by the famous expressionist sculptor Ernst Barlach. But Hermann Bahlsen went further than that. In collaboration with DWB architect Bernhard Hoetger (1874-1949), Bahlsen intended to build a new model company town as a sort of *Gesamtkunstwerk* by the end of the First World War. Unfortunately, the town, which was to be named 'TET-Stadt' and built near Hannover, with a factory, offices, warehouses, worker housing, theatres, schools, and a church, would never be achieved.[43]

The ideas of the DWB exerted substantial influence on the founding of a number of new worker settlements.

Firstly, there was Krupp's worker settlement, Margarethenhöhe, designed by DWB architect Georg Metzendorf (1874-1934) for 16,000 inhabitants.[44] Metzendorf developed his own architectural style, a mixture of the Berlin avant-garde and the more traditional South German School, and applied it at Margarethenhöhe. Metzendorf belonged to the so-called *Westdeutscher Impuls* (West German Impulse), a group of architects who developed a new industrial architecture, building romantic worker settlements in brick stone. Margarethenhöhe, a settlement built as a small world in itself in two distinctive phases between 1909-1934, consisted of a number of two- and three-storey family houses (*Kleinwohnhäuser*), apartments, squares, greens, and gardens. The partly cottage styled one-family houses, blocks and row

42 Jefferies 1995: 190-194. See about glass architecture and the curtain wall also Wilhelm 1983: 59-66.

43 On AEG's turbine factory see Jefferies 1995: 127-131; on Fagus Werke, *Ibid.:* 143-145; on Bahlsen, *Ibid.:* 119-123.

44 About Margarethenhöhe see for example: Metzendorf & Mikuscheit 1997; Kallen 1984; Mämpel et al. 2006; Bolz 2010: 108.

houses had a scullery, a living room, a kitchen, several bedrooms, a cellar and a garden. The mostly curbed streets were partly lined with trees. Surrounded by woodlands, Margarethenhöhe also had a main access street with a large bridge spanning the Mühlenbachtahl and a monumental city gate leading to the central market place. This so-called *Trabantenstadt* or *Gartenvorstadt* (garden suburb) also had a school, a hotel, a police station, a *Konsumanstalt* (Krupp grocery store), several other shops, and housed a community of artists as well.

Margarethenhöhe was not a typical Krupp worker settlement. It was inhabited by at least 50 per cent non-Krupp employees. Also, the demographic composition of its inhabitants was mainly middle class.

Margarethenhöhe embodied the architectural ideal of a model worker settlement "with its well-built houses and their gardens laid out on streets that led down to the market place, its physical form suggests those qualities of the stable communities of medieval market towns that served as sources of inspiration for its design."[45] Furthermore, the Deutsche Werkbund expressed and propagated this ideal at a DWB exhibition in Cologne in 1914. There, Metzendorf and other German architects constructed the 'Neue Niederrheinische Dorf', a romantic model village in which traditional regional architecture was combined with progressive ideas. One of the buildings Metzendorf constructed there was his exemplary Essen workingman's home, the so-called *Essener Arbeiterwohnhaus.*[46]

A second notable example, in which the DWB, as well as two other life reform movements, the Deutsche Gartenstadtgesellschaft and the Dürerbund, exerted substantial influence, was the first official German garden city Hellerau, near Dresden[47]. Karl Schmidt Hellerau (1873-1948), a crafts-furniture manufacturer in Dresden, initiated and founded Hellerau. Schmidt was an enlightened reformist entrepreneur and co-founder of the Deutsche Werkbund. He believed strongly in harmonious and just labour relations in his factory. In order to be able to expand his factory, in 1909 Schmidt moved his Deutsche Werkstätten für Handwerkskunst GmbH, with 500 workers, to a new green site, about ten kilometres from Dresden. Jugendstil architect and Schmidt's brother-in-law Richard Riemerschmid (1868-1957) designed the factory and also made a blueprint of the new garden city with curbed streets, greens, gardens, and a marketplace. Hellerau was divided into four

45 Bullock & Read 1985: 81.

46 Hagspiel 1984: 186-191.

47 About Hellerau see: Hartmann 1976: 46-101; Jefferies 1995: 80-81; Neumeyer 1978: 137-138; Schweitzer 1997; Van Zee 2012: 41-67.

Image 5 View of Margarethenhöhe, Essen, about 1912, Krupp, Esssen, Germany

Courtesy of the Krupp Archive: Historisches Archiv Krupp, Essen (WA 16i, 9.41.19)

separate parts: the factory quarter, a workingman's housing quarter for Schmidt's blue- and white-collar employees and artists, a villa quarter, and a public quarter with a school, a theatre, shops, and public welfare and recreational facilities. The houses and other buildings were designed by a number of architects. In addition to Riemerschmid, other renowned DWB members were involved; namely, Hermann Muthesius (1861-1927), Heinrich Tessenow (1876-1950), and Theodor Fischer (1862-1938). Fischer also built worker colonies on behalf of BASF ('Limburger Hof' in Ludwigshafen), and 'Gmindersdorf' for textile factory Gminder in Reutlingen.

A wide variety of housing types was applied at Hellerau, varying from romantic one-family cottages to tighter row housing and apartments. Moreover, Hellerau was considered as a social reform experiment, and incorporated the important DWB principles. By connecting city and land it should function as an alternative to industrial city life, characterized by rental barracks in unhealthy circumstances. At the same time, it should reconcile industry and art by producing a new generation of furniture. Also essential in this respect were the experimental theatre, the 'Festspielhaus', and the artistic school, the so-called 'Bildungsanstalt Jacques Dalcroze'.

Strictly seen, Hellerau was not a pure worker colony. There was, for example, no obligation for inhabitants to work for the Deutsche Werkstätten. Moreover, from the outset, Schmidt transferred ownership of the land to the independent Gartenstadtgesellschaft GmbH.

5.5 Quality production and joy in work

From its founding in Munich in 1907, *Qualitätsarbeit* or quality work, encompassing both the quality of production and joy in work, became one of the key concepts of the Deutsche Werkbund, alongside eclectic 'functionalism' in industrial architecture. In 1922 and 1924, the DWB made 'joy in work' and 'work and life' main topics of its annual conferences.

'Qualitätsarbeit' would not only contribute to sustainable economic growth and an increase in German exports, but also to the self-respect and dignity of workers as well as social harmony.[48] Therefore, in the eyes of many Werkbund affiliates, 'Qualitätsarbeit' could solve the actual labour question.[49] In fact, Friedrich Naumann and others had already developed the quality work concept before the effective founding of the Deutsche Werkbund.

Contrary to the convictions of Carlyle, Ruskin, and Morris in Britain, the German concept 'Qualitätsarbeit' expressed an explicit belief in the compatibility of the machine age and mass production, on the one hand, and 'primary quality' and 'aesthetics' of products as well as workers' 'joy in work', on the other hand. As in the case of industrial architecture, 'Qualitätsarbeit' also required collaboration between industry and the applied arts. In the background, the corporatist idea of *Gemeinwirtschaft,* propagated by industrialist and politician Walther Rathenau (AEG), played a supportive role.

Naumann considered 'Qualitätsarbeit' to be a typically national German phenomenon very suited to the second German industrial revolution and the manufacturing of finished products. As it chiefly required skilled work, the usage of pure and high quality materials as well as aesthetical design of products, 'Qualitätsarbeit' also attracted industrial designers and architects united in the Deutsche Werkbund. Likewise, Naumann believed in harmonious labour relations and supported industrial democracy in enterprises by means of introducing work's councils and profit sharing

48 Jefferies 1995: 102.
49 Campbell 1989a: vii

schemes. In this respect, he was impressed by pioneering initiatives in the 1890s by some progressive employers, such as Berlin manufacturer of Venetian-blinds Heinrich Freese and Ernst Abbé of optical firm Carl Zeiss in Jena.[50]

Rathenau, a versatile personality, also published several political books. Accepting the inevitability of the new mechanical age, he wanted to prevent its negative, alienating consequences with respect to work and society by propagating an ideal-typical corporatist society in which a small number of elite industrialists had to play a responsive leading role.[51] In his main work, *Von kommenden Dingen* (1917), Rathenau developed the concept of *Gemeinwirtschaft,* or economic commonwealth. This embodied an alternative collective, classless, non-capitalist type of society, incorporating not only an active state, but also a network of active representative social groupings, mainly professional and sectorial associations. In short, in his opinion, the economy ought not to be a private, but a social affair.[52] Additionally, in his book *Die neue Gesellschaft* (1919), Rathenau advocated *Arbeitsausgleich,* or equalization of work. This implied that each worker should carry out daily both manual work and mental work by means of job rotation. This way of organizing work prevented an unavoidable division between manual and mental labour. Moreover, it offered manual workers the opportunity to develop their individual talents in the form of a *Gegenberuf,* or alternate occupation.[53]

'Qualitätsarbeit' was introduced in various forms in a number of member enterprises of the Deutsche Werkbund. This was not only the case at the Deutsche Werkstätten, Fagus-Werk, and Bahlsen. Leading DWB firms that adopted 'Qualitätsarbeit' were, for example, the electrical machine firms Siemens Group, AEG, Bosch, and chemical giant Bayer. The new American mass-production system also exerted a significant attraction in this respect. And not only the Deutsche Werkbund and DWB member firms, but also the national government, employer organizations and trade unions were fascinated by the principles of and practical American experiences with scientific management, Fordism, and welfare work. This fascination was embedded in a broader rationalization movement that gained extra momentum after the First World War, when German industry had to recover from war damage. More in particular, after the stabilization

50 Jefferies 1995: 160-161.
51 Hughes 1990: 15.
52 Rathenau 1917 (1964): 7-234. See also Gall 2009: 197-209; Révész 1927.
53 Rathenau 1919 (1964): 278-358; Campbell 1989: 122-124.

of the national currency in 1925 until the Great depression in 1929, a real rationalization boom occurred in Germany. However, broadly accepted definitions of the content of rationalization did not exist. Its meaning varied from cost-saving techniques, efficient work organization, introduction of welfare work programmes, elimination of waste, and increased profits to the wider process of *Entzauberung der Welt* (world disenchantment), a concept coined by the renowned German sociologist Max Weber. In 1927, the 'Reichskuratorium für Wirtschaftlichkeit' (RKW), or National Productivity Board, defined rationalization as "the adoption and employment of all the means of increasing efficiency which are furnished by technical science and systematic organization. Its aim is to raise the general level of prosperity by cheaper, more plentiful and better quality goods." A shorter, more practical definition of rationalization applied by the RKW was *Verbesserung und Verbilligung* (improvement and economization) of industrial production.[54]

'The father of rationalization', Walther Rathenau, had previously contended that capitalism could only survive if "[…]the profit motive was leavened by the entrepreneurial duty of trusteeship."[55] Moreover, rationalization in the Weimar Republic "above all was associated with extensive corporation activity, the formation of cartel-like arrangements."[56]

Before and after the Great War a small number of firms experimented with scientific management, such as Bosch and Berlin machine factories Borsig, L. Loewe & Co., as well as the Siemens Group.[57] During the First World War, rationalization also received impetus from the efforts of Walther Rathenau, at that time also heading the Reich's 'Kriegsrohstoffenabteilung', the War Raw Materials Department. This important department was responsible for the provision and distribution of raw materials in Germany's war economy, by means of the so-called *Kriegsrohstoffengesellschaften*. These self-administrating war raw materials societies, organized in a large number of sectors, also implemented rationalization measures'.[58]

After the war, Carl Friedrich von Siemens, CEO of the Berlin based Siemens Group, became the main national proponent of rationalization, together with his assistant Dr. Carl Köttgen, also director of the Siemens Schuckert Werke (SSW). Von Siemens chaired the heavily state funded Reichskuratorium für Wirtschaftlichkeit, founded by him and Köttgen in

54 Shearer 1995: 487. This shorter definition of rationalization was formulated by Carl Friedrich von Siemens, founder and chairman of the RKW, and also CEO of the Siemens Group.

55 Brady 1932: 527, 531.

56 Maier 1970: 54.

57 See for example Homburg 1978: 170-194.

58 Gall 2009: 175-197.

1921. The RKW, involving by voluntary cooperation industry, trades, public administration, and industrial interest organizations, would fervently promote further rationalization of German industry in the 1920s, along Taylorist and Fordist lines. In this respect, the RKW propagated the so-called *Gemeinschaftsarbeit.* This implied narrow collaboration between German industrial firms under the leadership of big firms as regards rationalization policies, encompassing, for example, time-and-motion studies, psychotechnics, and standardization of industrial norms. In Berlin, Siemens, AEG, Borsig, L. Loewe, and other firms participated in the *Gemeinschaftsarbeit,* together with consultative practitioners and scientists.[59]

All things considered, in the decade after the First World War, rationalization or Americanization of the German economy was not a decisive success in Weimar Germany. Although many firms considered scientific management and Fordism worth copying to some extent, one could also speak of a certain 'Germanization of Americanism'. Only selective elements of American ideas that fitted with exclusive German labour relations were emulated.[60]

Apart from the RKW, the 'Deutsches Institut für Technisches Schulwesen' (Dinta), founded in Düsseldorf in 1925 by engineer Karl Arnhold, was also influential in this respect. This private right-wing institution opposed the introduction at the company level of scientific management and Fordism in Germany. Instead, like the DWB, Dinta stressed the importance of German work and German quality work. Dinta received strong support from conservative politicians and industrialists in the Ruhr region.

By the turn of the century, the Bayer Company in Leverkusen, which had almost 8,000 workers in 1914, already had a central Welfare Department. This department was responsible for workingman's housing, canteens, work accidents insurance, and old-age insurance for blue- and white-collar workers.[61].

In 1886, Robert Bosch (1861-1942) established an electrical components enterprise in Stuttgart. The company started as an electrical repair shop and producer of motor ignition systems. From 1912 onwards, Bosch played a central role in the Deutsche Werkbund. He also strongly supported Naumann's ideas and became a key DWB members. By 1914, Bosch employed 4,700 and by 1917, 7,000 employees. As an enlightened employer, in 1894 he introduced a nine-hour working day. Bosch also introduced a profit sharing scheme

59 Homburg 1991: 672-675. On the RKW see also Shearer 1997: 569-602.

60 Nolan 1994: 11-12.

61 Chandler 1990: 477-478.

in his company, paid rather high wages and financially supported social housing schemes for the poor. Trade union membership was also permitted for his workers. In 1900, his nephew, Hugo Borst (1881-1967), became business director. Borst, an individual member of the Deutsche Werkbund and an art collector, was a strong supporter of Taylorism and successfully introduced principles of scientific management and Fordism in the Bosch firm. In his opinion, the quality of the product and the working conditions should be guaranteed by "healthy, clean, light, dust-free, well heated and ventilated workrooms with happy colours, pictures or flowers," "together with the usual array of welfare facilities."[62]

Company-wide, Siemens introduced extensive welfare work policies from an early stage. By 1913, the Siemens Group employed 57,000 workers in Germany alone and 81,795 worldwide.[63] Based on the principle of 'sound egoism', company founder Werner von Siemens had already introduced a form of profit sharing in the 1850s. This was followed in 1872 by a pension savings system and, from the 1880s, financial support for both blue- and white-collar workers, and educational and recreational facilities. In 1907, a Siemens white-collar workers union was established organizing sports activities, choirs, etc. In 1908, the firm introduced sickness insurance. In 1910, it constructed a holiday home for white-collar workers. In 1911-1912 the company founded a kindergarten in Siemensstadt. Additionally, allotments, holiday colonies, a library, and company schools were created. In 1916, Siemens donated three million marks to a new foundation responsible for future workingman's housing. By the end of the First World War, the corporation also organized clinics for infant care and lung patients. A centralized personnel department was established in 1919. In 1928, Siemens established its own in-company medical service. Apart from the provisions mentioned, many other worker provisions were introduced over time, for example in the area of family care and for female workers. An in-company labour exchange office was also organized.

In its welfare work policy, Siemens made a distinction between skilled and unskilled workers, as well as between blue- and white-collar workers. Especially workers belonging to the loyal skilled and managerial *Stammarbeiter* elite or core workforce received special welfare work privileges.

Finally, by 1919, Siemens founded the intermediate social workingman's housing society 'Wohnungsgesellschaft Siemenstad GmbH', and started building Siemensstadt near the factory premises at Rohrdamm. Later, two other independent building societies got involved in the construction of

62 Jefferies 1995: 238. About Robert Bosch and his nephew also: 174-175, 185-190.
63 For a brief history of Siemens, see Kocka 1971: 133-156; Chandler 1990: 393-592.

Siemensstadt. Ultimately, by 1934, Siemensstadt encompassed more than 1,600 rental houses with one-1.5 to four-5.5 rooms.

In conclusion, the implementation of scientific management at Siemens in 1919-1922 as well as implementation of Fordist techniques, including an assembly line, initially in 1925-1928 and again in 1935-1938, remained experimental. Moreover, these initiatives were always coupled with an enlargement of welfare work policies directed at improving the qualifications, performance motivation, and loyalty of workers.[64]

Dinta, in turn, put its energy mainly into constructing a new (largely male) German quality worker, distinct from the 'alienated' Fordist American worker. This new German Worker ought to be a disciplined, skilled, and productive worker, loyal to his company and, finally, also possessing a professional ethos. All this could be achieved by developing and organizing extensive vocational training programmes at the firm level, supporting companies by developing corporate social policy programmes, as well as by publishing and editing company newspapers. By the end of the 1920s, Dinta ran training programmes in 150-300 German and Austrian firms. It also published more than 50 company newspapers. Companies served by Dinta included Gutehoffnungshütte, Hoesch, and Thyssen.[65]

5.6 Conclusion

Like Great Britain and the United States, Germany developed a strong tradition of welfare work between 1880-1930. In this period, private companies built numerous worker colonies and worker settlements in various sectors and in many regions. Likewise, many companies also introduced other welfare work programmes. Compared to the US, the number of model company towns remained rather limited. Only Krupp's Margarethenhöhe in Essen and the garden city Hellerau near Dresden can be considered, to some extent, model company towns. However, in both cases, the dwellings were not exclusively available for Krupp workers or workers of the Deutsche Werkstätten. Moreover, Hellerau was not exclusively developed by a company, but by intermediate parties.

Krupp's efforts with respect to workingman's housing and other welfare work initiatives had a nationwide impact and were copied by other enterprises, not only in the Ruhr region.

64 Homburg 1991: 586-661.
65 Nolan 1990: 187; 196.

The role of independent parties in constructing workingman's housing was repeated on a wider scale in Berlin. There, the number of company-owned worker colonies and worker settlements remained negligible, mainly because of cost considerations and a lack of free space. Siemensstadt, for example, was not strictly seen as a company town, although the company kept financial stakes in the building societies involved. Another reason for the deviating pattern of workingman's housing in Berlin is the degree of emancipation of the mostly skilled Berlin workers as well as the influence of the trade unions. Overly paternalistic welfare work, as initiated in the Ruhr, was not a viable option in the Berlin context.

Of note is the role and influence of the Deutsche Werkbund. The DWB, which originated from the broader Lebensreform movement, exerted a strong influence on factory architecture, the architecture of workingman's housing, design of products and on quality work. The Deutsche Werkbund succeeded in involving a number of renowned industrial architects and designers, such as Metzendorf, Poelzig, Behrens, and Gropius. With respect to factory architecture and workingman's housing the 'DWB-style' evolved over time from a romantic Heimat-style (for example, Metzendorf's Margarethenhöhe and the Essener workingman's home) into a modern, functional style (for example, Fagus shoe last factory, Turbinefabrik AEG, Siemens Werner Werk M, and Siemensstadt). The idea of quality work gained a renewed influence after the First World War and in the 1920s when the need for rationalization of the German industry became pressing. Many companies, such as Bosch and Siemens, adopted elements of scientific management and Fordism; at the same time, Americanization of production processes and welfare work remained limited. There was also a strong idea of the specific value of *Deutsche Arbeit,* compared to quality work elsewhere in the world. German quality work should not only contribute to worker satisfaction, worker involvement, and loyalty to the company, but equally to high quality products.

Unlike in the United States, the Great Depression did not end welfare work initiatives in Germany. Indeed, the Nazi regime embraced the idea of *Deutsche Arbeit* and redefined it for its own purpose. The regime also continued building some new company towns. The National Socialist German Labour Front (DAF), as well as the Dinta, which, under the leadership of Karl Arnhold, joined the DAF in 1933 as the Office for Vocational Education and Firm Leadership, promoted welfare work and social rationalization measures during the Nazi period.[66]

66 Campbell 1989: 312-336; Nolan 1990: 234-235.

6 France

From the Mulhousian welfare work model to the Taylorist Turn

6.1 Introduction

Industrial paternalism in France emerged in the context of the industrial development of the country from the 1830s onwards. Initially, providing workingman's housing was the main and most important element of welfare work, particularly in case of companies in rural regions with appropriate natural resources (water, timber, coal), where no or inappropriate workingman's housing facilities were available. Later, a number of companies also introduced profit sharing and other welfare work programmes. The apex of industrial housing provided by private companies was reached by 1889, when, at the 'Exposition Universelle' in Paris, on the occasion of the centenary of the French Revolution, extensive attention was paid to workingman's housing. At the same time, the 1889 Parisian world exhibition can be considered a turning point with regard to the development of building cheap housing for workers in France. Although the first private or cooperative building societies that constructed workingman's housing had been established earlier (from the 1860s), their role became more pronounced after 1890. At the outbreak of the First World War, building workingman's housing had mainly become a public affair, based on housing legislation. An important explanation for this development is the emerging social question in France in the nineteenth century and the way social reformers and the state tried to tackle it. Although there was a strong belief until 1889 in the problem solving qualities of industrial enterprises with respect to providing cheap and adequate workingman's housing, thereafter this belief gradually faded and the significance of building societies and the state predominated in the Third Republic (1870-1940).

To understand this development, first, I will pay attention to the characteristic development of the industrial revolution in France, which differed somewhat from the industrial revolution in the three other countries under examination. Then, in addition to the remarks made in chapter 2, I will return to the significance of labour utopias in the French context, in particular based on Fourier's ideas with respect to the phalanstère and, to a lesser extent, on Ebenezer Howard's ideas regarding the garden city. Also relevant were the ideas of the writer Émile Zola on solving the social question, and architect Tony Garnier's design of the futuristic *Cité Industrielle*.

Subsequently, the development of welfare work policy in private companies before the advent of the Third Republic in 1870 will be summarized as well as social policy as developed during the first phase of the Third Republic until about 1900. This so-called *économie sociale* would have a crucial impact on the specific development of welfare work in France between 1880 and 1930, in particular with regard to building workingman's housing and the introduction of scientific management and Fordism in French industry. Significant in this context is the key role played by intermediary organizations such as the 'Société Française des Habitations à Bon Marché' (HBM), the 'Musée Social', and, after the First World War, the employer initiative 'Rédressement Français'.

After describing this relevant context, more specific cases of welfare work in France will be dealt with in more detail, for example: industrial workingman's housing (*cités ouvrières*) by the 'Société Industrielle de Mulhouse' at Mulhouse and its imitations; welfare work in company towns (*cités industrielles*) Le Creusot (Schneider) and nearby Monceau-les-Mines (Compagnie des Mines de Blanzy); Guise (Godin); company town Decazeville (Société Anonyme des Houllières et Fonderies de l'Aveyron); company town Anzin (Compagnie des Mines d' Anzin); Baccarat (Cristalleries de Baccarat); Noisiel (Menier chocolate factory and worker village); and Magasins du Bon Marché (department store). To conclude, I will pay attention to welfare work initiatives after the First World War until the 1930s. Then, in France, too, the need to rationalize production processes by introducing Taylorist and Fordist elements of task and work organization supplanted the more traditional paternalistic welfare work programmes such as company housing.

6.2 The French industrial revolution

Compared to England, France's industrial development in the nineteenth century is generally considered as less advanced. There are various reasons for this. Firstly, France at that time was an overwhelmingly agricultural country with a strong and stable agrarian economy based on conservative values. Another important reason for the initially slow industrial development was almost certainly the regular political upheaval as a consequence of the French Revolution of 1789, bringing to an end the Ancien Régime and the subsequent Napoleonic wars. Other significant factors were, inter alia, the relative scarcity of coal and its mediocre quality, as well as the striking controlling and regulating presence of the state in economic affairs.[1] With notable exceptions in banking, transport, and retail, these various factors also created a typical nineteenth-century French entrepreneur, which still has some relevance today. Firstly, the 'average' French entrepreneur was a small businessman "acting for himself or at most on behalf of a handful of partners." Secondly, the French entrepreneur was "a fundamentally conservative man, with a firm distaste for the new and unknown." Thirdly, the French entrepreneur, his enterprise very often family based, valued his independence and strived for self-sufficiency. Often, the successful nineteenth-century entrepreneur belonged to France's protestant elite.[2]

If one can speak at all of a first industrial revolution in France, it came very slowly. The situation was similar in relation to the country's second industrial revolution. While the second industrial boom in Germany had already started by the end of the 1880s, in France such a notion had not even been perceived before 1906, mainly as a result of zero demographic growth.[3] The main larger corporations in the nineteenth century were textiles (for example, at Roubaix and Saint-Quentin), coalmining (for example Anzin, Monceau-les-Mines), iron and steel works (for example, Schneider at Le Creusot), and railways. Also some big department stores were established (La Belle Jardinière, Le Bon Marché, Les Magasins du Louvre, La Samaritaine). During the second industrial revolution the automobile industry (Renault, Citroën, Renault), car tyres (Michelin), chemical industries and the electricity industries dominated.[4]

6.3 The impact of Fourier's labour utopia in France

In a practical sense, Fourier's ideas with respect to the Phalanstère had little material impact in France with one notable exception, the Social Palace or 'Familistère', constructed in 1859 by cast-iron heater producer Jean-Baptiste Godin adjacent to his factory at Guise in the north of France. This example will be dealt with more extensively in section 6.5. Here, I will focus on the no less important 'inspirational' impact of Fourier's ideas on the writing of the most important and influential naturalist French writer

1 Woronoff 1998: 627-630.

2 About the relationship between French entrepreneurship and economic growth see the seminal article economic historian David Landes wrote about this. Landes 1949: 47-49; 59.

3 Caron 1981: 34.

4 See also: Asselain 1984.

of the Belle Époque, Émile Zola. After realistically describing the French social or labour question at the time of the Second Empire in his seminal 1885 novel *Germinal,* in which he dealt with an ultimately tragic and fatal strike about wage matters in a mining company in Northern France, Zola portrayed in one of his last novels *Travail* (1901) – the second volume of his *Les Quatre Évangiles* – a utopian phalanstère-like company town (*cité idéale*).[5] This fictitious company town, called La Crêcherie, was strongly based on Fourier's 'Phalanstère', as well as on Ebenezer Howard's industrial garden city. Almost at the same time, architect Tony Garnier designed in various steps his futuristic, albeit never realized, *cité industrielle* (1901, 1904, 1917).[6] Likewise, Garnier's *cité industrielle* had much in common with the ideas of both Fourier and Howard.

In advance of writing *Germinal,* Zola (1840-1902) visited the Anzin mines to get a good and reliable picture of the mining production process and the working conditions of the miners. In preparing and planning *Travail* he did something similar. After first considering visiting the large Schneider plant and company town at Le Creusot (Saône-et-Loire), Zola ultimately went to the large production site of another big French steel producer, Unieux, in industrial city St. Étienne in February 1900. Zola befriended entrepreneur Paul Ménard-Dorian who owned Unieux. In the same context, Zola also paid a visit to Godin's 'Familistère' at Guise and read not only Fourier and Howard, but also Edward Bellamy's book *Looking Backward.*

Travail is the story of idealistic entrepreneur Luc Froment and his steel factory and utopian community, La Crêcherie, erected adjacent to the more traditional industrial town of Beauclair, owned by steel producer Quirignon. Compared to Beauclair, La Crêcherie was an attractive workingman's paradise based on principles of justice. Based on a mixture of Fourier's and Howard's ideas, the harmonious utopian community or worker town in *Travail,* not only possessed attractive workingman's housing (initially 50 small white family houses with gardens), but also a central square and, identical to Fourier's phalanstère, a large communal building (*la maison commune*), containing a meeting room, a library, schools, a theatre, a restaurant, cooperative shops, bathing facilities, etc. The working conditions at La Crêcherie were also very agreeable, and included relatively high wages, an eight-hour working day (ultimately, four hours), professional training, and regular job rotation.

5 Zola, Émile (1991): *Germinal* (1885); *Travail* (1901) in *Les Quatre Évangiles*. Paris: Fasquelle..
6 Wiebenson 1960, 1969.

To Zola, La Crêcherie embodied the ideal of reformist social policy of the Third Republic at, and after, the turn of the century. Readers generally received *Travail* positively, but the critics were more sceptical. Only the Fourierists supported his novel without reservation, and even organized a banquet celebrating its publication.[7]

In the same period, architect Tony Garnier (1869-1948) born in Lyon and, from 1905, the city's architect, designed a futuristic *cité industrielle*, with some 35,000 inhabitants. He produced a first study of the 'cité' in 1901 and exhibited a second version in 1904 at the École des Beaux Arts in Paris. It took until 1917 for Garnier to publish his ultimate design for the *Cité Industrielle* in two volumes, in the form of loose sheets and an explanatory preface. Like Zola, Garnier was strongly inspired by Fourier's phalanstère. Overall, the *cité industrielle* had much in common with La Crêcherie; however, instead of small family houses with gardens it had apartments in, on average, two-storey living blocks in tree-lined streets. Garnier explicitly paid tribute to Zola by ornamenting his central assembly building with literary citations from Zola's novel *Travail*. Garnier's other inspirers were the father of modern town planning, Patrick Geddes (1854-1932) and, again, Ebenezer Howard. As a result, the *cité industrielle* was a planned and zoned city with abundant green spaces between the various physically separated, but related zones (residential, public, cultural, agricultural, manufacturing). The city should also have a communal *salle d'assemblées* (the above-mentioned assembly building), different categories of schools, hospitals, and a railway station. Places of worship were not envisaged. In the imagined city, the various functions of living, working, free time and traffic were strictly separated. Above all, it had to be "a socialist city, without walls or private property, without church or barracks, without police station or law court; a city were all unbuilt surface was public parkland."[8]

Though imaginary, the futuristic *cité industrielle* was not completely fictitious. It had to be constructed not far from Lyon, somewhere in the southeast of France on "a plateau with high land and a lake to the north, a valley and a river to the south." The residential quarter was going to be the main area of the city, "composed of rectangular blocks of 150 meters, running east-west." The main industry, a large metallurgic factory and

7 Mitterand 2002, Tome III: 713. See also: Seng & Saage 2012: 25-26; Febles 2008: 286-304; Buck 2002.

8 Frampton 1980: 102.

related mines, was situated on the east side of the city. There was also a hydroelectric station and a dam to generate electricity.[9]

Compared with the impact of Ebenezer Howard's *Garden Cities of To-Morrow* (1898), Garnier's *Cité* had only a limited impact. Howard's garden city model has directly influenced the development of garden cities and post-Second World War new towns in England, beginning with, Letchworth Garden City in 1903. There has been nothing comparable in France with respect to the *Cité Industrielle.* However, elements of the principles of the cité were expressed in Garnier's later works in Lyon, such as the abattoirs (1906-1932), the Grande Blanche hospital (1909-1930) and the Quartier des États-Unis (1924/1935).[10]

6.4 Paternalism and social policy in France before 1900

The pinnacle of enlightened capitalism in France was reached by 1889 when the centennial of the French Revolution was celebrated by organizing the fourth successive international Exposition Universelle in Paris.[11] More precisely, social reform in France in the 1880s turned out to be a result of a:

> mixed legacy of social reform that included a strong but limited tradition of enlightened paternalism, a contested liberal tradition, a centralized state, a largely agrarian social structure, industrial concentration in select segments of the economy, a historic ambivalence of elites towards industrial growth, and a tradition of criticizing industrialism.[12]

The 1889 Universal Exhibition was a clear demonstration of that legacy and devoted extensive attention to the actual state of the *économie sociale* and, in particular, welfare work reforms by a great number of private companies in France within the wider context of the industrializing world. The social exhibit located on the Esplanade des Invalides, covered a quarter of the total exhibiting space, and consisted of two main parts: the *Cité sociale* "conceived as a grandiose worker's village', and the Galérie de l' économie sociale displaying 'documents on recent industrial experiments in social

9 Wiebenson 1960: 16.

10 Frampton 1980: 103-104.

11 Before, three other Expositions Universelles were organized in Paris, in 1855, 1867, and 1878. After 1889, the two last Parisian world exhibitions took place in 1900 and 1937 respectively. See: Ory 1982, 1989.

12 Horne 2002: 53.

welfare." Part of the *Cité social* was the Workers' Housing Street with four full-scale models of cheap workingman's houses, "some of which were decorated with domestic furnishings typical of a working-class household and, in one case, adorned with workers themselves, dressed in their traditional blue overalls and accompanied by their hard-working families." Included in the Galérie de l' économie sociale were displays of 131 French companies with profit-sharing schemes, such as the Familistère de Guise, the Bon Marché department store, and Maison Leclaire. Other companies present at the exhibition were, for example, chocolate factory Menier near Paris and the Anzin mining company. Both companies displayed model working-class houses. Anzin also displayed its mortgage plans "based on long-term employer loans to personnel for the construction of individual homes or the acquisition of property." Furthermore, there was an exhibit of workingmen's clubs demonstrating "discussion circles, libraries, trade-related evening courses, and groups promoting leisure activities for male workers." The Galérie de l'économie sociale, in addition, displayed a number of welfare work experiments in companies in the form of "diagrams, wall murals, charts, books, and brochures."

Finally, awards were granted to the Anzin mining company for its model workingman's housing, the Baccarat crystal works for its professional training schools and medical service, and to Le Bon Marché for its profit sharing scheme. The social exhibit at the 1889 Exposition Universelle expressed the state of enlightened capitalism in France, by demonstrating and promoting successful paternalistic company welfare work practices to date. At the same time, the exhibit stressed the significance of guided self-help for workers in solving the social question in France, for example in the form of profit-sharing schemes, mutual aid programmes and, workingman's clubs or circles.[13] At the fringe of the 1889 exhibition, an important intermediary lobby- and propaganda organization was founded by a diverse group of eminent Third Republic social reformers, including Jules Simon, Jules Siegfried, Émile Cheysson, Jean Dollfus, Léon Say, Charles Gide, George Picot, and Charles Robert. This was the 'Société Française des Habitations à Bon Marché' (HBM). HBM became involved in the building of future cheap workingman's housing by strongly influencing the enactment of future social housing legislation. Another important, mid-term, spin-off of the 1889 exhibition with regard to future social policy in France, including social housing policy, was the privately sponsored Musée Social, ultimately

13 *Ibid.:* 2002: 69-76.

founded in 1894 in Paris.[14] By and large, the same group of reformers linked with the HBM played a role. Company owners, representatives of trade unions and cooperative organizations, civil servants and workers were also involved in the founding of the Musée. The core idea behind the Musée Social was to create a permanent exhibit of the documents and displays of the social economy section at the 1889 Universal Exhibition, as well as to create a publicly accessible thematic library. A second objective of the Musée was to carry out sociological studies and research into the social question in France and abroad, based on ideas of sociologist and engineer Frédéric Le Play. Le Play was advisor on social policy to Napoleon III and founder of the 'Société d' Économie Sociale' (1856).[15] In order to be able to administer the research projects and, subsequently, to influence employers and the government, seven research sections were created, among which: employer-sponsored social welfare services; labour and cooperative associations; and social insurance. But already by 1900 the first section had been abolished "since the general public no longer believed that entrepreneurial forms of welfare could resolve the country's pressing social problems." In 1908, a new section on urban and rural hygiene was added. This section was going to play an important role with respect to future housing legislation.[16] In France, the Musée Social also became, for a while, a great advocate of mutualism as the ideal form of social policy in France.

The idea of mutualism already had a rather long history in France, and even had mediaeval roots. Subsequently, Napoleon III legalized mutual aid societies in 1852 as vehicles for social betterment. During the Third Republic, these societies were succeeded by the legal Mutualist Charter in 1898, giving ample leeway to the French mutualist movement to get involved in the formation of future national social policy.[17]

The Musée likewise promoted the garden cities idea, with its most notable practical achievement the realization of 'Les Cités Jardins du Grand Paris'. This ring of garden cities around Paris had been constructed directly after

14 Count René Aldebert de Chambrun financed the Musée. He also became the principal owner by marriage of the Cristalleries de Baccarat, a company with extensive welfare work programmes.

15 Le Play had been the Exhibition-director of the Exposition Universelle in 1867 in Paris. Also this Exhibition paid major attention to workingman's housing by displaying onsite models of, and plans for workingman's housing in France, England, Prussia, Belgium and Austria. According to Bullock & Read, this exhibition confirmed the consensus reached among reformers in favour of the individual workingman's house with garden instead of urban flats. See Bullock & Read 1989: 380. On the founding history of the Musée Social see also: Horne 1995: 46-69.

16 Horne 2002: 150.

17 *Ibid.*: 196-198.

the First World War by the 'Office Publique des HBM du Département de la Seine'.[18]

The conviction that entrepreneurial welfare work could not resolve the social question in France and that, ultimately, civil society and the state had to play a decisive role had already received significant support from the 1840s, also from the entrepreneurial side. However, this was temporarily opposed by political developments, such as the failure of the Second Republic in the aftermath of the Revolution of 1848, the Franco-Prussian War of 1870, and the Paris Commune of 1871.[19] To some extent this is noteworthy, because during the first phase of the industrial revolution in France between 1820-1848 industrial paternalism and thus welfare work programmes had been extensive, particularly in the textile industry, coalmining, and the metallurgical industries.

There is evidence that before 1848 at least 461 companies in these sectors began to develop welfare work programmes, and at least 134 companies built rental workingman's housing, including all new mining and metallurgical companies as well as many textile companies. More specifically, the mines of Anzin provided housing for a quarter of its 5,000 workers, whilst in mining company town Decazeville half of the labour force lived in company housing.[20]

Bullock and Read summarized a number of important initiatives by industrial companies building workingman's housing from the 1880:[21]

- Steel manufacturer Schneider at Le Creusot, with 8,500 workers in 1867, started constructing housing from the 1830s. This resulted in eighteen blocks of flats with four storeys for 662 families by 1852. The company also offered over 2,300 loans by 1889. Later, Schneider preferred to build single-storey terraced houses with two rooms.
- Compagnie des Mines de Blanzy at Monceau-les-Mines, with 3,500 workers by 1867. This company built flats and individual houses; also sold lots and offered mortgage loans without interest to its miners and workers with the possibility to design their own houses. This resulted in 99 houses by 1866.
- André Koechlin Mulhouse built three-storey houses, with a flat on each storey, from the 1830s.

18 Bullock & Read 1985: 371-373.
19 Cf. also Donzelot 1984.
20 Stearns 1978: 89-106.
21 Bullock & Read 1985: 419-431.

- Hartmann Company Mulhouse constructed five-storey flats, each with two rooms, from the 1830s.
- Jean Zuber paper factory at Mulhouse, built company housing in the 1840s.
- Compagnie des Mines d'Anzin owned over 1,000 dwellings by the end of the 1840s, a number of which had four rooms.
- Godin built the Familistère at Guise in 1859, a community with family dwellings of a reasonable size and all kinds of communal amenities and provisions such as a school, a theatre, and a heated swimming pool.
- Foundation of the 'Société Mulhousienne des Cités Ouvrières' (SOMCO) in 1853. By 1867, this society had built a small worker town with 800 houses, with gardens, on twenty acres at Mulhouse. The houses were owned by its 5,500 residents. The town also had bathing facilities, a swimming pool, a laundry, schools, shops, a library, and offered free medical services. Called *la solution Muhousienne,* in subsequent years Mulhouse, and not Guise, became a major inspirational source for many other company-housing and reformers' initiatives, especially in cities like Le Havre, Lille, Nancy, and Bolbec.
- The spinning mill of Bourcart et Fils at Guebwiller, near Mulhouse, built 49 houses in 1854, designed by Émille Muller; and, from 1860, on a second site, 90 two-storey back-to-back houses were built in collaboration with a housing society in which the firm participated financially.
- Antoine Herzog, Colmar, founded a housing society in 1866 to build 150 houses.
- The Société des Mines de Carmeaux constructed semi-detached houses in a terraced form, with a ground-floor habitable space of 31 square metres in the 1860s.
- The Scrive Brothers, near Lille, founded a housing society to finance housing for their workers.
- Japy Frères built company owned housing in 1862 at Beaucourt; and semi-detached, single-storey houses with three rooms, kitchen and additional attic space went on sale in 1864.
- Compagnie des Mines d'Aniche in the North of France constructed two groups of houses for sale.
- The Manufacture de Peugeot Jackson at Doubs (800 workers) built houses for sale and offered loans with five per cent interest, resulting in 38 loans by 1867.
- Compagnie des Cristalleries de St. Louis, Moselle, built single-family houses with a garden for sale.

- Menier chocolate works at Noisiel, near Paris, built 500 houses in the mid-1870s in a rectilinear street plan, designed as a self-contained community with a central square with shops, a restaurant, and a school. The village additionally had a town hall, a fire station, a post office, and an old people's home.
- The Compagnie des Mines de Dourges, in the North, constructed in 1907-1908 the first French Garden City with only 74 picturesque houses in curving tree-lined streets, supported by the 'Association des Cités Jardins de France' and the 'Section d'Hygiène Urbaine et Rurale' of the Musée Social.

Some of the companies built rental housing, while others built housing for sale, often combined with long-term mortgage loans. In exceptional circumstances, workers were allowed to design their own house. Companies built multiple-storey apartments as well as single-family houses. In due course, single-family houses with a garden owned by the resident became the preferred workingman's housing model in France. This also became the reformers' ideal from mid-century. The quality of the housing varied from barracks to houses and improved over time. Usually, mining companies built houses close to the pits in the form of so-called *corons,* straight rows of houses, almost without amenities. The problem with *corons* was the lack of social cohesion between the residents. The mines of Anzin tried to break this pattern by building small groups of housing adjacent to each other, with a small number of facilities, like a bakery, for each group. The small town of the Dourges mine company also broke the monotonous pattern of the *corons* by laying out curving streets in a green setting.

From the mid-1890s, the initiative to construct workingman's housing gradually shifted from employers to private, urban, and cooperative building societies, in which a number of employers participated. The first housing law in France, the *Loi Siegfried* (1894), enabled this development.[22] As noted, by 1914, housing policy had become a fully public affair and was no longer a matter for employers.

All things considered, enlightened capitalism in the nineteenth century, but also at the beginning of the twentieth century, was rather well developed in France. One of the most important reasons for this was the chronic shortage of industrial workers. For many workers, agriculture remained more attractive, or they combined, at best, agricultural work on farms with industrial work in factories. Therefore, in order to become an

22 The next, more extensive housing legislation was adopted by Parliament in 1906 and 1908.

attractive employer, industrial entrepreneurs not only had to pay relatively high wages to workers, they also had to provide additional free meals, fuel, and other goods. They were also urged to construct workingman's housing and offer workers other welfare work benefits directed at preventing or alleviating material problems in case of sickness, work accidents, or old age (pensions). In a number of cases, and particularly in larger companies, company doctors, drugs, and infirmaries were provided. It was not unusual for larger firms to establish schools, company shops, and bakeries. For example, clockmaking Établissements de Japy Frères et Cie. at Beaucourt (Haut-Rhin), in addition to housing and mutual aid groups, "[...] set up a system of bonuses; in 1813 the company built a cemetery at company expense; in 1818 a church and a school; in 1842, a library and a kindergarten; in 1845, a company bakery."[23]

In this period, French paternalism was not only characterized by instrumental motives – such as binding the worker to the company – or based on calculated self-interest. A primary motive was also moralizing and controlling the company's workforce. Sometimes, beneficial motives were at stake, often based on religious principles, as in the protestant company town of Mulhouse. In due course, a number of welfare work programmes got elements of employer-guided self-help for workers, as was the case with employer savings banks, long-term mortgage loans, mutual social security aid groups, and cooperative company stores. In 1847, for example, in Mulhouse some 8,000 workers took part in various employer-sponsored aid groups.[24] Propagating self-help was part of a set of broader reform proposals put forward by employers and their associations in the 1840s, including proposals to regulate child labour and pensions collectively with the help of the state.[25]

The end of the Second Empire and the advent of the Third Republic partly implied the gradual end of traditional enlightened capitalism, shaped in France between 1820-1848, in favour of, at first, mutualism as one of the most striking expressions of self-help, and then, in the twentieth century, state sponsored welfare state provisions or, as it is called in France, *L'État Providence.*[26]

23 Stearns 1978: 98.
24 *Ibid.:* 169.
25 Regulated by law in 1841.
26 See Ewald 1986.

6.5 Welfare work and social betterment before 1914

Like the US, France had many company towns. Early precursors were La Saline Royale at Arc-et-Senans (1775), and the Fonderie Royale at le Creusot, predecessor of the Schneider steelworks (1780s). Most company towns were founded in the mining and metallurgy sectors, and the textile sector in the North of France, in the Alsace and the Burgundy region. Initially, two rather opposite models developed. First, and most successful, was the Mulhouse model or *solution Mulhousienne* consisting of *cités ouvrières* with worker-owned single-family houses with a garden. This model was also widely advocated by housing reformers and employers in the second half of the nineteenth century as the ideal French workingman's home and copied in several French cities, such as Lille and Nancy. The other model was based on the ideas of Fourier and the phalanstère. In this case, it was not the single-family house that was the ideal workingman's home, but a group of apartments in a collective building. The welfare work concept of the phalanstère differed fundamentally from the Mulhouse model. In this case, the workingman's living and working community was paramount, rather than a harmonious family life. As noted, Godin's Familistère at Guise best embodied the phalanstère idea.

Mulhouse was one of the first and, at the same time, one of the most eminent nineteenth century French company towns.[27] Situated in the Alsace border region, Mulhouse had been an independent city from the fifteenth century until 1798 before it became part of France. The town rapidly transformed into one of the most important industrial centres of France in the nineteenth century. Next to Rouen, Mulhouse may be considered as one of the two main cotton towns in the country, comparable to Manchester in England. A protestant aristocracy, consisting of a few closely-knit families, such as the Schlumberger's, the Koechlin's, the Dollfus's, and the Zuber's, also owned the cotton mills. They dominated the town for generations.

In 1826, a number of entrepreneurs in Mulhouse and the surrounding region founded the 'Société Industrielle de Mulhouse '(SIM). SIM's objectives were to enable further industrial development of the industry and entrepreneurship in the region, including the advancement of public welfare and welfare work. Examples of welfare work were: the Schlumberger Company's model bakery; savings banks in various companies, and a regional pension

27 On Mulhouse and its *cité ouvrière* see: Bullock & Reed 1985: 318-324; Ermenc 1957: 129-135; Fox 1984: 127-168; Jonas 1994; Kott 1987: 640-659.

savings bank for factory workers; mutual aid provisions; free medical services; libraries; a theatre; a gymnasium; a swimming pool; and the creation of vocational training schools for chemistry, design, weaving, spinning, and commerce. Primary education for boys and girls was obligatory.

One of SIM's ideas, inspired by Henry Roberts' *The Dwellings of the Labouring Classes,* was to create a *cité industrielle* on the outskirts of town of Mulhouse.[28] In order to realize this, Jean Dollfus and eleven other entrepreneurs, all members of SIM, founded a separate housing corporation, the 'Société Mulhousienne des Cités Ouvrières de Mulhouse' (SOMCO). The project started in 1853. It encompassed the construction of 384 differing single-family houses for sale to the workers of their factories. The houses, for example with two rooms and a kitchen on the ground floor, were designed by engineer and architect Émile Muller. Houses in groups of four, built in rows, provided in-house floor space varying from 30-55 square metres. By 1864, some 616 houses with gardens had been constructed. Then, by 1867, some 800 dwellings had been realized on twenty acres for 5,500 people. By 1876, the project resulted in almost 1,000 single-family houses with gardens and additional amenities and provisions, such as bathing facilities, a public laundry, cooperative stores, schools, and a workingman's club.[29] In 1895, the number of houses in the *cité* had increased to 1,240. The number of inhabitants had increased to 10,000 people. Overall, house-purchasing terms were *bon marché* (economical). Alongside a down payment of ten per cent, low interest loans were offered to the workers.

The *cité ouvrière* at Mulhouse may be considered as a major welfare work performance at the time of the Second Empire and the first half of the Third Republic, as well as during its further development throughout the period of the German annexation after 1870. What is notable is not only the development of the *cité ouvrière* so early in time, its extensiveness and quality, but also the fact that it involved a cohesive group of religiously motivated Calvinistic employers. The choice for building single-family houses for sale, set in a garden, was, in this respect, a fundamental one. It expressed the primary significance of family and house-ownership for the improvement of morality in the Mulhousian welfare policy.

The other model of workingman's housing in France was based on Fourier's phalanstère and the principles of association and cooperation. Apart from a few attempts, such as the 1849 Parisian *Cité Napoleon,* a worker's flat

28 Roberts 1850.

29 Between 1870-1918 the Alsace and Lorraine were annexed by Germany.

building designed by architect Gabriel Veugny, and Victor Calland's project proposal 'Le Palais de Famille' (1855), this model hardly had any practical impact on French employers. Only Godin's Familistère or Social Palace, constructed next to his stove heater factory at Guise (Aisne), approached the ideal model of the phalanstère.

Jean-Baptiste Godin (1817-1888), entrepreneur and idealist, founded his successful enterprise in 1846. Initially, he employed some 30 workers. By the 1880s, this number had increased to 2,000.[30] Godin's main objective was to improve the living conditions of workers. He started constructing his Social Palace in 1859 and it was completed in 1880. The building's appearance was like a phalanstère:

> [T]he centre of the Palace was bordered by two wings placed toward the front, so as to form a courtyard in the middle. Each of the three blocks had an inner courtyard covered by a huge glass dome supported by a majestic structure. The three pavilions were connected at the angles in such a way as to have as many doors and windows as possible. Inside the Familistère there were many conveniences. On each of the three stories, as well as on the ground floor, individual apartments gave out onto balcony-galleries. Every entrance door opened onto a vestibule that serviced two apartments (the smallest twenty square meters) and a small pantry. Thanks to the windows, which opened, one on the gardens and orchards, the other over the inner courtyard, there was cross ventilation. Piping in the walls arrived directly from the air galleries in the basement, allowing temperature control in the apartments. Water fountains were available on each floor of the Palace. Also, on the exterior as well as the interior of the Familistère, sewers and tanks collected and circulated refuse and sewage.[31]

Apartments could be doubled depending of family size.

As previously noted, Godin had also provided a number of amenities and provisions to the workingman's families, such as: a cooperative company stores; a laundry; bathing facilities; a roofed swimming pool heated by wastewater from the factory; a school; a crèche; a nursery; a restaurant; and a large theatre. The theatre and the school were located just opposite

30 On Godin's Social palace and his welfare work see: Godin 1871 (2010); Delabre 2010; Lallement 2009; Lallement 2012: 31-49; Bullock & Read 1985: 315-317; Paquot & Bédarida 2003.

31 Lallement 2012: 38.

Image 6 Vue d'ensemble du Familistère ou Palais social - Overview of the Familistère or Social Palace, Guise, France

From: J.B.A. Godin, *Solutions sociales*, Paris-Bruxelles 1871

the courtyard. In the park surrounding the Social Palace a bandstand was erected. As Godin was principally secularist he did not construct a church.

The apartments in the Social Palace were for rent and housed some 1,500 people. Rents were rather low and services were usually free of charge. Godin and his wife occupied a large apartment in the Social Palace. In sum, for its time, the Social Palace offered Godin's factory workers and their families rather good, healthy, and hygienic living conditions.

As at Mulhouse, welfare work at Godin not only included workingman's housing, but also a number of other welfare work programmes. Godin, for example, had already founded a mutual aid society for his workers in 1846. The workers themselves administered the various funds forming part of the mutual aid society. Contributions were paid by the employer as well as by individual workers. Financial aid was given in cases of sickness, disability, as well as to widows, orphans and the aged. In addition to this form of self-help, Godin also introduced some form of industrial democracy. In 1877, consultation circles consisting of factory workers were created. These circles were charged with the improvement of the still hard and unpleasant working conditions in the factory as well as with the improvement of the living conditions in the Social Palace. A second, more fundamental step was taken in 1880, when Godin founded the 'Association coopérative du capital' (association of capital and labour). His ultimate aim was to transfer factory ownership to the workers. This was achieved six years after Godin's death in 1894. From then on, the Association owned both the factory and the Social Palace.[32]

'Schneiderville' (Le Creusot)

By the end of the nineteenth and the beginning of the twentieth century, the Schneider metal works and mining company at Le Creusot in rural Burgundy (Saône-et-Loire), nicknamed 'Schneiderville', was considered as a major showpiece of French enlightened capitalism. At that time, Le Creusot had become one of the largest and most important company towns in France, uniting both town and the factory. By 1900, the town had 32,000 inhabitants. The Schneider Company employed some 15,000 people. Founding father, Eugène I. Schneider (1805-1875) and his brother Alphonse (1802-1845), after acquiring the already existing steel plant Le Crozot, established Schneider

32 By the end of the 1960s, Godin was taken by another company (Le Creuset). Today, the partly restored Social Palace belongs to the French industrial heritage. It is also a museum, which can be visited.

frères et Cie. in 1836. The company planned to build railroads, locomotives, steam engines, steamboats, arms, and other steel products.[33]

The Schneider family, fervent supporters of Napoleon III, was also politically active. During the Second Empire, Eugene I was mayor of Le Creusot (1866-1870), minister of agriculture in 1851, deputy, member and, in 1867, president of the 'Corps Législatif'. Likewise, his son Henry was mayor of the town of Le Creusot between 1871-1896 and deputy. Eugène II also became deputy and mayor of Le Creusot (1896-1900).

From the start, Schneider introduced many comprehensive welfare work programmes, including:

- Subsidized social activities
- Allowances for families of men on military service
- Allowances for large families
- Cheap loans for the purchase of company built homes
- Architectural service for workers interested in building their own homes
- A provident fund for financial assistance to sick and injured workers, widows, and orphans (1838)
- A free hospital with 130 beds and complementary home health services (1894)
- A free maternity hospital
- Old age pensions (1893)
- A home for the elderly (1887)[34]

In addition to these programmes, the firm created cooperative stores, started a company restaurant (in 1917), built churches, and organized sports like a bicycle club, a gymnastic club and a nautical club. The core of welfare work at Le Creusot was a combination of educational and workingman's housing programmes.

The company organized its own school system with the intention of insulating its labour force from external labour market influences. As a result, it was not uncommon for several generations of workers of the same family to work for the Schneider Company. A third of the workers worked for the company for more than twenty years, and a smaller group for more than thirty years. Elementary schools were created by the company from 1837

33 On Le Creusot an its welfare work policy see: Rabinow 1989: 97-103; Bullock & Read 1985: 421431; Beaud 1990: 9-18; Reid 1994: 1-22; Reid 1993: 129-143; Reid 1985: 579-607; Ermenc 1957: 133-134; Floquet & Laroche 2013: 117-136; Bretin Maffiuletti 2009: 49-66; Gacon & Jurrige 2014: 27-45; Le petit journal des grandes expositions 1995: 1-16.

34 Ermenc 1957: 134.

and were based on the principle that company jobs could only be offered to literate people, older than the age of fourteen. In 1841, 100 sons and daughters of Schneider workers started education at the first elementary company school. The number of pupils, wearing special Schneider school uniforms, had increased to a total of 4,000 by 1867. After graduating from elementary school, boys usually went to work at Schneider or were selected to attend a special school, founded in 1856. From 1872, the company also provided secondary education. In addition, some of the most promising pupils were sent to government engineering schools at the cost of the company. The regular workforce had an opportunity to upgrade its skills by following special courses offered by the company. In 1867, some 500 workers followed special courses. From 1899, Schneider introduced its own ambitious three-year course for training engineers, called *le Caboulot.* It produced 152 graduates between 1899-1919.

Before 1848, workingman's lodging was provided in the form of barracks. Thereafter, workingman's single-family houses, surrounded with gardens, were built at Le Creusot. With the exception of building housing for higher-ranking employees, it was not the intention of the firm to build its own company housing complexes for rent. Schneider's housing policy was different. Workers were stimulated to build and design their own houses with financially attractive company loans. By 1869, about a quarter of the workforce owned their housing, and by 1889, 2,300 loans had been provided. As a result of this alternative policy, Le Creusot was not a traditional company town with exclusively company built and company-owned housing. The company was, nevertheless, still able to steer the quantity and quality of housing production, including the city planning of Le Creusot. In the context of the Universal Expositions in Paris in 1867 and 1878, the company built only two complexes for workers with single-family houses. One of these was La Cité Villedieu with 105 houses on identical geometric lots. The size of the largest room in the houses, the *salle commune,* was 25 square metres, including a fireplace for cooking. This room was used both as a living room during daytime and as a dormitory during the night.

Not all workers had the same welfare rights. Best off were the so-called *titulaires.* This was the group of employees educated at the Schneider company schools with fixed contracts and not older than age 35 years when hired by the company. This was also the group of most skilled workers. Then, there was a second group, the *auxiliaires.* This was a group of less skilled workers without company education and older than age 35 when hired by the company. The third group of workers were the unskilled or *journaliers.*

This group had no work security and did not have access to the company's welfare work programmes.

The company strived to achieve a sustainable skilled and disciplined workforce, organized as one big Schneider family, the so-called *Crusotiens*. Labour conflict did not play a significant role until the 1930s. Strikes were limited to 1850 and 1899. In 1848, the company was hit briefly by a general strike in France. The national troubles of 1871 contributed to a reduction of working hours at Le Creusot, from eleven to ten hours per day, as well as to an increase of wages. The provident fund established in 1838 and based on financial worker contributions was abolished in 1872 and subsequently replaced by contribution-free worker benefits. A minimum old-age pension for workers with at least 30 years of company service was introduced in 1893. After the 1899 strike, the firm established a company-backed trade union, as well as a system of elected worker delegates.

In 1875, Eugene I's son, Henry (1840-1898), succeeded the founding father of the Schneider Company and, in 1891, Eugène I's grandchild Eugène II (1868-1942), nicknamed the 'king of the company', became the leader of the Schneider Company. The paternalism of the Schneider family was greatly influenced by their Christianity as well as by the social paternalistic ideas of Saint-Simon and by Frederic Le Play's convictions about workingman's housing, morality, and hygiene. Le Play was against state intervention, supported job security, and considered family life to be the basis of social order. He wrote an influential book about this, *La Réforme sociale en France* (1854). Social reformer Émile Cheysson, social director at Le Creusot at the beginning of the 1870s, introduced Le Play's ideas in the firm's welfare work policy. Cheysson was particularly responsible for the distribution of housing and the resolution of workingman's complaints about supervisors. He also gave more weight to the intermediary managerial role of engineers between the company owner and the workers, instead of foremen.

The coalmines of Anzin, Monceau-les-Mines and Decazeville

Coalmining has been very important for the industrial development of France. Coal was primarily used as raw material for the production of iron and steel, initially for the purpose of the production of railways. Often coal mining was combined with metallurgical industry on the same site. This was also the case at Decazeville in the Aubin Basin in Southwest France (Aveyron). Compared to skilled metal work, work in coalmines was semi-skilled.

In France, coal excavation was concentrated in the North, in the Loire region, and in the Aubin Basin. The largest coalmine in the nineteenth century was the Anzin coalmine near the Belgian border. Also significant were the coalmines in Monceau-les-Mines near Le Creusot (Saône-et-Loire) and Decazeville. Many new company towns were constructed in the various coal regions in the first half of the nineteenth century.[35] Almost all mining companies developed extensive housing programmes by building *corons* for their miners. This was different in Decazeville where, compared to Anzin and Monceau-les-Mines, paternalism and company housing remained less developed.[36] This was caused partly by the rather turbulent economic and conflicting history of labour relations in the coalmines and steelworks in the Aubin Basin.

Usually coalmines were not family-owned, but founded by small groups of investors in the form of a *Société Anonyme* or joint stock company. Decazeville started the extraction of coal in the 1820s and, before the turn of the century, the company changed owner three times. Duke Decazes and a group of Parisian financiers founded the 'Société Anonyme des Houillères et Fonderies de l'Aveyron' in 1826 at Firmy and Lassalle. Lassalle was renamed in the 1830s as Decazeville. By 1833, Decazeville had 1,123 inhabitants and by 1856 about 8,000. After an economic collapse of the industry in the 1860s, the first Société Anonyme was succeeded by the 'Société Nouvelle des Houillères et Fonderies de l'Aveiron', which had strong financial ties with the Schneider steelworks at Le Creusot. In 1892, a third new owner, Comambault ('Société Anonyme de Commentry-Fourchambault'), took on the Decazeville Company. Its general director at that time was Henri Fayol, a mining engineer and internationally renowned theorist of business administration. Summarizing the development of welfare work at Decazeville it can be argued that, instead of extensive workingman's housing programmes, the core of welfare work at Decazeville, from the start of the firm until 1914, was the founding of a mutual aid fund and a large company store.

The mutual aid fund was introduced as early as 1832. The workers themselves filled the fund by means of an obligatory levy of two per cent on their wages. Further financial contributions came from the company. Benefits were given to workers and their families in cases of sickness or work injuries.

35 Other examples of mining towns are: Carmaux, Aniche, Aubin, Lens, Dourges.

36 On Decazevile see: Reed 1985 (II); on Anzin see: Tilly 1985: 403-417; Reed 1985: 592-601; Bullock & Reed 1985: 419-431; Barker 1961: 161-178; on Monceau-les-Mines: see Bullock & Reed 1985: 419-431; Bretin Maffiuletti 2009: 49-66.

The mutual aid fund also contributed to the cost of educating children of company workers. The company store, based on the truck system, was established in the 1830s and consisted of a bakery, a butcher, a grocery, a clothing store, and a canteen. The workers themselves were involved in the administration of both the mutual aid fund and the company store. In time, the company store was transformed into a number of worker-owned cooperative stores. Finally, in the 1870s, a hospital was built for the Decazeville workers and their families. With respect to housing, the company's policy was directed at stimulating workers to take care of themselves and to build their own houses by providing the required materials. By 1850, the company was solely responsible for the construction of some 200 dwellings at Decazeville.

The history of welfare work at the Anzin Company, established in 1757 and owned by a small group of noble families, is totally different from the history of Decazeville. In the case of Anzin, the building of workingman's housing was the core piece of welfare work in the nineteenth century. Housing at Anzin was also constructed in *corons,* but with a somewhat different set-up. Here, the houses were built in groups of 60 to 80 houses. Each group of houses had its own facilities, such as a bakehouse, well, and kindergarten. By 1900, Anzin had built more than 2,800 houses, providing housing for about 90 per cent of its workforce.[37]

In order to create a stable and sustainable workforce, the Anzin Company offered a wide array of other welfare work programmes. The Anzin Company took care of the workers and their families from the cradle to the grave. It not only offered jobs to fathers, but also to other younger and older family members. As a result, it was not uncommon that more generations of the same family and other relatives worked for the company in the pits (*au fond*) as well as at the surface (*au jour*) at the same time. Pit work was carried out in small work teams and negotiated with the company management (the *marchandage* system). Other welfare work measures at Anzin concerned the supply of coal and fuel for heating, schools, instruction courses for workers, elaborate old age and survivors' pensions, free medical care, cooperative shops, and a consumer cooperative for the miners.

Like Anzin, paternalistic welfare worked was strongly developed at Monceau-les-Mines. At Monceau, the Compagnie des Mines de Blanzy built a substantial amount of single-family houses. Along with other mining companies, Blanzy exhibited its housing at the Universal Exposition in Paris in 1867. By 1891, Blanzy had realized some 1,000 houses. On display

37 Bullock & Reed 1985: 427 and 430; and Tilly 1985: 410.

were semi-detached houses, each house having four rooms with, in total, 39 square metres of habitable space. The company also offered the miners additional welfare work provisions, such as pensions, free medical services, cheap fuel and bread, and sports facilities.[38]

Welfare work at the glassworks of Baccarat, the Menier Chocolate Works and other companies

As has been noted, many other French companies introduced welfare work programmes in the golden age of capitalism. The general pattern of these programmes was similar, although the focus of welfare work could be different for each company. Department store Magasins du Bon Marché was well known for its profit sharing scheme. On the other hand, there was the exemplary Mulhousian welfare work model. Indeed, this model was emulated widely by a substantial number of companies in various industrial cities. Also in the Mulhousian region itself, this model was later copied by a number of potash mining companies. Between 1908 and 1930, these companies created some eighteen industrial villages with "a great architectural and social quality."[39] Another regular inspirational source was the ideas of Le Play and his 'Société d'Économie Sociale'. For example, the glassworks of Baccarat near Nancy and Lunéville in the Alsace, owned by the founder of the Musée Social, Count De Chambrun, was renowned for its *système Baccarat* as well as for the quality of its medical services, hygiene and savings programmes. The Baccarat system was based on a combination of paternalistic principles and social justice.[40] Also worth noting in this respect were the chocolate works at Noisiel (Seine et Marne) near Paris, owned by the wealthy Menier family. At that time, Menier was one of the most important chocolate works in the world. By 1900, the company employed more than 2,200 workers. By 1874, following the English example and according to the ideas of Le Play, Menier built a *cité ouvrière* on 20 hectares alongside the banks of the Marne River. The cité encompassed a number of, at that time, rather luxury single workingman's houses with running water, plumbing, and gardens. Menier also built a primary school for the worker's children, organized a savings scheme and a consumer's cooperative, introduced cantines, offered medical services,

38 Bullock & Read 1985: 425 and 429; Bretin Maffiuletti 2009: 49-66.

39 Jonas 1994.

40 Birck 1990: 29-55; Moriceau 2005: 53-70.

and regularly organized festivities or banquets for his workers and their families.[41]

6.6 Welfare work during and after the First World War until the 1930s

During and after the First World War, traditional employer paternalism remained strong in France. New company towns were still being built in the 1920s, such as the industrial garden city Ungemach at Strasbourg. But, as in Germany, traditional welfare work became mingled with American-style neo-paternalistic welfare work.[42] Increasingly important in this respect were efforts to rationalize production and labour relations in firms by introducing elements of scientific management and Fordism. The adoption of Fordism concerned, in particular, the assembly line and chain production and focused lesson on the social dimension.[43] However, despite direct personal contact between the founder of scientific management Frederick Winslow Taylor and important French industrialists, in particular the brothers André and Edouard Michelin, the Americanization of French industrial production was rather slow and, moreover, was selective. In other words, in France's case, it is no exaggeration to speak of a *rationalisation à la Française.*[44] It took until the end of the 1920s for Americanization of production processes and labour relations to gain more convincing momentum.

One of the first industrialists who adopted and promoted the principles of scientific management and Fordism in France was car tyre manufacturer Michelin in Clermont-Ferrand in the south of France (also at Milltown, NJ, in the United States), followed by car manufacturer Renault and some other companies representing the 'new' chemical, electrical, mining, and

41 Dellalande 2008: 9-33.
42 For the introduction of scientific management in France see in particular: Maier 1970; Frost; Fridenson 1987; Moutet 1997; Harp 2001, Chapter 6, Advocating Americanization? Taylorism and Mass Consumption in the Interwar Years: pp.187-224.
43 Moutet 1997.
44 Frost (2014), based on Moutet (1997): 4. Also Taylor's various works were translated at an early stage in France. In the academic world the most important propagator of Taylor's ideas was engineer Henry le Chatelier, professor at the Collége de France and the Sorbonne University. Michelin was very active in propagating Taylorism and Americanization in France by publishing many brochures about various aspects of Taylorism and its application. Michelin also created the Comité Michelin organizing seminars, conferences and a library, and published a magazine, called *Prospérité.*

armament industries.[45] Referring to the, comparatively seen, rapidly increasing wealth of American workers it was believed that new technologies, in particular scientific management and Fordism, could also contribute to an increase in worker welfare and to a solution for the social division in France. Company engineers in France were increasingly considered as 'social managers'. For many a 'new social economy' based on mass production and consumerism lay ahead.[46]

Michelin, by 1926 employing some 18,000 employees in Clermont-Ferrand, had already introduced a comprehensive profit sharing plan in 1898, resulting in bonuses for about forty per cent of its workforce in the 1920s. The company also paid rather high salaries, introduced a suggestion box, and was also actively engaged in constructing subsidized housing for its workers (*cités ouvrières Michelin*). In 1909, the company established the Society of Cheap Housing ('Société des Habitations à Bon Marché') at Clermont-Ferrand. This implied the use of external contractors. All houses had gas, water, and lavatories. From 1919, Michelin decided to build company housing exclusively for its own workforce and, in this respect, even applied rationalized methods based on the ideas of Frank Gilbreth. A number of six-room houses were constructed. The number of housing units built by Michelin increased from 181 in 1909-1911 to 1752 in the period 1925-1929.[47]

Michelin, established in 1889, as well as car manufacturers André Citroën, Louis Renault and the Peugeot brothers, were the first French firms using assembly lines. In subsequent years, the French automobile sector underwent almost a complete *tournant taylorien* (taylorist turn).[48] During the First World War, Michelin introduced the first assembly line for the production of gas masks and Breguet-Michelin airplanes. Preceded by Renault in 1912-1913, Taylorist time-and-motions studies at Michelin were only carried out after the First World War. Then, in the early 1920s, Michelin taylorized a significant part of its production process without introducing a piece rate system. The first diffusion of Taylorism in France after about 1910 was also stimulated after two important strikes in 1912 and 1913 at Renault. These strikes concerned the employer's attitude to the Taylor system.[49]

By the end of the 1920s and in the 1930s, the process of Americanization of production and labour relations intensified, at least in larger companies.

45 With respect to rationalization in coalmining see: Hardy-Hémery 1972: 3-48.

46 Maier 1970: 38.

47 Tesi 2009: 1-16.

48 Fridenson 1987.

49 Moutet 1975: 33-43.

This can be partly explained by the increasing need for cost reduction and efficiency in the context of the upcoming economic depression of the 1930s. Another significant factor was the spread of Michelin engineers over other companies after being laid-off as a consequence of the economic crisis.[50]

Significant proponents of Americanization in these years formed the 'Rédressement Français', and among its number were influential politicians such as Georges Clemenceau, André Tardieu, and Albert Thomas. Rédressement Français was an association, led by industrialist Ernest Mercier, with the objective of acting as a party-neutral technocratic network for the institutional and industrial modernization of France.[51] At the same time, there was still substantial resistance in French society against further Americanization of production and labour relations in companies from the side of the trade unions and a number of Catholic paternalistic industrialists and engineers. In their view, traditional French paternalistic industrial traditions did not merge well with Anglo-Saxon materialism, embodied in scientific management and Fordism.[52]

6.7 Conclusion

In assessing welfare work developments in France until the 1930s, one is struck by the special strength and vast scale of industrial paternalism in the nineteenth century in this country. The specific character of the nineteenth-century French entrepreneur goes a long way to explain this. He often belonged to the protestant elite and valued highly his own family interests as well as the need for a stable family life for his workers. The need to solve the social question in France was also relevant. Equally striking is the typical French embracing of Taylorism or *taylorisation a la Française,* after the First World War, mainly in the new industries and mining. This encompassed a mingling of traditional welfare work programmes with time-and-motion studies, the use of the stopwatch, and the introduction of assembly lines in the production processes of enterprises. This did not, however, include the social dimension of Fordism that encompassed higher wages in order to enable workers to enjoy the benefits of productivity gains.

On the entrepreneurial side, the creation of a family dynasty was not an exception, as the case of the Schneider dynasty at Le Creusot suggests.

50 In 1936, the Michelin workforce in Clermont had shrunk to 7,000. Harp 2001: 206.

51 Maier 1970: 57-59; Frost (2014): 7.

52 Frost (2014): 10.

Closely-knit entrepreneurial (family) networks, as in Mulhouse or like the *sociétés anonymes,* also played an important role. A clear manifestation of the significance of family life and family interests on the side of the, by origin often agrarian, workers and their families is the almost exclusive choice to live in worker-owned single-family houses with a garden. This was, of course, also in the interests of the employer. It turned out to be an appropriate way to bind not only the nuclear family but, if necessary, also the extended multi-generational family to the company.

The social philosophy that best expressed the importance of the family life of workers as well as the resolution of the social question was Le Play's *économie sociale.* This philosophy appealed to many entrepreneurs during the Second Empire and the Third Republic. Both the *solution Mulhousienne* and the Fourierist Familistère at Guise already comprised important elements of the *économie sociale* developed by Le Play, Cheysson and others.

Apart from a key role for the family in the factory life of workers, other important building blocks of the social economy were hygiene, health and safety at home as well as in the workplace, and self-help for workers. Self-help for workers in France was translated into forms of mutualism, often guided by the employer.

By 1910, the old idea of an *économie sociale* was gradually exchanged for another powerful philosophy in the context of French welfare work: rationalization, or put differently a 'new social economy'.

7 A comparison of welfare work between Great Britain, the US, Germany, and France

7.1 Introduction

Having completed the description of welfare work in the Golden Age of capitalism in the four countries under examination, I will now compare these four countries, briefly, in a more systematic way with respect to the most important aspects of paternalistic corporate welfare work and its development. These are: (a) inspirational origins; (b) relevant economic, social, and political context; (c) precursors and the unfolding of welfare work; (d) traditional paternalism and employer motives; (e) neo-paternalism and Taylorism/Fordism; (f) performance and worker satisfaction; (g) significance of product quality and applied arts for welfare work; (h) the 1930s and beyond; and finally, (i) conclusions with respect to systemic differences and similarities between the four countries under examination.

In advance, it is important to realize that this book is based on various interrelated scientific approaches and notions, such as: the history of industrialization in North-Atlantic countries; the history of paternalistic welfare capitalism; labour and industrial relations; social history; transnational social and labour policy; business history; and, finally, business and management theories. Together, these approaches constitute the building blocks of the history oriented sociology of work approach I have intentionally tried to apply here. This contrasts with the currently fashionable a-historical mainstream HRM approach.

In combination with the introductory chapter, this chapter can also be read as a compact and comprehensive summary of the book. In the last chapter, chapter 8, the question of what can be learnt from past experience, will be dealt with by comparing welfare work at the time of enlightened capitalism with post-Second World War developments with respect to work and employment.

7.2 Country comparison of welfare work

As has been noted, the period 1880-1930 has been an important period of intensive policy learning across national borders and across the North-Atlantic world with respect to welfare work. It was not uncommon for Europeans to travel to America and Americans to Europe to see what kind of welfare work innovations employers had introduced in their enterprises. Foreign experiences were subsequently emulated. An outstanding example is Cadbury's romantic workingman's village constructed adjacent to its new factory near Birmingham. A number of foreign visitors went to Bournville, prominent among them American chocolate manufacturer Simon Hershey and Margarethe Krupp, spouse of Krupp-owner Friedrich Alfred Krupp. Both emulated Bournville's example at Hershey and Margarethenhöhe, respectively. The international exchange of ideas and experiences was supported by various universal exhibitions in Europe and America, in the second half of the nineteenth century, for example in Paris and Chicago, also paying attention to best welfare work practices.

(a) inspirational origins

To a significant extent, utopian thinking, albeit in the form of profane or purist ideas, influenced or even motivated a number of enlightened capitalist entrepreneurs in shaping their own welfare work. Although there have been many utopian thinkers and ideas, in particular Robert Owen and François Fourier have been important in this respect, next to Quakerism. Owen practised his welfare work ideas from early on in his own textile factory at New Lanark. Subsequently, he went to America to root his ideas there. Fourier inspired many sectarian groups in America by applying his ideas on the phalanstère in the New World. One of his most ardent followers in France was entrepreneur Jean-Baptiste Godin, who established his phalanstère-like Familistère, adjacent to his stove factory at Guise. French naturalist writer Émile Zola based his novel *Travail* on Fourier's ideas. This also applies to French architect Tony Garnier and the utopic *cité industrielle* that he designed. At the onset of enlightened capitalism, purist Protestantism also played a significant role. A significant number of enlightened employers had a Quaker background and wanted to apply Quaker ideas on social justice in their companies. This was the case with the British chocolate entrepreneurs Cadbury, Fry, and Rowntree and the American chocolate manufacturer Hershey. More in general, Calvinism and the protestant ethic were important, as the example of the Société Industrielle de Mulhouse in France shows.

Part of the inspirational origins of welfare work is based on dystopian thinking and protest against the negative consequences of the process of industrialization. Particularly in Britain there was a strong resistance in the circle of influential writers, reformers, and artists against the negative consequences of the mechanization of work and the loss of craftsmanship. For example, William Morris, William Carlyle, and John Ruskin fulminated against mechanization. Their influence on welfare work reached as far as the construction of romantic workingman's villages like Bournville and Port Sunlight and, subsequently, the emergence of the British garden city movement. Comparable feelings about the negative consequences of industrialization can be found in the circle of German reform movements, like the Heimatschutz movement, the German garden city movement, and, initially, also the modernist German Werkbund (DWB). These movements had an obvious impact on the architecture of workingman's housing, for example in Margarethenhöhe and Hellerau. Anti-industrialism is also embodied in the many religious sects that experimented with new ways of life and working in the United States. Among them are not only Fourierist experiments, but also experiments inspired by the ideas of William Morris as well as many purist initiatives. Important in this respect is the juxtaposition of city and land. In all four countries under examination this juxtaposition contributed to a long-time idealization of the pastoral idea, which was reflected in the building of workingman's housing. Many rejected *Mietskasernen* and big apartment buildings for workers in favour of single-family houses with fruit and vegetable gardens.

In sum, utopian profane and purist ideas, as well as pastoral ideas and ideas about the preservation of craftsmanship, all stood at the origin of corporate welfare work as it manifested at the end of the nineteenth century and the beginning of the twentieth century. Most obviously, these ideas influenced the building and architecture of company housing as well as the emergence of the garden city movement, both of which were influential on other forms of welfare work.

(b) relevant economic, social, and political context

The development of corporate welfare work emerged in the wake of the Industrial Revolution that began in Great Britain after the invention of the steam machine. The United States, Germany, and France followed suit. One of the first industries to play an important role regarding welfare work was the textile industry, followed by railroad construction, coalmining, metallurgy, and other industries. Often, new companies were established near places where water and raw materials were abundant. These were not necessarily existing villages or towns. Initially, the workers came from surrounding rural areas. Later, workers migrated from other parts of the country, or, as in the case of America, emigrated from Europe. Accompanying the Industrial Revolution was the emergence of the social question, encompassing increasing poverty and bad living and working conditions of workers.

From the 1890s onwards, with a number of new inventions such as electricity and cars, the second industrial revolution succeeded the first industrial revolution. New industries emerged, mainly in urban areas, like electronics, the chemical industry, the pharmaceutical industry, and the machine industry. The second industrial revolution also brought with it innovations regarding the organization of work in enterprises, such as the introduction of scientific management and the assembly line.

Politically seen, the period 1880-1930 was also a time of progressive politics and social reform in Britain, the US, Germany, and France. This implied that the well-being of workers also gradually improved on the basis of new labour protection legislation and, to a lesser extent, worker's insurance. In the United States, welfare work got an additional boost from the introduction and dissemination of Fordism (in this case, the stimulation of consumption by higher wages). Until Franklin Roosevelt's New Deal in the 1930s, the role of trade unions was especially disputed in the US. There, corporate welfare work was the most important alternative to trade union influence and their access at the company level.

(c) *precursors and the unfolding of welfare work*

In all four countries under examination, there were early precursors of later more systematically organized corporate welfare work. This early welfare work was largely based on comparable ideas and motives, as in the case of nineteenth-century traditional paternalism. Examples in this respect are the Fuggerei in Augsburg, Germany; the Royal Salt Works at Arc-et-Senans, near Besançon; the early factory villages and workhouses for the poor in England; and the founding of Paterson, near Philadelphia in the United States. These examples were succeeded by some more comprehensive and sophisticated welfare work initiatives by the end of the eighteenth century and the beginning of the nineteenth century, such as Owen's New Lanark and Saltaire in Britain, and Lowell in Massachusetts in the United States. One may conclude that the initial groundwork for later welfare work was already laid before, or at least at the onset of the first industrial revolution. In a number of cases, this early welfare work was related to relief, disciplining, and uplifting of the poor. Labour market motives also played a significant role.

(*d*) *traditional paternalism and employer motives*

In principle, the content of welfare work programmes in the golden age of capitalism has been broad and diverse. From the outset, many companies focused on constructing workingman's or company housing. Soon, other programmes were added, initially directed at improving income security of workers. Examples in this respect are: old-age pensions; disability and survivor's pensions; sickness benefits; profit sharing schemes; and stock ownership. Also common were health and worker's well-being provisions, like medical services by company doctors, (sometimes) company hospitals, and social services. Likewise, educational provisions, such as nurseries, primary schools, and company schools became important. Many entrepreneurs built one or more churches to serve their workforce. Also, sports- and recreational facilities became an obvious part of welfare work programmes. Constructing a theatre and a (heated) swimming pool, as was the case at Guise in France, was certainly no exception. Worker representation or worker participation was practised early, again at Guise, where the workers themselves eventually became owners of Godon's stove factory. Cadbury in Britain also introduced worker representation at an early phase. After the First World War, worker representation became a normal part of welfare work programmes in America and Europe. Finally, the shortening of working hours and company wage and consumption policies could be seen as part of welfare work programmes. For example, in a number of cases, women and children worked fewer hours than men. Henry Ford was the first entrepreneur to introduce higher wages (the five-dollar day) with the idea of stimulating consumption at the same time.

Perhaps the most appealing aspect of welfare work programmes was company housing. This varied from building simple shacks to professionally designed workingman's villages and company towns with all kinds of amenities, shops, gardens, greens, and parks. Exemplary, but certainly no exceptions, were Pullman in the United States, Cadbury and Port Sunlight in Great Britain, Margarethenhöhe in Germany, and Godon's Familistère in France. Company housing also raised some important questions, such as what was the most ideal workingman's home, a single-family house or an apartment in apartment buildings? Should company housing be for rent or for sale? For which category of workers should company housing be built? Should company housing also be accessible to people who did not belong to the company's workforce? Who should govern the village or town, the company itself or the workers and their families? In France, Germany, and Britain, intermediary building organizations soon took on the initiative of building company housing. In the beginning, companies often also established and participated actively in these intermediary organizations. Overall, this shift of responsibility ultimately implied a shift from single-family houses in separate workingman's villages to garden cities in Britain and Germany, and apartment housing, for example in Siemensstadt in Berlin.

Usually, it was a mix of utilitarianism and benevolence that motivated employers to introduce welfare work programmes, but a substantial number of these enlightened employers was primarily motivated by idealism or religion. They all shared the idea that offering welfare work could contribute to solving or softening the social question. Frequently, it was also a question of necessity and welfare work programmes were offered because of labour market reasons.

The basic attitude of employers was and remained paternalistic. Initially, many enlightened employers wanted to keep trade unions out or at least at a distance from the company, to prevent trade union influence and labour unrest. After the First World War this gradually changed. Particularly in the US, the idea arose that employers and workers could, in principal, have or simply did share common interests.

Welfare work and enlightened capitalism has always been a paternalistic affair of mixed intentions. Sometimes idealistic motives prevailed, more often, however, business and labour market motives predominated.

(e) neo-paternalism and Taylorism/Fordism

An important drive behind the second industrial revolution was attempts to improve the productivity of work. This received extra impetus after the First World War, particularly in Europe, as there was a need to repair war damage as soon as possible. Most significant in this respect has been the adoption and further spread of scientific management or Taylorism, as well as the introduction of Fordism. Both originated in the US and subsequently found broad support, albeit reluctantly at first, in industrialized European countries. The chief objective of scientific management was to improve individual productivity by measuring exactly how much time a worker needed to carry out the various parts of his task. Time-and-motion studies were applied to sort out the 'best way' to carry out a task. Fordism, invented in the Ford factories, started from a different principle. An assembly line was used to bring the work to the workers, who subsequently composed the final product, for example, a car, in a sequential order. Fordism not only improved the productivity of workers and factories, essentially it was also the translation of productivity gains into higher wages, and ultimately into increased consumption and wealth of workers and their families. In this way, both employer and workers could benefit equally from productivity gains, and former class conflicts could be neutralized.

For these reasons Taylorism and Fordism were connected to welfare work from the outset. Apparently, they fitted miraculously well with the increasingly important idea among enlightened American employers that employers and workers had common shared interests. Taylorism and Fordism also found wide acceptance in Europe, particularly in the new industries, like car production, electrotechnics, and machine manufacturing. However, in European countries, elements of both Taylorism and Fordism were handpicked and mixed more pronouncedly with traditional welfare work. As a result, the character of the emerging neo-paternalism during the second industrial revolution in European countries turned out to be less pronounced than in the United States. It did not appeal convincingly, for example, to small- and medium-sized businesses in France. In Germany, it competed with firmly supported corporatist ideas on how to organize production.

However, it is no exaggeration to conclude that Taylorism and Fordism had changed for good the nature of traditional welfare work in America and Europe. Despite remaining differences between the two continents, welfare work gained a new and important dimension, in the sense that it got a more pronounced relationship with productivity improvement than before.

(f) performance and worker satisfaction

It is not so easy to get a reliable and representative picture of employer performance with respect to welfare work. Overall quantitative research data are scarce and good objective yardsticks fail. Most evaluative research has been carried out in the United States by governmental bodies or committees and some scientists (Brandes 1976; Brody 1993; Jacoby 2004). From this we know, for example, that in the 1920s a substantial number of American workers was covered by one or more welfare work programmes, and that after housing and profit sharing the accent in American welfare work shifted in the first decades of the twentieth century to worker participation and democracy. Contrary to the lack of overall research, many qualitative case studies have been carried out, varying from muckraking reports to business and historical case studies (Harpers Review; Nelson 1995; Tarbell 1916; Günter 1980, etc.). On the other hand, indirect indicators make clear that, in many cases, employees were satisfied with welfare work in their enterprises and preferred welfare work above trade unionism. Some iconic enterprises like Krupp in Germany, Schneider in France, and Cadbury in England, remained free from significant labour unrest and strikes for decades. Lisabeth Cohen's research regarding enterprises in the Chicago area showed overall satisfaction of workers with welfare work in many enterprises (Cohen 1990). Finally, statistical health indicators in some areas made clear that companies with extensive welfare work programmes, like Cadbury and Lever, performed much better with respect to longevity and mortality rates of workers than surrounding firms without or with less extensive welfare work programmes.

Some caution is required in relation to the more precise quality of corporate work when measured by today's standards. There were big differences between individual companies or groups of related companies in terms of size and quality of the welfare work programmes supplied. Some companies, like Krupp, Schneider, Lever (Port Sunlight), Cadbury, and other chocolate factories in Britain (Rowntree, Fry) and France (Menier), organized their welfare work almost from cradle to grave. The vast majority of enlightened companies were more modest. In addition to enlightened companies there a large number unenlightened 'soulless' companies or, in more extreme cases, 'satanic mills' remained.

The sustainability of welfare work and, by extension, work and workers security was usually cyclical and depended greatly on the economic performance of the companies concerned, or, as in case of Pullman, judicial restrictions and negative public opinion. At least in the period of traditional paternalism, over-paternalism by company owners sometimes turned out to be counter-productive.

Usually, managerial staff, white-collar-, and skilled workers were better off than unskilled, and blue-collar workers.

However, there is evidence that, with some exceptions, until the First World War, workers in vanguard enterprises were rather satisfied with welfare work and, ultimately, seemed to prefer the benefits of corporate welfare work above those of trade unionism.

An important remaining question is to what extent the transition from traditional paternalism towards neo-paternalism in the 1920s had a significant impact on worker satisfaction with respect to welfare work. Employer motives shifted significantly towards the putative concordance of productivity growth and the increase of worker wealth. Likewise, non-charismatic external managers and engineers replaced in large numbers traditional family based charismatic leadership of firms. New management theories (Taylorism, Fordism) became increasingly mixed with welfare work practices.

To what extent, too, did architects and artists contribute to worker satisfaction, particularly in Germany and the United States? There is some evidence that workers in vanguard welfare work enterprises accepted and supported these changes. See also (g) and (h) hereafter.

(g) significance of product quality and applied arts for welfare work

An interesting phenomenon is the development, in particular in Germany after the turn of the century, of a rather unique way of organizing work and production, embodied in the idea of 'German work'. German work expressed a strong link between corporate welfare work, quality work, and product quality. Thus, Germany wanted to simultaneously solve the problem of work alienation and the international competitiveness of its industry. In this context, the German Werkbund (DWB) has played a crucial role. The Werkbund consisted of a group of high profile German employers, politicians, social reformers, scientists, architects, and artists. The DWB succeeded in making strong links between industry, mass production, applied science, and applied arts. This resulted not only in a better quality of products, but also in a more pronounced role for the applied arts in the workplace. As with Taylorism and Fordism in America, the ideas behind German work changed welfare work in a fundamental way in Germany. And, as with Taylorism and Fordism, the ideas behind German work were followed, to some extent, abroad, particularly in the United States. Here, too, the involvement of independent professional architects in designing and developing the so-called new company towns, as well attention to product design has some relationship with comparable developments in Germany at that time.

(h) the 1930s and beyond

It has been contended several times in this book that the heyday of corporate welfare work ended in the early 1930s as a consequence of the worldwide Great Depression. In general, this statement is right. But it is also true that during the Great Depression governments increasingly embraced the basic ideas behind corporate welfare. For example, in the United States, Roosevelt's New Deal policies legally reinforced worker rights and worker income security. Something similar occurred in France and Germany. In France, Leon Blum's short lived Popular Front also reinforced collective worker rights. In Germany, in the 1930s, the Nazis embraced existing ideas of welfare work and German work. Additionally, they also constructed a number of new company towns (Campbell 1989a). In the decades after the Second World War, the collectivization of corporate welfare work continued in America and Europe and culminated in collective welfare states in the 1960s and 1970s. Nevertheless, also after the Second World War, corporate welfare work or enlightened capitalism did not vanish completely and was revived, albeit less comprehensively, in what we now call human resources management (HRM).

(*i*) *conclusion*

At the threshold of the 1930s, corporate welfare work experienced a fundamental transformation if compared to the nineteenth century. Most significant was the move from the extensive building of company housing and company towns, at least in the three European countries under examination, to attempts to improve worker productivity without losing attention for worker's well-being. The over-paternalism of the nineteenth century was replaced by softer, less encompassing forms of neo-paternalism, in which the leading role of entrepreneurial families was replaced by professional managers and engineers. A second fundamental change, at least in Germany and to a lesser extent also in the United States and Great Britain, was the increased importance of applied arts in welfare work with respect to product design, quality work, factory architecture, the design of American company towns, as well as the design of garden cities in Great Britain and Germany. In Europe, company towns were replaced by workingman's housing, developed by intermediate building organizations. Professional architects would play a remarkable role in this respect.

In sum, if the Great Depression of the 1930s had not hit so clearly corporate welfare work as it was at the start of that decade in America and Europe, the actual picture of postwar corporate welfare work might well have been more in line with developments in the 1920s.

Alongside to substantive shifts across time of welfare work and the transition of traditional welfare work to neo-paternalistic welfare work, an intriguing final question is whether, and to what extent, one can still speak about divergent paths of welfare work in the four countries under examination? Is it possible to discern particular national models?

Beyond doubt is that the welfare work developments in Great Britain, the United States, Germany, and France had much in common. Mutual policy learning across the North Atlantic world and emulation was en vogue by the end of the nineteenth and first decades of the twentieth centuries. At the same time, some form of historical national path dependency might be discerned based on national socio-economic and cultural developments as well as on the moments the first and second industrial revolutions took off. In chapter 4, I devoted space to the validity of the concept of American exceptionalism and concurred with Daniel Rodgers that 'the American way' is perhaps a better analytical concept than American exceptionalism

(Rodgers 1998). Apart from many similarities between the four countries, I would also like to underline the incidence of a more specific national course of development of welfare work caused by already existing specific national circumstances. In this respect, it is legitimate to consider the British approach to welfare capitalism as firmly influenced by the free market and the strongly supported idea of laissez-faire; the American approach as erratic industrialization in a short time period combined with much room for private employers and companies to manoeuvre, leading to a great variety of company towns and welfare work programmes; the German approach as being strongly inclined to corporatism and economic collaboration between companies (cartelization); and the French approach as one of an agricultural-based economy and continued economic centralism.

8 Learning from past experience

The success of paternalistic welfare work in the period of enlightened capitalism can be partly explained by the reciprocal interest of many employers, social reformers, and politicians in best – welfare work – practices abroad, even across two continents in the North Atlantic world. In particular, Krupp's welfare work and housing policy as well as Cadbury's Bournville acted as shining examples to many in Europe and America for quite a long time. During and after the First World War, American influence on European employers became more manifest. Welfare work in Europe became more Americanized by the introduction of elements of Taylorism (time-and-motion studies, use of the stopwatch) and Fordism (the assembly line).

Today, horizontal policy learning and borrowing of ideas across borders and continents has become a regular affair. However, the question arises about whether, apart from horizontal learning across space, also vertical learning across time could be relevant with respect to future welfare work. In other words, could employers, employees, trade unions, politicians, and reformers learn from past welfare work experience?

Strictly seen, enlightened paternalistic welfare work did not completely crumble during the Great Depression of the 1930s. Some companies succeeded rather well in maintaining a substantial part of their welfare work programmes through the 1930s and the Second World War. Other companies succeeded in modernizing their welfare work programmes through this period. For example, non-unionized enterprises Kodak, Sears Roebuck, and Thompson Products in the United States modernized welfare work by making their programmes less paternalistic and welfare work more professionalized. More in general in the United States, as labour historian Jacoby contended, "with modern welfare capitalism, the emphasis shifted from control to consent; this was a kinder, gentler sort of paternalism."[1] However, American welfare work was no longer comparable to the rather unique joint movement of employers and reformers, often supported by workers, which it had been between 1900 and 1930. After the Second World War, the context in which these respective enterprises maintained welfare work differentiated radically from the context before the Great Depression and the Second World War. In all four countries, the role of the state had become

1 Jacoby 1997: 5.

more important. The same was true with respect to the power of unions. In the United States, for example, since Franklin Roosevelt's New Deal, trade unions were recognized by the state. From that moment, unions in the US got easier access to former non-unionized companies and competed overtly with, or challenged paternalistic corporate welfare work programmes. By contrast, in the three European countries unions acquired more influence at the national level and became actively involved in creating the new postwar welfare states. In this case, the nascent postwar European welfare states became direct competitors to what remained of corporate welfare work. This was, moreover, not the first time that this had occurred. In France, Britain. and Germany from the 1910s intermediary-housing companies had taken the initiative from private employers to build workingman's housing. At the same time, the state took a more pronounced legislative role in this field. In sum, what remained of pre-war welfare work programmes at the company level was much more modest if compared with former times. In Europe, in the decades after the Second World War, welfare work at the company level became the handmaiden of the newly emerging welfare states. In the United States, based on a long time cultural tradition, the direct role of employers in welfare work – for example, concerning healthcare, pensions, and building company towns – remained more important. From the 1960s, this resulted in a new type of modernized company town, the so-called corporate campus. A corporate campus is a more or less self-sufficient company village "with a post-industrial, white collar twist," encompassing a group of office buildings around a square or courtyard, a bell-tower, shops, dining rooms, health facilities, a parking lot, etc.[2] Renowned architects often designed corporate campuses, including Finnish-American architect Eero Saarinen (IBM), and British architect Norman Foster (Apple). Companies like Bell Labs, IBM, and PepsiCo built the first corporate campuses. Other notable examples are FedEx's Collierville (Tennessee), with jogging trails, a wellness centre, a library, and coffee bars in all office buildings; and Google's Googleplex at Mountain View (California), with exercise, relax and massage facilities, dry cleaning, other personal services, and gourmet meals. Norman Foster designed the futuristic Apple headquarters at Cupertino (California). This perfectly shaped circular shaped glass building is reminiscent of past utopian building complexes, such as Ledoux's Arc-et-Senans and Fourier's phalanstère.[3] Finally, Facebook has decided to build a new company town, Anton Menlo, adjacent to its campus at Menlo Park (California). The

2 Grandin 2009: 4, 187-202.

3 Rauterberg 2012: 43.

town will encompass about 400 dwellings, for sale at market prices. The apartments, for about ten per cent of its employees and a limited number of non-Facebook employees, will be at walking distance from the office buildings. Anton Menlo will also provide a number of amenities, such as: a café; a convenience store; a bicycle repair shop; a pet spa with doggy day care and pet walking services; a pool and spa; and sports and entertainment facilities.[4]

One has to keep in mind that, contrary to enlightened welfare work in past times, modern welfare work in campus-like surroundings by companies like Apple, FedEx, Google, and others is focused on a very limited group of core, mostly high-skilled employees. The majority of the workers in these companies often do not have a regular labour contract with the mother company, but instead have a variety of less secure flex and temp contracts with subcontractors. As a consequence, the welfare work entitlements of these workers are substantially less than the entitlements of the core employees. Apple, for example, employs worldwide 63,000 workers directly and more than 750,000 workers through subcontractors. Apple is not an exception. Economist David Weil refers to a worldwide trend of fragmenting or fissuring of former fixed lifetime employer-employee contracts, very often also including carving up of jobs, in both industries and services. Instead, the main employer or 'lead business' henceforth concentrates on its absolute core competences and, by extension, increasingly contracts out work to subcontractors, franchisers, or other organizations lower in the supply chain. Overall, this development results in lower costs and larger revenues for the lead business, but also in less-secure employment, lower wages, lower safety standards, and worse working conditions for workers.[5]

In order to be able to answer the question about whether and what can be learnt in this respect from past paternalistic welfare work experience, it is necessary to diagnose more closely the current 'new capitalism'.

Sociologist Richard Sennett made one of the first comprehensive diagnoses of the new capitalism of our time. The main characteristic of the culture of the new capitalism, according to Sennett, is flexibility. Flexibility consists of three elements: discontinuous reinvention of institutions, flexible specialization, and concentration of power without centralization.

In various subsequent interrelated studies, he analyzed the cultural consequences of the new capitalism in comparison with pre-capitalist times and the times of social capitalism, which generally covers the period

4 Albergotti 2013.

5 Weil 2014: 7-27; Kuttner 2014: 52-53.

1880-1930. Pre-capitalist times are characterized by an individualistic, self-disciplined work ethic, and craftsmanship. By contrast, the work ethic of the new capitalism is one of a superficial group or team ethos. Social capitalism's vice is the "iron cage of solidarity" whereas the vice of the new capitalism is "indifference".[6] The accompanying political and social rationale of social capitalism is inclusion, and for the new capitalism, it is efficiency. Likewise, former strong social ties are exchanged for weak social ties in the new capitalism.

The new capitalism has been enabled by the following three developments: a shift from managerial capitalism to shareholder capitalism, investors' desire for short-term, rather than long-term financial results, and new communication and manufacturing technologies. The main consequences of these developments are a delayering or de-pyramidization of organizational structures, non-linear sequencing of production processes, and a casualization of the labour force by subcontracting parts of the production or services as well as by stimulating temporary labour contracts. Taken together, according to Sennett, the new capitalism turns out to be a winner-takes-all economy with – sometimes extreme – inequality, low craftsmanship, constantly shifting tasks, low mutual commitment, low institutional loyalty of both workers and managers, low informal trust, and a weakening of institutional knowledge. In the eyes of Sennett, the new capitalism is volatile and, specifically, "not long term."[7] Sennett's observations are confirmed by empirical evidence. For example, in a meta-analysis of survey data and hundreds of case studies carried out in the period between 1970 and 1993, Eileen Appelbaum & Rosemary Batt concluded that, in those years, the American system of mass production underwent a great transformation towards flexibilization and so-called high performance systems.[8] Two models were en vogue in American companies: lean production versus a team-based model. Both models borrowed extensively from experiences abroad, such as from the Japanese lean production model, the Swedish sociotechnical systems approach, Italian flexible specialization, and German diversified quality production. In the end no single best way emerged in reforming mass production, but rather two distinctive, more or less opposite, strategies.

6 Sennett 2006: 164.

7 See in particular Sennett 2006. This study summarizes and links Sennett's various research and writings about labour over the years. See also: Sennett 1998, 2008.

8 The same occurred in Europe.

These were the so-called American human resources approach and a low-cost approach.[9]

New manufacturing technologies are not the only constituting blocks of the new capitalism. Sennett also referred to the shift from managerial capitalism to shareholder capitalism and to the related wish for short-term financial gains of investors, as well as to the increase in, sometimes extreme, inequality. In another book about the emergence of the private equity industry, Appelbaum & Batt also supply evidence concerning negative consequences of the first two developments. It turns out that the private equity industry is transforming family and managerial capitalism by buying out former management, loading companies with large debts, and degrading the working and wage conditions of workers.[10] With respect to the increase of inequality, French economist Thomas Piketty recently provided extensive quantitative evidence. On the basis of time series and other statistical data covering the nineteenth and twentieth centuries, he analyzed the evolution of income (re-) distribution, as well as the distribution of private financial, real estate, and industrial assets in and between a number of countries, including the United States, Britain, Germany, and France. After several decades of reducing inequalities between 1900 and 1920, as well as after the Second World War – the *Trente Glorieuses* – Piketty observed increasing inequalities with respect to income in the period of the new capitalism, from the 1980s onwards, and likewise with respect to private wealth from the 1950s onwards. This development is most conspicuous in the United States, but the trend is similar in Britain, France, and Germany.[11]

In sum, the new capitalism is characterized by, respectively, flexibility, a fissured workplace, an increase of the private equity industry, and an increase in inequality, contributing to a drastic change in the social contract between workers and their employers. If one adds to this the on-going dismantling of the welfare state, the resulting picture points to increasing voids in worker security as well as to an emerging 'precariat', an increasing group of blue- and white-collar workers without a fixed job and low incomes.[12] It is in this context that former experiences with enlightened capitalism might become a powerful inspirational source for solving problems of workers' well-being.

9 Appelbaum & Batt 1994: 3-25.
10 Appelbaum & Batt 2014.
11 Piketty 2013: 15-68.
12 Standing 2014.

What, then, could the transfer potential be of former enlightened welfare capitalism?

Firstly, it would make sense to redefine the contextual social contract between workers, employers, and the state. The balance between these three interrelated actors has shifted several times since the onset of enlightened welfare work. Initially, welfare work was unique to enlightened employers or the private market. Later, workers and the state also got a voice in the social economy. Then, after the Second World War, the state became the principal actor in terms of welfare work. Finally, since the emergence of the new capitalism, both the state and employers leave and have already left significant voids in welfare work and worker security. As a result, the postwar social contract between the three principal actors is vanishing. According to the eminent theorist of social policy and social welfare the late Robert Titmuss, from the start of enlightened capitalism welfare work evolved from a residual model (traditional paternalism) to first, an industrial achievement-performance model (neo-paternalism), and then to an institutional redistributive model (welfare state).[13] In this period of new capitalism, the institutional redistributive model experiences is experiencing a serious drawback. Without a deliberate renewal of the social contract, the balance will, in time, tilt towards the 'lowest' point, a residual model of welfare capitalism, at least for the majority of the workers. Therefore, it is recommendable to rethink the pros and cons of a modernized industrial achievement-performance model that takes into account both the positive experiences of the past and the limitations of the new capitalism. Another often used term for the industrial achievement-performance model is the 'Handmaiden Model', indicating that this model is based on merit and performance with respect to needs and still requires a significant role for social welfare institutions or the state.

The negative limitations of the new capitalism are, in principle, far-reaching and encompass, in addition to retrenching welfare states, aggressive international business competition and private austerity. On the other hand, enlightened capitalism also possesses some notable qualities, which could, in principle, be re-applied in a sensible way. On the limitations side, paternalism must be mentioned first. Future welfare work should be free from any paternalistic elements, save perhaps from some aspects that contribute positively to the creation of a joint company spirit. The voice of workers should be equal to the voice of employers. Secondly, cradle to grave protection should be avoided given its unintended negative effects

13 Titmuss 1974: 30-31.

as well as the fact that all three principal actors should bear a fair share of responsibility for welfare work. Additionally, the principle of subsidiarity could be helpful here. When employers and workers are not able to organize welfare work in a responsible or minimally acceptable way, and consequently underperform, state institutions could come into play temporarily.

On the merit side of corporate welfare work, in principle many things can be mentioned, varying from substantive material matters to the ways it was organized. In future, corporate welfare work could, for example, retake from the state a part of occupational income security and employment security, pensions, profit sharing, health and family care, occupational training, and occupational education. Also, organizing worker participation should be primarily a matter for employers. Equally important is the way employers organize welfare work. In this respect, much can be learned still from the Mulhousian model in which a group of employers collaborated in organizing welfare work at the regional level. Also models of self-help or guided self-help, as practised in various countries, are still of interest here. Think, in this respect, of the mutalities idea practised in France or the cooperative idea practised in various countries.

Finally, perhaps the most important lesson to be learned from enlightened capitalism is the social conscience of many progressive employers of that time. Therefore, future welfare work should become again, at least in part, a matter of social conscience for employers and not only a legal or bureaucratic obligation. It was, in particular, this deliberate social commitment by a large number of enlightened entrepreneurs in many countries, and not primarily the cash nexus, that made and still makes the main ideas behind enlightened capitalism contagious.

Bibliography

Albergotti, Reed (2013). *Facebook's Company Town. Social Network is Building a 394-Unit Housing Community near its Offices.* Dow Jones Reprints (updated Oct. 3).

Albert, Sidney P. (1999). 'Evangelizing the Garden City'. *Shaw*, vol. 19, pp. 41-77.

Anderson, Stanford (2000). *Peter Behrens and a New Architecture for the Twentieth Century.* Cambridge: The MIT Press.

Appelbaum, Eileen & Rosemary Batt (1994). *The New American Workplace. Transforming Work Systems in the United States.* Ithaca: ILR Press.

Appelbaum, Eileen & Rosemary Batt (2014). *Private Equity at Work: When Wall Street Manages Main Street.* New York: Russell Sage Foundation.

Ashworth, William (1954), *The Genesis of Modern British Town Planning. A Study in Economic and Social History of the Nineteenth and Twentieth Centuries.* London: Routledge and Kegan Paul Ltd.

Asselain, Jean-Charles (1984). *Histoire économique de la France. Du XVIIIe siècle à nos jours.* Paris: Éditions du Seuil.

Bahmueller, Charles F. (1981). *The National Charity Company. Jeremy Bentham's Silent Revolution.* Berkeley: UCLA Press.

Barker, Richard J. (1961). 'French Entrepreneurship During the Restoration: The Record of a Single Firm, the Anzin Mining Company'. *The Journal of Economic History,* vol. 21, no. 2, pp. 161-178.

Beaud, Claude (1990). 'Les Schneider au Creusot: Un modèle paternaliste en réponse aux impératifs du libéralisme et à la montée du movement socialiste'. In: Erik Aerts, Claude Beaud & Jean Sengers (eds), *Liberalism and Paternalism in the 19th Century. Proceedings Tenth International Economic History Congress Leuven,* August. Session B-13, pp. 9-18. Leuven: Leuven University Press.

Bell, Colin & Rose (1972). *City Fathers: The Early History of Town Planning in Britain.* Harmondsworth: Penguin.

Bellamy, Edward (1887). *Looking Backward. 2000-1887.* Cambridge: The Riverside Press. Kindle e-book.

Berke, Gerald (1994). *Alternative Tracks. The constitution of American industrial order, 1865-1917.* Baltimore: The Johns Hopkins Press.

Bernstein, Irving (1960). *The Lean Years. A History of the American Worker 1920-1933.* New York: Da Capo Press, Inc.

Birck, Françoise (1990). 'Entre le patronage et l'organisation industrielle. Les Cristalleries de Baccarat dans le dernier quart du XIXe siècle'. *Genèse,* no. 2, A la découverte du fait social, pp. 29-55.

Bloch, Ernst (1973). *Das Prinzip Hoffnung.* Frankfurt am Main: Suhrkamp.

Blokker, D.S.J. (2012). 'Avant Texas, au Texas, après Texas. Un exposé sur le projet phalanstérien de Victor Considerant, 1820-1860'. Unpublished student paper VU University: Amsterdam.

Bollerey, Franziska (1977). *Architekturkonzeption der utopischen Sozialisten. Alternative Planung und Architektur für den gesellschaftlichen Prozess.* Munich: Heinz Moos Verlag.

Bolz, Cedric (2010). 'From "Garden City Precursors" to 'Cemeteries for the Living': Contemporary Discourse on Krupp Housing and Besucherpolitik in Wilhelmine Germany'. *Urban History,* vol. 37, no. 1, May 2010, pp. 90-116.

Borges, Marcelo & Susana B. Torres (eds.) (2012). *Company Towns. Labor, Space, and Power Relations Across Time and Continents.* New York: Palgrave Macmillan.
Boyle, T.C. (1999). *Riven Rock.* New York: Penguin Press.
Brady, Robert A. (1932). 'The Meaning of Rationalization: An Analysis of the Literature'. *The Quarterly Journal of Economics,* vol. 46, no. 3, May, pp. 525-540.
Brandes, Stuart D. (1976). *American Welfare Capitalism 1880-1940.* Chicago: University of Chicago Press.
Bretin Maffiuletti, Karen (2009). 'Les loisirs sportifs en milieu de grande industrie: sport, patronat et organisations ouvrières au Creusot et à Monceau-les-Mines (1879-1939)'. *Le Mouvement Social.* No. 226: pp. 49-66.
Briggs, Asa (1968), *Victorian Cities.* London: Penguin Books.
Briggs, Asa (1994). *A Social History of England. From the Ice Age to the Channel Tunnel.* London: Weidenfeld and Nicholson.
Brinkley, Douglas (2004). *Wheels for the World. Henry Ford, His Company, and a Century of Progress 1903-2003.* London: Penguin Books.
Brody, David (1993). *Workers in Industrial America. Essays on the Twentieth Century struggle.* New York: Oxford University Press.
Bryson, John. R & Philippa A. Lowe (2002). 'Story-telling and History'. *Historical Geography,* 28, 1, pp. 21-41.
Buck, Imke (2002). *Der späte Zola als politischer Schrifsteller seiner Zeit.* Phd dissertation. Universität Mannheim (pdf).
Buddensieg, Tilmann & Hennig Rogge (1979). *Industriekultur. Peter Behrens und die AEG 1907-1914.* Berlin: Gebr. Mann Verlag.
Buder, Stanley (1975). *Pullman. An Experiment in Industrial Order and Community Planning 1880-1930.* New York: Oxford University Press.
Bullock, Nicholas & James Read (1985). *The Movement for Housing Reform in Germany and France 1840-1914.* Cambridge: Cambridge University Press.
Burk, Kathleen (2007). *Old World New World. The Story of Britain and America.* London: Abacus.
Busch, Wilhelm & Thorsten Scheer (ed.) (2002). *Symmetrie und Symbol. Die Industriearchitektur von Fritz Schupp und Martin Kremmer.* Cologne: Verlag der Buchhandlung Walther König.

Cadbury, Deborah (2010). *Chocolate Wars. From Cadbury to Kraft: 200 Years of Sweet Success and Bitter Rivalry.* London: Harper Press.
Cadbury, Edward (1912) (2013). *Experiments in Industrial Organization.* London (New York 1979): Hardpress Limited
Campbell, Joan (1989a). *Der Deutsche Werkbund 1907-1934.* Munich: Deutscher Taschenbuch Verlag DTV.
Campbell, Joan (1989b). *Joy in Work, German Work.* Princeton, NJ: Princeton University Press.
Candee, Richard M. (1992). 'Early New England Mill Towns of the Piscataqua River Valley'. In: John S. Garner (ed.) *The Company Town: Architecture and Society in the Early Industrial Age.* New York: Oxford University Press, pp. 111-138.
Carlson, Linda (2003). *Company Towns of the Pacific Northwest.* Seattle: University of Washington Press.
Carlyle, Thomas (1843). *Past and Present.* Amazon Kindle e-book. Publisher unknown.
Chadwick, Sir Edwin (1842) (1965). Report on an Inquiry into *the Sanitary Condition of the Labouring Population of Great Britain.* London: W. Clowes and Sons. Reprinted as *Report on the Sanitary Conditions of the Labouring Population of Great Britain,* edited with an introduction by M.W. Flinn. Edinburgh: Edinburgh University Press.

Chandler, Alfred D., Jr. (1977). *The Visible Hand. The Managerial Revolution in American Business.* Cambridge: The Belknap Press.

Chandler, Alfred D., Jr. (1990). *Scale and Scope. The Dynamics of Industrial Capitalism.* Cambridge: The Belknap Press.

Child, John (1964). 'Quaker Employers and Industrial Relations'. *Sociological Review,* 12, pp. 293-315.

Child, John (1969). *British Management Thought. A C*

Claeys, Gregory (1991). *Introduction.* In: Robert Owen. *A New View of Society and Other Writings.* Harmondsworth: Penguin Books.

Claeys, Gregory (2002). *Citizens and Saints. Politics and Anti-Politics in Early British Socialism.* Cambridge: Cambridge University Press.

Cohen, Lizabeth (1990). *Making a New Deal. Industrial Workers in Chicago, 1919-1939.* Cambridge: Cambridge University Press.

Conway, Moncure D. (1886). 'An Iron City Behind the Ruhr'. *Harpers' New Monthly Magazine,* Vol LXXII, no. 430, March, pp. 495-518.

Coolidge, John (1993). *Mill and Mansion. A Study of Architecture and Society in Lowell, 1820-1865.* Amherst: University of Massachusetts Press.

Crawford, Margaret (1995). *Building the Workingman's Paradise. The Design of American Company Towns.* London: Verso.

Crawford, Margareth (1999). 'The "New" Company Town'. *Perspecta, Settlement Patterns,* vol. 30: 48-57.

Cronon, William (1991). *Nature's Metropolis. Chicago and the Great West.* New York: W.W. Norton & Company.

De Bruyn, Gerd (2012). 'Die aus dem Lot geratene Idylle. Franz Heinrich Ziegenhagen und "Delirious New York"'. In: *L'Architecture Engagée. Manifeste zur Veränderung der Gesellschaft.* Munich: DETAIL-Institut für Internationale Architektur, pp. 40-51.

De Gier, Erik (2010). 'Paradise Lost: GM & the UAW in Historical Perspective'. Research paper, *Digital Commons,* Ithaca: Cornell University ILR School.

De Gier, Erik (2011). 'New Deal Labor Reforms and their Aftermath: The Flawed Evolution of the American Labor-Management Model as regards Center Firms, 1945-1980'. Research paper, *Digital Commons,* Ithaca: Cornell University ILR School.

De Gier, Erik (2012). '"Looking Backward"'. Over de actualiteit van arbeidersparadijzen rond 1900'. *De Academische Boekengids* 94, September 2012, pp. 17-19.

De Gier, Erik (2015). Avant-garde Welfare Capitalism. Corporate Welfare Work and Enlightened Capitalism in Great Britain, the United States of America, Germany and France (1880-1930). In: *Warsaw Forum Of Economic Sociology* 6:1 (11) Spring. pp. 117-129.

Delabre, Guy (2010). 'Une Introduction à Solutions Sociales'. In: *Jean-Baptiste André Godin. Solutions sociales* (1871). Guise: Les Éditions Du Familistère. Reprint, pp 9-23.

Dellalande, Nicolas (2008). 'Émile-Justin Menier, un chocolatier en République. Les controversies sur la légitimité de la compétence politique d'un industriel dans la France des années 1870'. *Politix,* vol. 14, no. 84, pp. 9-33.

Dellheim, Charles (1982). 'The Creation of a Company Culture: Cadburys, 1861-1931'. *The American Historical Review,* vol. 92, no. 1 (February), pp. 13-44.

Dickens, Charles (1969). *Hard Times.* London: Penguin Books.

Dinius, Oliver J. & Angela Vergara (2011). *Company Towns in the Americas. Landscape, Power, and Working-Class Communities.* Athens: University of Georgia Press.

Disraeli, Benjamin (1845). *Sybil, or the Two Nations.* Amazon Kindle e-book. Publisher unknown.

Donzelot, Jacques (1984). *L'Invention du social. Essai sur le déclin de pasions politiques.* Paris: Fayard.

Dos Passos, John (1966). *U.S.A.* Harmondsworth: Penguin Books.

Dyos, H.J. & Michael Wolff (1973), *The Victorian City.* London: Routledge & Kegan Paul.

Eisen, Marcus (2012). 'Das sozialdemokratische Ideal: Die Hufeisensiedlung in Berlin-Britz, Das "Neue Frankfurt", Das "Rote Wien". In: *L'Architecture Engagée. Manifeste zur Veränderung der Gesellschaft.* Munich: DETAIL-Institut für Internationale Architektur, pp. 252-275.

Ely, Richard T. (1885). 'Pullman. A Social Study'. *Harper's Monthly,* LXX, pp. 452-466.

Engels, Friedrich (1993), *The Condition of the Working Class in England.* Oxford: Oxford University Press.

Ermenc, J.J. (1957). 'Avant-Garde Capitalism in France'. *The French Review.* vol. 31, no. 2, December: pp. 129-135.

Esch, Elisabeth (2011). 'Whitened and Enlightened. The Ford Motor Company and racial engineering in the Brazilian Amazon'. In: Oliver J. Dinius & Angela Vergara. *Company Towns in the Americas. Landscape, Power, and Working-class Communities.* Athens: University of Georgia Press, pp. 91-110.

Ewald, François (1986). *L'Etat providence.* Paris: Bernard Grasset.

Febles, Eduardo A. (2008). 'The Anarchic Commune as World's Fair in Émile Zola's Travail'. *Nineteenth-Century French Studies,* vol. 36, no. 3 & 4, Spring-Summer, pp. 286-304.

Fitton, R.S. & A.P. Wadsworth (1958). *The Strutts and the Arkwrights 1758-1830. A Study of the Early Factory System.* Manchester: Manchester University Press.

Floquet, Matthieu & Patrice Laroche (2013). 'The Impossible Tradition from "Absolute Monarchy" toward Industrial Democracy in France: The Experience of Worker's Representatives at Schneider, 1899-1936'. *Labor History,* vol. 55, no. 1, pp. 117-136.

Foglesong, Richard E. (1986). *Planning the Capitalist City. The Colonial Era to the 1920s.* Princeton, NJ: Princeton University Press.

Fox, Robert (1984). 'Science, Industry, and the Social Order in Mulhouse, 1798-1871'. *The British Journal for the History of Science,* vol. 17, no. 2, July, pp. 127-168.

Frampton, Kenneth (1980). *Modern Architecture. A Critical History.* London: Thames and Hudson.

Fridenson, Patrick (1987). 'Un tournant Taylorien de la société Française (1904-1918)'. *Annales. Histoire, Sciences Sociales,* vol. 42, no. 5, September-October, pp. 1031-1060.

Frost, Robert. 'Fordism and the American Dream in France, 1919-1939'. Retrieved on 29-10-2014 from *Digital Fordism. Chapters Center for Digital Discourse and Culture,* Virginia Tech (www2cddc.vt.edu/digital fordism/fordism), pp.31.

Gacon, Stéphane & François Jurrige (2014). 'Les trois ages du paternalisme. Cantines et alimentation ouvrières au Creusot (1860-1960)'. *Le Mouvement Social.* vol. 247, pp. 27-45.

Gall, Lothar (2009). *Walther Rathenau. Portrait einer Epoche.* Munich: Verlag C.H. Beck.

Garner, John S. (1971). 'Leclair Illinois. A Model Company Town (1890-1934)'. *Journal of the Society of Architectural Historians,* vol. 30, October, pp. 219-227.

Garner, John S. (ed.) (1992). *The Company Town: Architecture and Society in the Early Industrial Age.* New York: Oxford University Press.

Gaskell, Elisabeth (1848), *Mary Barton.* Amazon Kindle e-book. Publisher unknown.

Gaskell, S. Martin (1979). 'Model Industrial Villages in S. Yorkshire/N. Derbyshire and the Early Town Planning Movement'. *Town Planning Review,* 50: 4, pp. 437-458.

Gaskell, S. Martin (1980). 'Gardens for the Working Class: Victorian Practical Pleasure'. *Victorian Studies,* vol. 23, no. 4, pp. 479-501.

Godin, Jean-Baptiste André (2010/1871). *Solutions sociales.* Guise: Les Éditions Du Familistère.

Grandin, Greg (2009). *Fordlandia. The Rise and Fall of Henry Ford's Forgotten Jungle City.* New York: Picador.

Green, Hardy (2010). *The Company Town. The Industrial Edens and Satanic Mills that Shaped the American Economy.* New York: Basic Books.

Grütter, Theodor (ed.) (2012). *200 Jahre Krupp. Ein Mythos wird besichtigt.* Katalog zur Ausstellung im Ruhr Museum. Essen: Klartext Verlag.

Günter, Roland (1980). 'Arbeitersiedlungen im Ruhrgebiet'. In: Eduard Trier & Willy Weyres (eds), *Kunst des 19. Jahrhunderts im Rheinland. Band 2.* Düsseldorf: Pädagogischer Verlag Schwann GmbH, pp. 465-495.

Günter, Roland & Bodo Herzog (1975). 'Die Entwicklung der grossbürgerliche Wohnkultur und Bruno Möhrings avantgardistische Siedlung für leitende Manager der Gutehoffnungshütte in Oberhausen (1910)'. In: Joachim Petsch (ed.), *Architektur und Städtebau im 20. Jahrhundert.* Berlin-West: Verlag für das Studium der Arbeiterbewegung GmbH, pp. 158-211.

Haber, Samuel (1964). *Efficiency and Uplift. Scientific Management in the Progressive Era 1890-1920.* Chicago: University of Chicago Press.

Haber, Samuel (2002). 'The Nightmare and the Dream: Edward Bellamy and the Travails of Socialist Thought'. *Journal of American Studies,* vol. 36. no. 3, pp. 417-440.

Hagspiel, Wolfram (1984). 'Das "Neue Niederrheinische Dorf"'. In: Wolf Herzogenrath & Dirk Treuber. *Der westdeutsche Impuls 1900-1914. Kunst und Umweltgestaltung im Industriegebiet. Die Deutsche Werkbund-Ausstellung Cöln 1914.* Cologne: Kölnischer Kunstverein, pp. 186-191.

Hardy-Hémery, Odette (1972). 'Rationalisation technique et rationalisation du travail à la Compagnie des Mines d'Anzin (1927-1938)'. *Le Mouvement Social,* no. 72, Jul.-Sept., pp. 3-48.

Harp, Stephen L. (2001). *Michelin. Advertising and Cultural Identity in Twentieth-Century France.* Baltimore: The Johns Hopkins University Press.

Harrison, J.F.C. (1969). *Robert Owen and the Owenites in Britain and America. The Quest for the New Moral World.* London: Routledge and Kegan Paul.

Hartmann, Kristiana (1976). *Deutsche Gartenstadtbewegung. Kulturpolitik und Gesellschaftsreform.* Munich: Heins Moos Verlag.

Hayden, Dolores (1976). *Seven American Utopias. The Architecture of Communitarian Socialism, 1790-1975.* Cambridge, MA: MIT Press.

Himmelfarb, Gertrude (1985). *The Idea of Poverty. England in the Early Industrial Age.* London/Boston: Faber and Faber.

Himmelfarb, Gertrude (1986). *Marriage and Morals among the Victorians and Other Essays.* London/Boston: Faber and Faber.

Hoagland, Alison K. & Margaret M. Mulrooney (1991). *Norvelt and Penncraft, Pennsylvania. Subsistence-Homestead Communities of the 1930s.* Washington D.C.: National Park Service. US. Department of Interior.

Hobsbawn Eric (1996). *The Age of Capital 1848-1875.* New York: Vintage Books.

Hobsbawn, E.J. & C.J. Wrigley (1999). *Industry and Empire. From 1750 to the Present Day.* London: Penguin Books.

Homburg, Heidrun (1978). 'Anfänge des Taylorsystems in Deutschland vor dem Ersten Weltkrieg. Eine Problemskizze unter besondere Berücksichtigung der Arbeitskämpfe bei Bosch 1913'. *Aufsätze/Geschichte und Gesellschaft. Zeitschrift für historische Sozialwissenschaft,* vol 4, pp. 170-194.

Homburg, Heidrun (1991). *Rationalisierung und Industriearbeit. Das Beispeil des Siemens-Konzerns Berlin 1900-1939.* Berlin: Haude & Spener.

Honhart, Michael (1990). 'Company Housing as Urban Planning in Germany, 1870-1914'. *Central European History,* vol. 23, March, pp. 3-21.

Horne, Janet (1995). 'Le Musée Social à l'origine: Les metamorphoses d'une idée'. *Le Mouvement social,* no. 171 (Apr.-June), pp. 47-69.

Horne, Janet R. (2002). *A Social Laboratory for Modern France. The Musée Social and the Rise of the Welfare State.* Durham: Duke University Press.

Hounshell, David A. (1985). *From the American System to Mass Production 1800-1932.* Baltimore: The Johns Hopkins University Press.

Howard, Ebenezer (1902), *Garden Cities of To-Morrow.* London: S. Sonnenschein & Co., Ltd. Amazon Kindle e-book.

Howe, Daniel Walker (2007). 'What Hath God Wrought. The Transformation of America, 1815-1848'. In: David M. Kennedy (General Editor). *The Oxford History of The United States.* New York: Oxford University Press.

Hughes, Thomas, P. (1990). 'Walther Rathenau: '"System Builder"'. In: Tilman Buddensieg, Thomas Hughes, Jürgen Kocka et al. , *Ein Mann vieler Eigenschaften. Walther Rathenau und die Kultur der Moderne.* Berlin: Verlag Klaus Wagenbach, pp. 9-31.

Hunt, Tristram (2009), *The Frock-Coated Communist. The Revolutionary Llife of Friedrich Engels.* London: Allan Lane/Penguin Books: London.

Hunt, Tristram (2010), *Building the New Jerusalem. The Rise and Fall of the Victorian City.* London: Orion Books (e-book).

Jacoby, Sanford M. (1997). *Modern Manors. Welfare Capitalism since the New Deal.* Princeton, NJ: Princeton University Press.

Jacoby, Sanford M. (2004). *Employing Bureaucracy. Managers, Unions, and the Transformation of Work in the 20th Century.* Mahwah, NJ: Lawrence Erlbaum Associates Publishers.

James, Harold (2012). *Krupp. A History of the Legendary German Firm.* Princeton, NJ: Princeton University Press.

Jeremy, David J. (1991). 'The Enlightened Paternalist in Action: William Hesketh Lever at Port Sunlight Before 1914'. *Business History,* 33: 1, pp. 58-81.

Jonas, Stéphane (1994). 'Les Villages ouvriers et Mulhouse 1830-1930. Villages ouvriers, utopie ou réalités? Actes du colloque international au Familistère de Guise, 16-17 October 1993'. *L'archéologie industrielle en France,* no. 24-25.

Jorns, Auguste &Thomas Kite Brown (2003). *Quakers as Pioneers in Social Work* (1931), Whitefish, MT: Kessinger Publishing.

Kallen, Peter W. (1984). 'Idylle oder Illusion? Die Margarethenhöhe in Essen von Georg Metzendorf'. In: Zdenik Felix. *Die Margarethenhöhe. Das schöne und die Ware. Der Westdeutsche Impuls 1900-1914. Kunst und Umeltgestaltung im Industriegebiet.* Essen: Museum Folkwang, pp. 48-95.

Kloppenberg, James T. (1986). *Uncertain Victory. Social Democracy and Progressivism in European and American Thought, 1870-1920.* New York: Oxford University Press.

Kocka, Jürgen (1971). 'Family and Bureaucracy in German Industrial Management, 1850-1914: Siemens in Comparative Perspective. *The Business History Review,* vol. 45, no. 2, pp. 133-156.

Kolakowski, Leszek (1976). *Geschiedenis van het Marxisme.* 1. Utrecht: Het Spectrum B.V.

Kott, Sandrine (1987). 'Enjeux et significations d'une politique sociale: La Société industrielle de Mulhouse'. *Revue d'histoire moderne et contemporaine,* vol. 34, no. 4, Oct.-Dec.): pp. 640-659.

Krueger, Susanne (1999). *Krupp und die Stadt Essen.* Essen: Route Industriekultur 5. Kommunalverband Ruhrgebiet.
Kuttner, Robert (2014). 'Why Work is More Debased'. *New York Review of Books,* October 23, pp. 52-53.

Lallement, Michel (2009). *Le travail de l'utopie. Godin et le Familistère de Guise.* Paris: Les Belles Lettres.
Lallement, Michel (2012). 'An Experiment Inspired by Fourier: J.B. Godin's Familistère in Guise'. *Journal of Historical Sociology,* vol. 25, no. 1 March: pp. 32-49.
Landes, David S. (1949). 'French Entrepreneurship and Industrial Growth in the Nineteenth Century'. *The Journal of Economic History,* vol. 9, no. 1, May, pp. 45-61.
Landes, David S. (1999). *The Wealth And Poverty Of Nations. Why Some are so Rich and Some so Poor.* London: Abacus.
L'Architecture Engagée. Manifeste zur Veränderung der Gesellschaft (2012). Munich: DETAIL-Institut für Internationale Architektur.
Leach, William (1993). *Land Of Desire. Merchants, Power, and the Rise of a New American culture.* New York: Vintage Books.
Le petit journal des grandes expositions (1995). *Les Schneider. Le Creusot. Une famille, une enterprise, une ville (1836-1960).* Paris: Réunion des Musées Nationaux.
Lillibridge, Robert M. (1953). 'Pullman: Town Development in the Era of Eclecticism'. *Journal of the Society of Architectural Historians,* vol. 12, no. 3, October, pp. 17-22.
Lind, Michael (2012). *Land of Promise. An Economic History of the United States.* New York: Harper Collins.
Lindsey, Almont (1971). *The Pullman Strike. The Story of a Unique Experiment and of a Great Labor Upheaval.* Chicago: University of Chicago Press.

MacCarthy, Fiona (1994). *William Morris. A Life for Our Time.* London: Faber and Faber.
MacCulloch, Diarmand (2003). *Reformation. Europe's House Divided 1490-1700.* London: Penguin Books.
MacQueen, Adam (1964). *The King of Sunlight. How William Lever Cleaned up the World.* London: Bantam Press.
Maier, Charles S. (1970). 'Between Taylorism and Technocracy: European Ideologies and the Vision of Industrial Productivity in the 1920s'. *Journal of Contemporary History,* vol. 5, pp. 27-61.
Mämpel, Wulf, Walter Buchholz, Frank-Rainer Hesselmann, Elisabeth Schulz & Liliane Zuuring (2006). *Margarethenhöhe. Das Jahrhundertwerk.* Essen: Margarethe Krupp-Stiftung für Wohnungsforsorge/Verlagsgruppe Beleke.
Marchand, Roland (1998). *Creating the Corporate Soul. The Rise of Public Relations and Corporate Imagery in American Big Business.* Berkeley: University of California Press.
Marx, Leo (1967). *Technology and the Pastoral Ideal in America.* New York: Oxford University Press.
McCreary, Eugene C. (1968). 'Social Welfare and Business: The Krupp Welfare Program, 1860-1914'. *The Business History Review,* vol. 42, no. 1, pp. 24-49.
McQuaid, Kim (1976). 'An American Owenite. Edward A. Filene and the Parameters of Industrial Reform'. *American Journal of Economics and Sociology,* vol. 35, no. 1, pp. 77-94.
Meakin, Budgett (1905). *Model Factories and Villages.* London: T. Fisher Unwin.
Metzendorf, Rainer & Achim Mikuscheit (1997). *Margarethenhöhe. Experiment und Leitbild. 1906-1996.* Essen/Bottrop: Margarethe Krupp-Stiftung/ Verlag Peter Pomp.
Mitterand, Henri (2002). *Zola. Tome III. L'honneur 1893-1902.* Paris: Fayard.

Mohl, Raymond A. & Neil Betten (1972a). 'Ethnic Adjustment in the Industrial City: The International Institute of Gary, 1919-1940'. *International Migration Review*, vol. 6, no. 4, pp. 361-376.

Mohl, Raymond A. & Neil Betten (1972b). 'The Failure of Industrial City Planning: Gary, Indiana, 1906-1910'. *Journal of the American Institute of Planners*, vol. 38, no. 4, pp. 203-214.

Moriceau, Caroline (2005). 'L'hygiène à la Cristallerie de Baccarat dans la seconde moitié du XIXe siècle. La santé ouvrière au coeur de la gouvernance industrielle'. *Le Mouvement Social*, no. 213, pp. 53-70.

Morris, Charles R. (2012). *The Dawn of Innovation*. New York: Public Affairs.

Morris, William (1891), *News from Nowhere*. London: Longmans, Green and Co. Amazon Kindle e-book: transcribed from the 1908 Longmans, Green, and Co. edition by David Price. Publisher unknown.

Mosher, Anne, E. (1995). '"Something Better than the Best": Industrial Restructuring, George McMurtrey and the Creation of the Model Industrial Town of Vandergrift, Pennsylvania, 1883-1901'. *Annals of the Association of American Geographers*, vol. 85, no. 1, March, pp. 84-107.

Mosher, Anne E. (2004). *Capital's Utopia: Vandergrift, Pennsylvania, 1885-1916*. Baltimore: Johns Hopkins University Press.

Mosher, Anne, E. & Deryck W. Holdsworth (1992). 'The Meaning of Alley Housing in Industrial Towns: Examples from Late Nineteenth and Early-Twentieth Century Pennsylvania'. *Journal of Historical Geography*, vol. 18, no. 2, pp. 174-189.

Moutet, Aimée (1975). 'Les origines du système de Taylor en France. Le point de vue patronal (1907-1914)'. *Le Mouvement Social*, no. 93, Oct.-Dec., pp. 15-49.

Moutet, Aimée (1997). *Les logiques de l'entreprise. La rationalisation dans l'industrie française de l'entre-deux-guerres*. Paris: Éditions de L'École Des Hautes Études En Sciences Sociales.

Müller, Sebastian (1974). *Kunst und Industrie. Ideologie und Organisation des Funktionalismus in der Architektur*. Munich: Carl Hanser Verlag.

Mumford, Lewis (1922), *The Story of Utopias*. Amazon Kindle e-book. Publisher unknown.

Nelson, Daniel (1995). *Managers & Workers. Origins of the Twentieth-Century Factory System in the United States 1880-1920*. Madison: University of Wisconsin Press.

Neumeyer, Fritz (1978). *Der Werkwohnungsbau der Industrie in Berlin und seine Entwicklung im 19. und frühen 20. Jahrhundert*. Phd Dissertation. Technische Universität Berlin.

Neye, David E. (2013). *America's Assembly Line*. Cambridge: MIT Press.

Nolan, Mary (1994). *Visions of Modernity. American Business and the Modernization of Germany*. New York: Oxford University Press.

Nordhoff, Charles (1875). *The Communistic Societies of the United States from Personal Visit and Observation*. Amazon Kindle e-book. Publisher unknown.

Noyes, John Humphrey (1870). *History of American Socialisms*. Amazon Kindle e-book: reprint of the 1870 edition. Publisher unknown.

Ory, Pacal (1982). *Les Expositions Universelles de Paris*. Paris: Éditions Ramsay.

Ory, Pascal (1989). *1889 La mémoire des siècles. L'Expo Universelle*. Brussels: Éditions Complexe.

Osterhammel, Jürgen (2010). *Die Verwandlung der Welt. Eine Geschichte des 19. Jahrhunderts*. Munich: C.H. Beck.

Oxford DNB, *William Hesketh Lever* (23 January 2013). www.oxforddnb.com.

Owen, Robert (1991). *A New View of Society and Other Writings*. Harmondsworth: Penguin Books.

Paquot Thierry & Marc Bédarida (eds) (2003). *Habiter l' utopie. La Familistère de Guise*. Paris: Éditions De La Villette.

Pierenkemper, Toni & Richard Tilly (2004). *The German Economy During the Nineteenth Century.* New York: Berghahn Books.

Piketty, Thomas (2013). *Le capital au XXIe siècle.* Paris: Éditions du Seuil.

Pollard, Sydney (1964). 'The Factory Village in the Industrial Revolution'. *The English Historical Review,* vol. 79, no. 312 (Jul.), pp. 513-531.

Pollard, Sydney (1968). *The Genesis of Modern Management. A Study of the Industrial Revolution in Great Britain.* London: Penguin Books.

Rabinow, Paul (1989). *French Modern. Norms and Forms of the Social Environment.* Chicago: University of Chicago Press.

Rabreau, Daniel (2002). *La Saline Royale d'Arc-et-Senans. Un monument industriel. Allégorie des Lumières.* Paris: Belin-Herscher (Les destinées du patrimoine).

Rathenau, Walther (1964a). 'Von kommenden Dingen'. In: Hans Werner Richter (ed). *Walther Rathenau Schriften und Reden.* Berlin: S. Fischer Verlag, pp. 7-233.

Rathenau, Walther (1964b). 'Die neue Gesellschaft'. In: Hans Werner Richter (ed.). *Walther Rathenau Schriften und Reden.* Berlin: S. Fischer Verlag, pp. 278-358.

Rauterberg, Hanno (2012). 'Die Diktatur der Einfachkeit. Wie das Apple-Design unser Dasein verändert – eine Ideologiekritik'. *Die Zeit,* no. 33, 9 August: p. 43.

Reid, Donald (1985a). 'Industrial Paternalism: Discourse and Practice in Nineteenth-Century French Mining and Metallurgy'. *Comparative Studies in Society and History,* vol. 27, no. 4, pp. 597-607.

Reid, Donald (1985b). *The Miners of Decazeville. A Genealogy of Deindustrialization.* Cambridge, MA: Harvard University Press.

Reid, Donald (1993). 'Schools and the Paternalist Project at Le Creusot, 1850-1914'. *Journal of Social History,* vol. 27, no. 1, pp. 129-143.

Reid, Donald (1994). 'In the Name of the Father: A Language of Labour Relations in Nineteenth-Century France'. *History Workshop Journal,* no. 38: pp. 1-22.

Reif, Heinz (1986). '"Ein seltener Kreis von Freunden". Arbeitsprozesse und Arbeitserfahrungen bei Krupp 1840-1914'. In: Klaus Tenfelde (ed.), *Arbeit und Arbeitserfahrung in der Geschichte.* Göttingen: Vandenhoeck & Ruprecht, pp. 51-91.

Révéz, Imre (1927). *Walther Rathenau und sein wirtschaftliches Werk.* Dresden: Carl Reissner Verlag.

Robertson, A.J. (1971). 'Robert Owen, Cotton Spinner: New Lanark, 1800-25'. In: Sydney Pollard & John Salt (eds), *Robert Owen. Prophet of the Poor. Essays in Honour of the Two Hundreth Anniversary of his birth.* London: Macmillan, pp. 145-165.

Rodgers, Daniel T. (1978). *The Work Ethic in Industrial America 1850-1920.* Chicago: University of Chicago Press.

Rodgers, Daniel T. (1998). *Atlantic Crossings: Social Politics in a Progressive Age.* Cambridge: The Belknap Press.

Rodgers, Daniel T. (2004). 'American Exceptionalism Revisited'. *Raritan Review* 24, Fall 2004, no. 2, pp. 21-47.

Roethlisberger, F.J. & William J. Dickson (1950). *Management and the Worker. An Account of a Research Program Conducted by the Western Electric Company, Hawthorne Works, Chicago.* Cambridge, MA: Harvard University Press.

Rosenbaum, Julia B. (2006). *Visions of Belonging. New England Art and the Making of American Identity.* Ithaca: Cornell University Press.

Rowlinson, Michael (1988). 'The Early Application of Scientific Management by Cadbury'. *Business History,* vol. 30, no. 4, pp. 377-395.

Rowlinson Michael & John Hassard (1993). 'The Invention of Corporate Culture: A History of the Histories of Cadbury'. *Human Relations,* vol. 46, pp. 299-326.
Ryan, James Emmett (2009). *Imaginary Friends. Representing Quakers in American Culture, 1650-1950.* Madison: University of Wisconsin Press.

Schlandt, Joachim (1970). 'Die Kruppsiedlungen. Wohnungsbau im Interesse eines Industriekonzerns'. In: Hans G. Helms & Jorn Janssen, *Kapitalistischer Städtebau.* Neuwied: Leuchterhand, pp. 95-111.
Schrofer, Lawrence (1975). *The Formation of a Modern Labor Force. Upper Silesia, 1865-1914.* Berkeley: University of California.
Schulze, Franz & Kevin Harrington (eds) (1993). *Chicago's Famous Buildings. A Photographic Guide to the City's Architectural Landmarks and other Notable Buildings.* Chicago: University of Chicago Press.
Schweitzer, Kerstin (1997). 'Hellerau, die erste deutsche Gartenstadt bei Dresden'. *Zeit-Online,* 28 March.
Seng, Eva Maria & Richard Saage (2012). 'Utopie und Architektur'. In: *L'Architecture Engagée. Manifeste zur Veränderung der Gesellschaft.* Munich: DETAIL-Institut für Internationale Architektur, pp. 10-37.
Sennett, Richard (1998). *The Corrosion of Character. The Personal Consequences of Work in the New Capitalism.* New York: W.W. Norton & Company.
Sennett, Richard (2006). *The Culture of the New Capitalism.* New Haven: Yale University Press.
Sennett, Richard (2008). *The Craftsman.* London: Penguin Books.
Shearer, J. Ronald (1995). 'Talking About Efficiency: Politics and the Industrial Rationalization Movement in the Weimar Republic'. *Central European History,* vol. 28, no. 4, pp. 483-506.
Shearer, J. Ronald (1997). 'The Reichskuratorium für Wirtschaftlichkeit: Fordism and Organized Capitalism in Germany, 1918-1945'. *The Business History Review,* vol. 71, no. 4, pp. 569-602.
Standing, Guy (2014). *The Precariat: The New Dangerous Class.* London: Bloomsbury.
Stearns, Peter N. (1978). *Paths to Authority. The Middle Class and the Industrial Labor Force in France, 1820-1848.* Urbana: University of Illinois Press.
Stemmrich, D. (1981). *Die Siedlung als Programm. Untersuchungen zum Arbeiterwohnungsbau anhand Kruppscher Siedlungen zwischen 1861 und 1907.* Hildesheim: Georg Olms Verlag.

Tarbell, Ida M. (1916). *New Ideals in Business. An Account of their Practice and their Effects upon Men and Profits.* New York: The MacMillan Company.
Tawney, Richard (1979). *Religie en de opkomst van het kapitalisme.* Nijmegen: SUN Reprint.
Taylor, Graham Romeyn (1915). *Satellite Cities. A Study of Industrial Suburbs.* New York: Arno Press & The New York Times.
Tenfelde, Klaus (ed.) (1994a). *Bilder von Krupp. Fotografie und Geschichte im Industriezeitalter.* Munich: Verlag C.H. Beck.
Tenfelde, Klaus (1994b). 'Krupp – der Aufstieg eines deutschen Weltkonzerns'. In: Tenfelde (ed.). *Bilder von Krupp. Fotografie und Geschichte im Industriezeitalter.* Munich: Verlag C.H. Beck.
Tesi, Francesca (2009). 'The Application of Taylorism in France: The Role of the Michelin Family in the Rationalization of French Work'. *Business and Economic History On-Line,* vol.7, pp. 1-16.
Tilly, Louise (1985). 'Coping with Company Paternalism. Family Strategies of Coal Miners in Nineteenth-Century France'. *Theory and Society,* vol. 14, no. 4, pp. 403-417.
Tilly, Richard H. (1990). *Vom Zollverein zum Industriestaat. Die wirtschaftlich-soziale Entwicklung Deutschlands 1834 is 1914.* Munich: Deutscher Taschenbuch Verlag (DTV).
Titmuss, R.M. (1974). *Social Policy. An introduction.* London: George Allen & Unwin Ltd.

Van Zee, Marynel Ryan (2012). 'Form and Reform: The Garden City of Hellerau-bei-Dresden, Germany between Company Town and Model Town'. In: Marcelo Borges & Susana B. Torres (eds.). *Company Towns. Labor, Space, and Power Relations across Timmes and Continents.* New York: Palgrave Macmillan, pp. 41-67.
Von Beyme, Klaus (2012). 'Der Frühsozialismus und die Stadtplanung'. In: *L'Architecture Engagée. Manifeste zur Veränderung der Gesellschaft.* Munich: DETAIL-Institut für Internationale Architektur, pp. 64-87.
Vernon, Anne (1958). *A Quaker Business Man. The Life of Joseph Rowntree 1836-1925.* London: George Alan and Unwin Ltd.

Ward Richardson, Benjamin (1876). *Hygeia. A City of Health.* Amazon Kindle e-book. Publisher unknown.
Weber, Max (2012). *Die protestantische Ethik und der Geist des Kapitalismus.* Altenmünster: Jazzybook Verlag Jürgen Beck, Amazon Kindle e-book.
Weil, David (2014). *The Fissured Workplace: Why Work Became so Bad for so Many and What Can be Done to Improve it.* Cambridge, MA: Harvard University Press.
Weinstein, James (1968). *The Corporate Ideal in The Liberal State 1900-1918.* Boston: Beacon Press.
Wells, H.G. (2005). *A Modern Utopia.* Edited by Gregory Clayes and Patrick Parrinder. With an introduction by Francis Wheen and notes by Gregory Claeys and Andy Sawyer. London: Penguin Books.
Wiebe, Robert H. (1967). *The Search For Order 1877-1920.* New York: Hill & Wang.
Wiebenson, Dora (1960). 'Utopian Aspects of Tony Garnier's Cité Industrielle'. *Journal of the Society of Architectural Historians,* vol. 19, no. 1, pp. 16-24.
Wiebenson, Dora (1969). *Tony Garnier: The Cité Industrielle.* New York: George Braziler.
Wikipedia, The free encyclopaedia (retrieved November 2012). www.wikipedia.org.
Wilhelm, Karin (1983). *Walter Gropius Industrie Architekt.* Braunschweig: Friedr. Vieweg & Sohn.
Wilson, Charles (1970). *The History of Unilever. A Study in Economic Growth and Social Change.* Volume 1. London: Cassell.
Wood, Gordon S. (2011). *The Idea of America. Reflections on the Birth of the United States.* New York: The Penguin Press.
Woronoff, Dennis (1998). *Histoire de l'industrie en France. Du XVIe siècle à nos jours.* Paris: Éditions du Seuil.

Zahavi, Gerald (1983). 'Negotiated Loyalty: Welfare Capitalism and the Shoeworkers of Endicott Johnson, 1920-1940'. *The Journal of American History,* vol. 70, no. 3, pp. 602-620.
Zola, Émile (1901). *Travail.* Paris: Gallimard.
Zola, Émile (1991). *Germinal* (1885). Paris: Fasquelle, Le Livre de Poche.

Index

For Product Safety Concerns and Information please contact our EU
representative GPSR@taylorandfrancis.com
Taylor & Francis Verlag GmbH, Kaufingerstraße 24, 80331 München, Germany

www.ingramcontent.com/pod-product-compliance
Ingram Content Group UK Ltd.
Pitfield, Milton Keynes, MK11 3LW, UK
UKHW022126190926
475702UK00013B/1674
9781041176558